The Cognition Workbook

Essays, Demonstrations, & Explorations

The Cognition Workbook

Essays, Demonstrations, & Explorations

Daniel Reisberg

Reed College

W. W. Norton & Company
New York • London

W. W. Norton & Company has been independent since its founding in 1923, when William Warder Norton and Mary D. Herter Norton first published lectures delivered at the People's Institute, the adult education division of New York City's Cooper Union. The firm soon expanded its program beyond the Institute, publishing books by celebrated academics from America and abroad. By midcentury, the two major pillars of Norton's publishing program—trade books and college texts—were firmly established. In the 1950s, the Norton family transferred control of the company to its employees, and today—with a staff of four hundred and a comparable number of trade, college, and professional titles published each year—W. W. Norton & Company stands as the largest and oldest publishing house owned wholly by its employees.

Editor: Aaron Javsicas

Project Editor: Jack Borrebach

Copyeditor: Jackie Estrada

Electronic Media Editor: Callinda Taylor

Editorial Assistant: Catherine Rice

Marketing Manager, Psychology: Andrea Matter

Production Manager: Ashley Horna

Photo Editor: Mike Fodera

Permissions Manager: Megan Jackson

Permissions Clearing: Bethany Salminen

Design: Lisa Buckley, Rebecca A. Homiski, and Matrix Publishing Services

Composition: Jouve International—Brattleboro, VT

Manufacturing: Quad/Graphics—Versailles, KY

ISBN: 978-0-393-91932-5

W. W. Norton & Company, Inc., 500 Fifth Avenue, New York, NY 10110-0017

wwnorton.com

W. W. Norton & Company Ltd., Castle House, 75/76 Wells Street, London W1T 3QT

1 2 3 4 5 6 7 8 9 0

Contents

CHAPTER 1

The Science of the Mind

Demonstrations

1.1 The Articulatory Rehearsal Loop

Cognitive psychology relies on a wide range of methods, many of which depend on precise measurement or complex analyses of subtle data patterns. However, some of the phenomena we observe in the lab can be demonstrated informally—either by you, the reader, working on your own, or in a classroom setting. In this workbook, therefore, I've provided a series of demonstrations illustrating some of the phenomena discussed in the text. I hope these demonstrations will help you sharpen your understanding of the data patterns; I hope the demonstrations will also make the data more concrete and more familiar, and hence more memorable.

As our initial example, Chapter 1 introduces the notion of the articulatory rehearsal loop, one of the key "helpers" within the working-memory system. As the chapter describes, many lines of evidence document the existence of this loop, but one type of evidence is especially easy to demonstrate.

Read these numbers and think about them for a moment, so that you'll be able to recall them in a few seconds: 8 2 5 7. Now, while you're holding onto these numbers, read the following paragraph:

> You should, right now, be rehearsing those numbers while you are reading this paragraph, so that you'll be able to recall them when you're done with the paragraph. You are probably storing the numbers in your articulatory rehearsal loop, saying the numbers over and over to yourself. Using the loop in this way requires little effort or attention, leaving the central executive free to work on the concurrent task of reading these sentences—identifying the words, assembling them into phrases, and figuring out what the phrases mean. As a result, with the loop holding the numbers and the executive doing the reading, there is no conflict and no problem. Therefore, this combination is relatively easy.

Now, what were those numbers? Most people can recall them with no problem, for the reasons just described. They read—and understood—the passage, and holding onto the numbers caused no difficulty at all. Did *you* understand the passage? Can you summarize it, briefly, in your own words?

Next, try a variation: Again, you will place four numbers in memory, but then you will immediately start saying "Tah-Tah-Tah" over and over out loud, while reading a passage. Ready? The numbers are: 3 8 1 4. Start saying "Tah-Tah-Tah" and read on.

> Again, you should be rehearsing the numbers as you read, and also repeating "Tah-Tah-Tah" over and over out loud. The repetitions of "Tah-Tah-Tah" demand little thought, but they do require the neural circuits and the muscles that are needed for speaking, and with these resources tied up in this fashion, they're not available for use in the rehearsal loop. As a result, you don't have the option of storing the four numbers in the loop. That means you need to find some other means of remembering the numbers, and that is likely to involve the central executive. As a result, the executive needs to do two things at once—hold onto the numbers, and read the passage.

Now, what were those numbers? Many people in this situation find they have forgotten the numbers. Others can recall the numbers but find this version of the task (in which the executive couldn't rely on the rehearsal loop) much harder, and they may report that they actually found themselves skimming the passage, not reading it. Again, can you summarize the paragraph you just read? Glance back over the paragraph to see if your summary is complete; did you miss something? You may have, because many people report that in this situation their attention hops back and forth, so that they read a little, think about the numbers, read some more, think about the numbers again, and so on—an experience they didn't have without the "Tah-Tah-Tah."

Finally, we need one more condition: Did the "Tah-Tah-Tah" disrupt your performance because (as proposed) it occupied your rehearsal loop? Or was this task simply a distraction, disrupting your performance because saying "Tah-Tah-Tah" over and over was obnoxious, or perhaps embarrassing? To find out, let's try one more task: Close your fist, but leave your thumb sticking out, and position your hand so that you're making the conventional "thumbs down" signal. With your hand in this shape, poke your thumb, over and over, into the top of your head. Keep doing this while reading the following passage. Once again, though, hold these numbers in your memory as you read: 7 2 4 5.

> In this condition, you're again producing a rhythmic activity as you read, although it's tapping rather than repeating a syllable. If the problem in the previous condition was distraction, you should be distracted in the same way here. And you probably look ridiculous poking your head in this fashion. If the problem in the previous condition was embarrassment, you should again be embarrassed here. On either of these grounds, this condition should be just as hard as the previous one. But if the problem in the previous condition depended instead on the repeated syllables blocking you from using your articulatory loop, that won't be a problem here, and this condition should be easier than the previous one.

What were the numbers? This condition probably was easy—allowing us to reject the idea that the problem lies in distraction or embarrassment. Instead, use of the articulatory loop really is the key!

Demonstration adapted from: Baddeley, A. (1986). *Working memory*. Oxford, England: Clarendon Press.

1.2   Sound-Based Coding

The chapter mentions that people often make sound-based errors when holding information in working memory. This is because working-memory storage relies in part on an auditory buffer—the so-called "inner ear." The inner ear, in turn, relies on mechanisms ordinarily used for hearing, mechanisms that are involved when you're listening to actual, out-in-the-world sounds. The use of these mechanisms essentially guarantees that things that sound alike in actual hearing will also sound alike in the inner ear, and this produces the confusions that we see in our data, with people remembering that they saw an "F" (and thus the sound "eff"), for example, when they really saw an "S" ("ess").

This proposal about the inner ear also has other implications, and we can use those implications as further tests of the proposal. For example, if sound-alike items are confusable with each other in memory, then these items may actually be harder to remember, compared to items that don't sound alike. Is this the case? Read the list of letters below out loud, then cover the list with your hand. Think about the list for 15 seconds or so, and then write it down. How many did you get right?

Here's the list of letters:

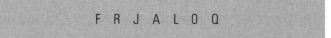

E   C   V   T   G   D   B

Now do the same with this list – read it aloud quickly, then cover it. Think about it for 15 seconds, then write it down.

F   R   J   A   L   O   Q

Again, how many did you get right?

It's possible that this demonstration won't work for you—because it's possible you'll recall both lists perfectly! But if you were equally accurate with the two lists, did you have to work harder for one list than for the other? And, if you made errors in your recall, which list produced more errors?

Most people find the first (sound-alike) list more difficult and are more likely to make errors with this list than with the second one. This is just what we'd expect if working memory relies on some sort of sound-based code.

Applying Cognitive Psychology

Research Methods: Testable Hypotheses

Research in cognitive psychology yields results that are both intriguing and useful. These results have value, however, only if they're based on sound methods and good science. If not, we may be offering practical suggestions that do more harm than good, and we may be making theoretical claims that lead us away from the truth, not toward it.

For students learning about cognitive psychology, therefore, it is important to understand the methods that make our science possible. This will allow you to see why our results are compelling and why we can, with confidence, draw the conclusions that we do. For this reason, I have written brief Research Methods essays, highlighting a methodological issue or focusing on a research example, for each of the chapters in the text. I hope these essays will broaden your understanding of our methods and deepen your appreciation for why our results can be (indeed, *must be*) taken seriously. More broadly, these essays will help you understand how our science proceeds.

First, though, we might ask: What *is* science, and what is it about cognitive psychology that makes it count as a science? The key lies in the idea that science cannot be based just on someone's opinions about the world or on someone's (perhaps biased) interpretation of the facts. Instead, a science needs to be based on the facts themselves, and that means the scientific community needs to check every one of its claims against the facts, to find out with certainty whether each claim is correct. If we learn that the evidence for a claim is weak or ambiguous, then we need to seek more evidence in order to achieve certainty. And, of course, if we learn that a claim does *not* fit with the facts, then we're obligated to set the claim aside, to make sure we only offer claims that we know are in line with reality.

Clearly, then, the notion of *testing* our claims, to make sure they match the facts, is central for any science, and this has a powerful implication for how we formulate our claims in the first place. Specifically, we need to make sure that all of our claims are formulated in a way that will allow the testing that is central to the scientific enterprise; said differently, science is possible only if the claims being considered are rigorously *testable*. But how do we ensure testability? How do we ensure that it will be *possible* to confront our claims with the facts? Among other points, we need to make certain our claims never rely on ambiguous terms or vague phrasing; we also need to avoid escape clauses like "Maybe this will happen" or "Sometimes we'll observe *X* and sometimes we won't."

To see how this plays out, consider the claim "No matter what day of the year you pick, someone famous was born on that day." Is this claim testable? Actually, it isn't. Imagine that the most prominent person you can think of, born on December 19, is Daniel Reisberg. Does this support the claim, because Reisberg is famous? (After all, thousands of students have read his books.) Or does it contradict the claim, because Reisberg isn't famous? (After all, most people have never heard of him.) Both of these positions seem plausible, and so our "test" of this claim about birthdays turns out to depend on opinion, not fact: If you hold the opinion that Reisberg is famous, then the evidence about the December 19 birthday confirms our claim; if you hold the opposite opinion, the same evidence *doesn't* confirm the claim. As a result, this claim is not testable—there's no way to say with certainty whether it fits with the facts or not.

Of course, we could make this claim testable if we could find a suitable definition of "famous." In that case, we could, with some certainty, decide whether Reisberg is famous or not, and then we could use this point to test our claim about birthdays. But until that is done, there is no way to test this claim in the fashion, not dependent on opinion, that science requires.

This example illustrates why a scientific hypothesis must be framed precisely— so that we can check the facts and then say with certainty whether the hypothesis is correct. But how do we check the facts? We'll explore this question in upcoming Research Methods essays in this workbook.

FOR DISCUSSION

We often recite so-called words of wisdom to remind each other of how events in the world work: "Good things come in threes." "Absence makes the heart grow fonder." "Opposites attract." Choose one of these common expressions (perhaps one of the ones just mentioned, or some other). Does this expression offer a testable claim? If not, why not? How could you rephrase or elaborate on the expression (or, perhaps, define the terms used in the expression) to turn it into a testable claim?

Cognitive Psychology and Education:
Enhancing Classroom Learning

There has long been a specialty known as *educational psychology*—a specialty that asks, in a scientific way, questions about how students learn, how they use what they learn, and what teachers can do to improve the educational process. Some of the questions within educational psychology are linked to issues of motivation: What is the best way to motivate students? Is praise effective? Should teachers give students certain performance goals? Growth goals? Should teachers reward students in some concrete way for reaching these goals?

Other questions in educational psychology are rooted in *developmental psychology*, as we try to figure out how the educational process can be tuned to match the developmental status of a growing child. Still other issues are tied to the broader field of *social psychology*: how students interact with each other and can help each other, how teachers can encourage cooperation and good morale in the classroom, and so on.

But, of course, many questions in educational psychology are directly tied to issues within *cognitive psychology*: How can students be more effective in learning new material? What can they do to retain the material they've learned? How can students become better at solving problems or drawing conclusions? Questions like these are directly tied to the issues in play in this book; therefore, I've written brief Cognitive Psychology and Education essays for each chapter, applying the claims and methods developed in that chapter to some important aspect of classroom learning.

Certain educational issues are covered directly in the text itself. Chapter 5, for example, talks about how material is entered into memory, and the studies described in the chapter have obvious and immediate implications for your classroom work. Likewise, Chapter 12 talks about different strategies you can use, during learning, to increase the chances that you'll be able to draw analogies from what you have learned, helping you to solve problems you encounter in the future. But in other cases the educational implications will be less obvious, and so these essays will provide a setting in which to explore those implications more fully.

I've tried to frame these essays so that they'll be useful for students reading this workbook as part of a college or university course. The reason, simply, is that I want to do all I can to help you become a better student! The content of the essays has also been guided by the questions that I've gotten over the years from my own students. Like all students, they want to maximize their performance, and they realize that my courses deal with issues that are directly relevant to their daily activities— their *reading* (and so they ask me about speed reading), *learning* (and so they ask me how to study), *taking tests* (and so they ask me about test strategies), and more. I address their questions in these essays, and in the process I hope to teach you more about cognitive psychology and also provide you with information you can immediately use.

FOR DISCUSSION

Throughout this text, we'll be describing strategies that will help you learn new materials and memorize new information. It may be useful, though, to establish a "baseline"—a description of the strategies and approaches you're using *now*. As you enter a new course, do you have specific study strategies that you try to implement as the term unfolds? Alternatively, if a younger student approached you for advice on better ways to study, what would you recommend? Then, with these ideas in view, think about what the *basis* for these suggestions might be. Did someone tell you that these were good ways to study? Did you choose them on your own? Do you have any basis for being certain that these strategies are, in fact, effective? Keep these strategies in mind as you move through this text, in order to ask how they might be similar to the ones recommended here, and how they might be different.

Cognitive Psychology and the Law:
Improving the Criminal Justice System

Research in cognitive psychology can help us understand deep theoretical issues, such as what it means to be rational or what the function of consciousness might be. But our research also has pragmatic implications, with studies often providing important lessons for how we should conduct our day-to-day lives. Some of those pragmatic lessons are obvious. (For example, it seems self-evident that our claims about memory might provide suggestions for how students should approach materials in the classroom.) Other implications of our work, though, are more surprising—for example, the implications of cognitive psychology for the criminal justice system.

Think about what happens in a criminal investigation. Eyewitnesses provide evidence, based on what they paid attention to during a crime and what they remember. Police officers question the witnesses, trying to maximize what each witness recalls—but without leading the witness in any way. Then the police try to deduce, from the evidence, who the perpetrator was. Then later, during the trial, jurors listen to evidence and make a judgment about the defendant's innocence or guilt.

Cast in these terms, it should be obvious that an understanding of *attention, memory, reasoning,* and *judgment* (to name just a few processes) is directly relevant to what happens in the legal system. Indeed, we can plausibly hope to use what we know about these processes to improve the courts' procedures—for example, to design more effective ways to question witnesses (*memory*), to help jurors do their job (*judgment*), and so on.

Drawing on these points, I provide Cognitive Psychology and the Law essays for every chapter of the textbook, describing how the materials in that chapter can help you to understand a specific aspect of the criminal justice system. These essays illustrate how cognitive psychology can be brought to bear on issues of enormous importance, issues that are in obvious ways rather distant from the laboratory.

I want to be clear, though, that cognitive psychology has implications for many domains, and so I could have generated essays to highlight our field's contributions to other real-world concerns—the practice of medicine, for example, or the training of firefighters, or the education of businesspeople. Why, therefore, do I focus on the criminal justice system? There are several reasons, but one prominent motivation is my own involvement with these issues: As a psychologist specializing in memory, I consult with police, lawyers, and the courts on questions about eyewitness evidence. This work allows me, as a scientist, to play a small part in improving the criminal justice system in my corner of the United States—a point that gives me enormous satisfaction, speaking both as an academic and as a citizen.

My work with the courts provides a powerful reminder for me that our science does indeed generate knowledge that is useful and deeply important. At the same time, though, my work with the courts sometimes reminds me of the *limitations* of our science, and that is also important. For example, when we study how someone pays attention to shapes on a computer screen, can we draw conclusions about how an eyewitness pays attention to a complex and rapidly unfolding crime? When we study how someone memorizes a list of words, does this tell us how a crime victim remembers a robbery? These are important questions, and the answers need to be thought through with care. As it turns out, we'll consider answers to these questions before we're done (and the answers are encouraging!). But, for now, let's focus just on these questions themselves and celebrate the fact that psychology's partnership with the criminal justice system forces us to take these questions very seriously—and that has to improve how, as scientists, we think about these issues.

FOR DISCUSSION

This essay mentions the role of *attention, memory, reasoning*, and *judgment* within the legal system. But the essay also suggests that these processes are crucial in other domains (including—the essay notes—the practice of medicine, the training of firefighters, and the education of businesspeople). Can you generate examples of settings in which these processes are in fact central in these various domains? Better still, think about the kind of work you'll do if you follow your currently preferred career path. Can you describe examples in which this domain draws on the processes central to cognitive psychology?

CHAPTER 2

The Neural Basis for Cognition

Demonstrations

2.1   Foveation

The chapter describes the basic anatomy of the eyeball, including the fact that the **retina** (the light-sensitive surface at the back of the eye) has, at its center, a specialized region called the **fovea**. The cells in the fovea are distinctive in several ways, but, perhaps most important, they are much better at discerning visual detail than cells elsewhere on the retina.

In fact, cells away from the fovea are not just *worse* at seeing detail in comparison to foveal cells, they are actually quite *bad* at seeing detail. As a result, if you want to see an object's details, you need to look straight at it; this movement positions your eyes so that the object's image falls on the fovea. If you want to see detail in other regions, then you have no choice: You need to reposition your eyes, so that new inputs will be in "foveal view."

Putting this more broadly, if you want to scrutinize an entire scene, you need to move your eyes a lot, and this point leads to another limitation, because eye movements are surprisingly slow: For the eye movements we use to explore the world—eye movements called *saccades*—you need almost 200 msec to change your eye position. Most of that time is spent in "planning" and "programming" each movement, but, even so, you're only able to move your eyes four or five times each second; it's just not possible to move your eyes more quickly than this.

This combination—the inability to see detail outside of the fovea, and the slowness of eye movements—places severe limits on your pickup of information from the world, and these limits, in turn, influence how the nervous system must use and interpret the information actually received. How severe are these limits? And just how distinctive is the fovea? Hold the book about 12 inches from your face. Point your eyes at the black dot in the middle of the display, and try not to move them.

Stare at the dot for a moment, to make sure you've got your eye position appropriately "locked" in place, and then, without moving your eyes, try to read the letters one row up or down from the dot, or a couple of positions to the left or right. You should be able to do this, but you will probably find that your impression of the letters is indistinct. Now—still without moving your eyes—try reading the letters further from the dot. This should be more difficult.

```
KAF   JKSU   IOV   IMPHR   AC

OATA   NEME   TNIP   ORYU   X

HMRR   OLW   ●   IANTC   GT

NNE   RHOHW   RETLA   GREBS

IER   VRNEL   I   UAKB   LQPTS
```

What's going on? When you point your eyes at the dot, you're positioning each eyeball relative to the page so that the dot falls on the fovea; therefore, the other letters fall on retinal positions away from the fovea. The other letters are thus falling on areas of the retina that are literally less able to see sharply.

Notice, however, that in the ordinary circumstances of day-to-day life, the entire visual world seems sharp and clear to you. You don't have an impression of only being able to see a small region clearly, with everything else being blurry. Your sense of the world, though, is produced in large part by the "construction" and "filling in" that you unconsciously do—relying on inference and extrapolation to supplement the surprisingly sparse input that is actually provided by your eyes.

2.2 Eye Movements

The previous demonstration was designed to remind you that only a small portion of the retina (the fovea) is sensitive to fine detail. This is, of course, one of the reasons that you constantly move your eyes: Every shift in position points the eyes at a new portion of the visual world, allowing you to pick up detail from that portion of the world. Eventually, with enough time, and enough changes in eye position, you can inspect an entire scene.

To explore the world, you rely on eye movements called *saccades*. These eye movements (mentioned in Demonstration 2.1) are abrupt and "jerky," as your eyes hop from position to position, and, in fact, the word *saccade* is taken from the French for "jerk" or "twitch." To see just how jerky these eye movements are, sit (or stand) close to a friend (within two feet or so), but just off to the side. (There's no need in this demonstration for you and your friend to be nose-to-nose.) Have your friend look off to the left, and then, when you say "go," have your friend move his or her eyes smoothly to the right. You'll easily see that—despite this instruction—the eye movements aren't smooth at all. Instead, your friend's eyes move left-to-right in a series of small jumps; these are the saccades. (Now reverse roles, so that your friend can see your saccades.)

Next, try a variation of this procedure: Again, position yourself to watch your friend's eye movements. This time, hold up a pen, positioning it off to your friend's left. Now, smoothly move the pen from your friend's left to your friend's right, and have your friend watch the pen's tip as it moves across his or her view. This time, you won't see jerky eye movements. Instead, when someone is tracking a moving object (such as the pen's tip), the person relies on a different type of eye movement called *smooth pursuit movements*. (And, once more, reverse roles so that your friend can watch your smooth pursuit.)

Obviously, therefore, people are capable of producing smooth (not jerky) eye movements. But which type do you use in your ordinary examination of the world? One last time, position yourself to watch your friend's eye movements. This time, have your friend look around, counting the *circular objects* that are in view. (If there are no circular objects around, choose some other target. In truth, the nature of the target doesn't matter; you just want some chore that will force your friend to inspect the immediate environment.) Which type of eye movements does your friend use— the jerky saccades, or smooth movements?

2.3   The Blind Spot and the Active Nature of Vision

Axons from the retina's ganglion cells gather together to form the optic nerve. This nerve leaves the eyeball and carries information first to the thalamus and then to the visual cortex. Notice, therefore, that there has to be a location at the back of each eyeball that can serve as the "exit" for the ganglion cells' axons, and the axons fill this "exit" entirely, leaving no room for rods or cones. As a result, this region contains no photoreceptors at all and thus is completely insensitive to light. Appropriately enough, this region is called the "blind spot."

Ordinarily, people are not aware of the blind spot—but we can make them aware with a simple procedure. Turn to p. 12 and hold the book about 18 inches from your face. Close your left eye. Stare at the center of the author's picture on the left. Gradually move the book toward or away from your nose. At most distances, you'll still be able to see the brain (on the right) out of the corner of your eye. You should be able to find a distance, though, at which the brain picture drops from view—it just seems not to be there.

What is going on? You've positioned the book, relative to your eye, in a fashion that places the author's picture on your fovea but the picture of the brain on your *blind spot* and so the brain simply became invisible to you.

Even when the brain "disappeared," however, you didn't perceive a "hole" in the visual world. In particular, the brain picture disappeared, but you could still perceive the continuous grid pattern with no interruption in the lines. Why is this? Your visual system detected the pattern in the grid (continuous vertical lines + continuous horizontals) and used this pattern to "fill in" the information that was missing because of the blind spot. But, of course, the picture of the brain is not part of this overall pattern, and so it was not included when you did the filling in. Therefore, the picture of the brain vanished, but the pattern was not disrupted.

2.4   A Brightness Illusion

The earlier demonstrations for this chapter emphasized the active nature of vision: We apparently "fill in" information outside of the retina, so that we feel like we're seeing a uniformly detailed scene even though we're actually picking up detail from only a small portion of the visual world. Likewise, we seem to "fill in" information that's missing from the visual input because of the blind spot. Vision's active role is also evident in many illusions—for example, in the faint gray "dots" you see where the white bars in this figure cross.

There are no dots at those intersections. The white bars are uniform in brightness from the far left to the far right, and from the top to the bottom. (If you don't believe this, cover the figure with two pieces of paper, adjusting the paper to *hide* the black squares and to expose only a single white bar.) Why do you see the dots? They are the result of lateral inhibition. In brief, the bits of white at the intersections are receiving more inhibition than the bits of white *away* from the intersections, and it's this "extra" inhibition that makes the white at the intersections look slightly darker.

Why is the white at the intersections receiving more inhibition? Bear in mind that lateral inhibition is produced by a cell's "neighbors," and, the more excited those neighbors are, the more inhibition they produce. With this basis, think about a cell that's picking up information from one of the intersections. Let's call this Cell X. Cells responsive to the bit of the page just *above* the intersection are also "seeing" white—and so these cells are excited, so they're trying to inhibit Cell X. Likewise for cells responsive to the bit of page just below the intersection, and also those responsive to the bits of page just left and right of the intersection. In short, Cell X is surrounded by other cells that are "seeing" white—cells "north," "south," "east," and "west" of it—and so Cell X is receiving inhibition from all sides.

Now think about a cell positioned so that it is picking up information *away from* the intersection. Let's focus on a cell that's a bit to the right of Cell X, and so it's in the middle of one of the horizontal white bars; we'll call this Cell Y. Cells responsive to the bit of page *left* and *right* of this position are seeing white and are therefore excited and trying to inhibit Cell Y. But cells responsive to the page *above* and *below* this position are seeing black, and so are less excited and thus not trying to inhibit Cell Y. Thus, Cell Y has excited neighbors only on two sides (to its left and to its right) and therefore is receiving inhibition from just two sides. In this way, Cell Y is receiving roughly half the inhibition that Cell X is.

As a result of all this, the white regions at the intersections literally send a weaker signal to the brain—and so are perceived as less bright. The visual system starts out receiving the same *physical input* from the white regions at the intersections (because, objectively, the brightness at these regions is exactly the same as the brightness elsewhere on the white bars). However, the visual system responds differently to this input depending on where in the pattern it is—thanks to the lateral inhibition. This produces the sense of the faint gray dots at the intersections—an instance in which the setup of the visual system is clearly shaping (and, in this case, distorting) what you see.

Demonstration adapted from Ewald Hering, The effect of distance between contrasting regions, in *Outlines of a Theory of the Light Sense*, pp. 150–51. Copyright © Springer-Verlag. Reprinted with kind permission of Springer Science + Business Media.

Applying Cognitive Psychology

Research Methods: Control Groups

In several passages in Chapter 2, we talk about this or that brain area as being activated during a particular activity—so that certain areas in the occipital lobe (for example) are especially active when someone is examining a visual stimulus, certain areas of the frontal lobe are especially active when someone is listening to a verbal input, and so on. We need to be clear, though, about what these claims really mean.

All cells in the brain are active all the time. When they receive some input, however, or when they are involved in a particular process, the brain cells *change* their activation level. Therefore, when we talk about, say, the occipital lobe's response to a visual input, we do not mean that the cells are active when an input arrives and dormant the rest of the time. Instead, we're saying that when a visual input arrives, the activity in the occipital lobe *increases* from its prior (*baseline*) level.

To measure these increases, we need a basis for comparison, and, in fact, this is a feature of virtually all scientific investigation: Usually, we can interpret a measurement or an observation *only with reference to some appropriate baseline*. This is true outside of science as well. Imagine that your school's football team wins 90% of its games when you're wearing your lucky socks. Does this mean the socks are helpful? We'd need to ask how often the team wins when you're *not* wearing your lucky socks; if that number is also 90%, then your socks have no effect at all. If the number is 95%, then your socks might actually be a jinx!

In scientific research, our basis for comparison, in evaluating our data, is typically provided by a *control condition*—a condition that allows us to see how things unfold in the absence of the experimental manipulation. If, therefore, we want to understand how the brain responds to visual inputs, we need to compare a condition with a visual input (the *experimental condition*) with a control condition lacking this input. The difference between the conditions is the *independent variable*—the thing that's varying and which differentiates the two conditions.

In our football example, the independent variable was the presence or absence of your lucky socks. Let's be clear that there's just one thing that's varying in this comparison—whether the socks are present or not—and so there is just one independent variable. However, there are two options for this variable (socks present vs. socks absent), and so the one independent variable creates two conditions.

Likewise, if we are asking how visual stimulation changes brain activity, there is again just one thing that's varying: whether the stimulus is present or absent. But here, too, there are two options for this variable, and so the single independent variable leaves us with two conditions. (In other, more complicated experiments, there might be three or more options for a variable—perhaps no visual input versus dim input versus bright input. Likewise, there might be more than one independent variable. We'll hold these complications to the side for now.)

The independent variable is sometimes called the *predictor variable*, because our comparison is asking, in effect, whether we can use this variable to predict the experiment's outcome. (Does the presence of your lucky socks predict a greater chance of winning? Is the presence of a visual input associated with greater brain activity, so that when the input is on the scene we can predict that the activity will increase?)

The variable we measure in our data collection is called the *dependent variable*, so that our study is asking, in essence, whether this variable depends on the predictor variable. In many cases, the dependent variable is straightforward (What was the score of the game? What is the level of brain activity?), but sometimes it is not. We will return to this topic in one of the Research Methods essays for Chapter 12.

We still need to ask, however, exactly how we should set up our study, and how in particular we should set up the control condition. Imagine, as one possibility, that participants in our experimental condition are staring attentively at a computer screen, eagerly awaiting (and eventually seeing) a visual stimulus, while the participants in our control condition are told merely to hang out, so that we can observe the functioning of their brains. If we found differences between these two conditions, we could draw no conclusions. That's because any differences we observe *might be* due to the presence of the visual stimulus in one condition and not the other, or they might be due to the fact that participants in one condition are attentive while those in the other condition are relaxed. With no way to choose between these options, we'd have no way to interpret the data.

Clearly, then, our control condition must be carefully designed so that it differs from the experimental condition in just one way (in our example, in the presence or absence of the visual stimulus). We want to make sure that the two conditions are essentially identical in all other regards. As part of this, we want to make sure that participants in the two conditions get similar instructions and have similar expectations for the experiment. Only then, with the independent variable "isolated" in this fashion, will the contrast between the conditions be meaningful, allowing us to interpret the data and thus to properly test our hypothesis.

FOR DISCUSSION

We know that people often experience *auditory imagery*—hearing a sound (a favorite song, perhaps) playing "in their heads," even though no actual sound is present in their environment. Subjectively, auditory images seem to resemble actual hearing—you experience the image as having a certain tempo, a certain sequence of pitches, and so on. But what is the biological basis for auditory imagery?

Imagine that you wanted to test this hypothesis: "Auditory imagery relies on brain areas similar to those used in actual hearing." What conditions would you want to study in order to test this hypothesis? First, you would need to think about what instructions you could give your research participants to make sure they were engaging in auditory imagery during the time in which you monitored their brain activity. Second, you would need to choose what task you'd give to research participants in the control condition. Actually, you might consider having *two* control conditions—one that involves actual *hearing* with an overt stimulus, and one that involves neither actual hearing nor auditory imagery. That way, you could show that the brain activity during imagery was *similar to* that of the "hearing" control group but *different from* that of the "not hearing" group. What might your other two control groups involve—what tasks would participants in these groups do, or what instructions would you give them, while you were monitoring their brain activity?

Cognitive Psychology and Education:
Food Supplements and Cognition

Advertisers offer a range of food supplements that supposedly will make you smarter, improve your memory, help you think more clearly, and so on. Unfortunately, though, these supplements have usually not been tested in any systematic way. (In the United States and in many other countries, new *medicines* are tested before they are put on the market, but new food supplements are not.) In most cases, then, the claims made about these supplements are unsupported by evidence.

One supplement, though, has been widely endorsed and rigorously tested; this supplement is *Ginkgo biloba*, an extract derived from a tree of the same name and advertised as capable of enhancing memory. Is *Ginkgo biloba* effective? The answer begins with the fact that, for its normal functioning, the brain requires an excellent blood flow and, with that, a lot of oxygen and a lot of nutrients. Indeed, it is sometimes estimated that the brain, constituting just 2% of our body weight, consumes 15% percent of our body's energy supply!

It's not surprising, therefore, that the brain's operations are impaired if some change in your health interferes with the flow of oxygen or nutrients. If (for example) you're ill, or not eating enough, or not getting enough sleep, these conditions will affect virtually all aspects of your biological functioning. However, since the brain is so demanding of nutrients and oxygen, it's one of the first organs to suffer if the supply of these necessities is compromised. This is why poor nutrition, or poor health, almost inevitably undermine your ability to think, to remember, to pay attention, and more.

Of course, the opposite is also true: A healthy diet, adequate exercise, and regular sleeping hours will improve the performance of all your bodily systems; but again, since the brain is so expensive to maintain, these different aspects of a healthy lifestyle are especially important for making sure your brain has the resources it needs to function well. The implications of this for students are clear.

But what about *Ginkgo biloba*? Evidence suggests that *Ginkgo* extract may improve blood circulation, reduce some sorts of bodily inflammation, and protect the nervous system from several types of damage. This is why researchers are examining this extract as a possible treatment for people who have troubles with blood circulation or who are at risk for nerve damage. In fact, results suggest that patients with Huntingdon's disease, Alzheimer's disease, and several other conditions may be helped by this food supplement—and, in particular, helped to remember more, and to think more clearly. Let's be clear, though, that *Ginkgo* is not making these patients "smarter" in any direct fashion. Instead, the *Ginkgo* is broadly improving the patients' blood circulation and the health status of their nerve cells, allowing these cells to do their work.

What about healthy people—people who are not suffering from bodily inflammations or damage to their brain cells? Will *Ginkgo* help them? Here the evidence is mixed. Some reviews offer the tentative conclusion that *Ginkgo* may improve the cognitive functioning of healthy young adults, but many studies have failed to observe any benefit from this food supplement, suggesting that *Ginkgo*'s effects, if they exist at all in healthy adults, are so small that they are difficult to detect.

Are there other steps that are more promising—steps that *will* improve the mental functioning of healthy young adults? We've already indicated part of a positive answer: Overall, good nutrition, plenty of sleep, adequate exercise, and so on will keep your blood supply in good condition, and this will help your brain to do its job. In addition, there may be something else you can do: The brain's functioning depends on an adequate fuel supply, and that fuel supply comes from the sugar *glucose*. Crucially, the body's neurons have no way to store glucose, and so, for their moment-by-moment functioning, they depend on the bloodstream to deliver a steady supply of this fuel.

You can protect yourself, therefore, by making sure that your brain has all the glucose it needs. This is *not* a recommendation to jettison all other aspects of your diet and eat nothing but chocolate bars. In fact, most of the glucose your body needs doesn't come from sugary foods; most comes from the breakdown of carbohydrates, and so you get it from the grains, dairy products, fruits, and vegetables you eat. Thus, it might be a good idea to have a slice of bread and a glass of milk just before you take an exam, or just before you walk into a particularly challenging class. These steps will help ensure that you're not caught by a glucose shortfall that could interfere with your brain's functioning.

We need to be cautious, though, in how we think about these points. As one concern, you don't want to gulp down *too much* sugar. If you do gobble up a candy bar just before your exam, or gulp down a large glass of sugary lemonade, you might produce an upward spike in your blood glucose followed by a sudden drop, and this can produce problems of its own. In addition, we should emphasize that the benefits of ingesting carbohydrates—even if you get the "dose" right—may be relatively small. This is because the glucose supply for the brain is tightly controlled by a number of different mechanisms inside the body, and these mechanisms usually guarantee that your brain gets the sugar it needs. As a result, the extra glucose you might obtain from a fast snack may just get "set aside" by the liver and not be sent to the brain at all.

In short, then, the evidence suggests that food supplements offer no "fast track" toward better cognition. *Ginkgo* is helpful, but mostly for special populations. A high-carb snack may help, but will be of little value if you're already adequately nourished. Thus, on all these grounds, the best path toward better cognition seems, in some ways, to be the one that common sense would already recommend—a balanced diet, a good night's sleep, and paying careful attention during your studies.

FOR DISCUSSION

This essay focuses on the interplay between your body's state (Are you adequately nourished? Getting enough sleep?) and your mental function. But, in addition to factors like nourishment and sleep, we can also consider your body's daily rhythm. In fact, your biological functioning involves multiple rhythms, and these govern your sleep, your digestion, and more. One rhythm governs your level of overall alertness during the day, although people differ in when their "peak" alertness occurs. This is why some people seem to be "morning people" (most alert before noon) and some people seem to be "night people" (most alert in the evening).

Are you a morning person, a night person, or something in between? Can you think through what adjustments you might make in your work schedule so that your daily routine will be in tune with your biological cycle? And what are your thoughts about situations in which, say, "night people" are required to take an 8:00 A.M. exam, or morning people are required to take an evening exam? Once we acknowledge that the body's state matters for cognition (and surely it does!), should we be troubled about these out-of-tune situations?

For more on this topic

Gold, P. E., Cahill, L., & Wenk, G. L. (2002). *Ginkgo biloba:* A cognitive enhancer? *Psychological Science in the Public Interest, 3*, 2–11.

Husain, M., & Mehta, M. A. (2011). Cognitive enhancement by drugs in health and disease. *Trends in Cognitive Sciences, 15*, 28–36.

Masicampo, E., & Baumeister, R. (2008). Toward a physiology of dual-process reasoning and judgment: Lemonade, willpower, and expensive rule-based analysis. *Psychological Science, 19*, 255–260.

McDaniel, M. A., Maier, S. F., & Einstein, G. O. (2002). "Brain-specific" nutrients: A memory cure? *Psychological Science in the Public Interest, 3*, 12–38.

Cognitive Psychology and Education:
The So-Called "Smart Pills"

In the previous essay, we looked at one means of enhancing cognition—through food supplements such as *Ginkgo biloba.* There is, however, another strategy that people have tried but that has been deeply controversial: the use of stimulants. Students working through the night have often turned to caffeine and nicotine to help them stay awake—drinking yet another cup of coffee, or smoking a cigarette. The same is true for military personnel who need to remain alert for a long mission; they, too, have turned to these stimulants. And, in recent years, grocery stores have been offering other (more potent) means of getting the same effects, in the form of heavily caffeinated "energy drinks" (and "energy bars," caffeinated candy, and even a caffeinated inhalant).

The controversy in this area, however, has focused on a different type of stimulation: In the last dozen years or so, people have turned to the (typically illegal) use of various prescription drugs to enhance their performance in school and in the workplace. Many of these drugs are stimulants used widely for treatment of attention-deficit/hyperactivity disorder (ADHD). These same drugs—including methylpenidate (marketed as Ritalin or Concerta) and various forms of amphetamine (e.g., Adderall)—have become popular, though, as "cognitive enhancers."

These drugs are effective as stimulants, and so, plausibly, do help to keep people alert as they work or study. Even so, many researchers are deeply troubled about the increasing use of these prescription medications. As one concern, many of the commonly taken drugs have side effects, including gastrointestinal upset or nausea, and these side effects can offset any potential benefits from the drug. (The drug might perk you up, but that's not going to be helpful if you're focusing all your attention on not vomiting.) In addition, people often come "crashing down" when the drug effects wear off, so whatever gain in productivity they experienced while influenced by the drug is canceled out by the *loss* in productivity they'll experience in the next few days, while dealing with the "crash."

More troubling, many individuals use these drugs repeatedly over long periods of time, and we know little so far about the long-term problems that this use may create. We do know that there's a risk of addiction associated with these medications, and that's certainly a substantial concern. It's also important that individuals who receive these drugs with a doctor's prescription (e.g., for ADHD) are given clear information about dosages, and they receive follow-up from the doctor. In contrast, individuals who use these drugs as stimulants often obtain the drugs through means other than a prescription, and so they improvise on the dose and receive no follow-up— factors that magnify any concerns about side effects and undetected drug dependence. Related, a doctor prescribing these medications would be alert to factors that, for that individual, might argue *against* using these drugs (so-called "contraindications," including other medical conditions the person might have, or other drugs the person might be taking). This safety net is obviously not in place if someone obtains these drugs without a doctor.

Ironically, alongside of these potential problems, the possible *benefits* of these drugs are questionable. We certainly know that getting information into memory requires that you pay attention and engage the material somehow, and this mental "work" won't happen if you're sleepy and unfocused. On that basis, a stimulant might help you to learn new material. Likewise, judgment and reasoning often depend on mental shortcuts that are efficient but open to error. To avoid these shortcuts, you need to rely on (what we'll call, in Chapter 11) System 2 thinking, and this sort of thinking is less likely if you're sleepy. So here, too, a stimulant might help you. And, for that matter, in Chapter 12, we'll distinguish between *fluid* and *crystallized intelligence*. Fluid intelligence is what you need for working on novel problems, especially problems that require some mental flexibility—and fluid intelligence is compromised when you are tired.

There's really no debate, therefore, about whether being alert and awake is helpful for cognition. There's likewise no debate about whether a stimulant helps you to be alert; plainly, it does. The question, then, is whether these prescription medications are superior to, say, caffeine in offering this stimulation, and also whether the prescription medications might offer other benefits beyond stimulation. If the answer to these questions is "no," then the prescription drugs are surely a bad bet—providing no benefits beyond caffeine, but with greater risk of side effects, and greater risk of drug dependence.

What is the evidence on these points? One recent report offers the encouraging (but "provisional") conclusion that the prescription stimulants help with the *consolidation* of memories. In other words, the stimulants enhance the processes that take place in the hours after a learning episode, processes that serve to "cement" a memory in place (Smith & Farah, 2011). There's indication, though, that this benefit for consolidation emerges only if just the right dose of the drug is delivered, at just the right moment. Otherwise, the drugs do little to help (and might even disrupt) consolidation. Indeed, these specifics might lead us to expect that any benefits of the drugs will be difficult to document, and that expectation is correct. One summary of the evidence, for example, concluded that the "use of stimulants in college students did not promote learning or academic achievement. Overall, it is still uncertain whether the medical use of stimulants enhances academic achievement" (Swanson, Wigal & Volkow, 2011, p. 745). Another 2011 paper argues that a conclusion offered by Rasmussen (2008) is still in line with the evidence: "Enhancements with stimulants are hard to demonstrate, especially when compared to caffeine, and seem to relate more to individual perception of increased ability rather than to objective improvement of function" (Elliott & Elliott, 2011).

Where, then, does this leave us? Many people (including your textbook's author!) can do little intellectual work prior to their morning's coffee. Intellectual work *is* "work" and requires an alert brain. Caffeine—a mild stimulant—helps promote this alertness, and so do the prescription stimulants. Whether the prescription stimulants can do more than this—and whether they can promote memory consolidation, or the brain's executive functioning, or some other specific process—is (at best) not yet clear. At the same time, the potential problems associated with the prescription meds are well documented. As a result, most researchers would advise against the use of these pills. The drug benefits are questionable, and their problems are real, and so there are surely better, healthier, safer ways to promote alertness and enhance your mental life.

FOR DISCUSSION

The use of the so-called "cognitive enhancers" raises scientific, political, and legal questions—questions that are made more urgent by the fact that the use of these medications is certainly widespread. Here's one quandary, though, that is surely worth discussing: The essay has highlighted *problems* that may be associated with these medications, and these problems are serious. Even if we hold the problems to the side, however, there's still room for debate about when, how, or whether we should use these drugs.

Let's say that someone named Joe has been diagnosed with ADHD. A medical doctor might argue therefore that some aspects of Joe's brain are "underperforming," and so the doctor might prescribe stimulants that will ramp up these aspects of Joe's brain function, so that they are performing "normally." On the other hand, let's say that Jim's status suggests no diagnosable condition, so his brain seems to be functioning "normally." For Jim, a doctor might hesitate to prescribe stimulants, even if the stimulants might enhance some aspect of Jim's mental life. It would seem, then, that how we use these drugs rests on some notions of what "normal" means, and whether we want to have different approaches to "lifting" someone toward (what we count as) normalcy, and lifting someone above normalcy. Does this seem right to you?

And, again, let's emphasize that this issue is tricky—but set aside for the moment the various problems caused by these drugs. Ultimately, though, our assessment of the drugs has to include all of the relevant factors—including the problems that, for this discussion question, we're holding aside!

For more on this topic

Elliott, G., & Elliott, M. (2011). Pharmacological cognitive enhances: Comment on Smith & Farah (2011). *Psychological Bulletin, 137*, 749–750.

Hills, T., & Hertwig, R. (2011). Why aren't we smarter already: Evolutionary trade-offs and cognitive enhancements. *Current Directions in Psychological Science, 20*, 373–377.

Rasmussen, N. (2008). *On speed: The many lives of amphetamine.* New York, NY: NYU Press.

Smith, M., & Farah, M. (2011). Are prescription stimulants "smart pills"? The epidemiology and cognitive neuroscience of prescription stimulant use by normal healthy individuals. *Psychological Bulletin, 137*, 717–741.

Swanson, J., Wigal, T., & Volkow, N. (2011). Contrast of medical and nonmedical use of stimulant drugs, basis for the distinction, and risk of addiction: Comment on Smith & Farah (2011). *Psychological Bulletin, 137*, 742–748.

Cognitive Psychology and the Law: Detecting Lies

It is obvious that people sometimes lie, and sometimes lie to the police. Of course, the police do all they can to detect this deception, and some police officers are confident that they can tell, during an interview, whether a suspect is lying to them. In truth, however, most people (and most police) aren't very skilled in making this determination. This is one of the reasons that law enforcement often relies on a machine called the *polygraph*, or, as it's more commonly known, the *lie detector.* This device is designed to measure moment-by-moment changes in someone's breathing, heart rate, blood pressure, and amount of perspiration. To use these measurements for lie detection, we rely on the fact that someone who's lying is likely to become anxious about the lie, or tense. These emotional changes, even if carefully hidden by the test subject, are associated with changes in the biological markers measured by the polygraph; thus, by using the polygraph to detect these changes, we detect the lie.

Unfortunately, though, this procedure is of questionable value. On the positive side, polygraphs are surely correct more often than they're incorrect. Even so, the polygraph often fails to detect lies, and—just as bad—the test often indicates that people are lying when they're not. The reason for these errors is simple: Sometimes liars are perfectly calm and not at all tense, and the polygraph will therefore miss their lies; sometimes truth tellers are highly anxious, and the polygraph will pick this up. In addition, it's often possible to "beat the test" by using certain strategies. One strategy is for the test subject to engage in fast-paced mental arithmetic during key parts of the test. (Most polygraph tests compare the subject's state when he's just been asked crucial questions—such as "Did you rob the bank?"—in comparison to his state when he's just been asked neutral questions—such as "What is your name?" If the test subject uses a strategy that increases his arousal during the *neutral* questions, this will make it harder to detect any difference between his state during these questions and during the crucial questions, making it harder to detect lies!)

A different lie-detection technique is less commonly used, but more promising. The *Guilty Knowledge Test* (GKT) doesn't rely on measurements of stress or tension in order to detect the lie. Instead, the test seeks to detect the *cognition* associated with lying. Specifically, the test relies on the fact that in many crimes there will be certain details that no one knows other than the police and the guilty party. This allows the police to ask questions like "Was the injured woman's scarf: (a) red? (b) green? (c) blue? (d) white?" A criminal might refuse to answer, claiming to have no knowledge; but even so, the criminal will almost certainly show an *orienting response* when the correct answer is mentioned. It is as if the criminal cannot help "perking up" in response to the one option that's familiar and cannot help thinking, "Yes, that was it," even though he overtly insists that he does not know the answer.

There are several ways to detect this orienting response; one method involves measurements of electrical activity in the brain, measurements that can be obtained through electrodes placed on the surface of the scalp. With these measurements, we can easily spot the shift in someone's brain waves when the familiar option comes along ("Yes, the scarf was *red*"), even if the criminal sits silently, or denies any knowledge of the crime.

The GKT seems quite promising, but the test does have a limitation: It can be run only if the police can identify an adequate number of test items (i.e., facts that the perpetrator would certainly know but that no one else would); the accuracy of the GKT falls if the number of test items is too small. Even with this limit, however, the GKT is being adopted by some law enforcement agencies, both in the United States and elsewhere.

Finally, one further type of biologically based lie detection has been proposed but is still unproven. Specifically, a number of investigators (and a handful of private companies, such as "No Lie MRI") suggest that fMRI scans can distinguish liars from truth tellers. Evidence based on this procedure has been offered in a number of U.S. court cases and has several times been *rejected* by the courts, with judges ruling that this technique is so far unreliable and unproven. For the moment, therefore, this type of brain measurement remains an intriguing, but so far undocumented, possible means of spotting lies.

Where does all of this leave us? Currently, the GKT seems our most promising option as a path toward lie detection. More broadly, though, it seems certain that our increasing understanding of the brain will aid law-enforcement professionals in their effort toward detecting lies, and this is a domain in which scientific developments will surely be translated into pragmatic tools.

FOR DISCUSSION

Imagine that you are in charge of law enforcement for your city or for your state or province. Given the information you just read, what policy or procedural changes would you want to consider—things you should start doing or things you should stop doing—to improve your agency's capacity for detecting lies? Or would you delay taking action until more data were available on this topic? What sorts of data?

You might also give some thought to the fact that most tests of the GKT are done *in the laboratory*: Volunteers in these studies are encouraged to lie about certain points, and then the researchers try to detect these lies by using the GKT. But, of course, volunteers in a lab might be different from perpetrators of actual crimes; thus, the GKT might detect (relatively minor) lies in the lab, but it might not detect (much more consequential) lies involving a real crime. What sort of steps might you take to make the lab studies as realistic as possible, in order to maximize the chances that the lab data could be generalized to real-world settings? What sorts of studies might you design "in the field"—perhaps with suspects in real criminal cases—that might tell you if the GKT works as proposed in an actual criminal investigation?

For more on this topic

Ben-Shakhar, G., Bar-Hillel, M., & Kremnitzer, M. (2002). Trial by polygraph: Reconsidering the use of the Guilty Knowledge Technique in court. *Law and Human Behavior, 26,* 527–541.

Honts, C., et al. (1994). Mental and physical countermeasures reduce the accuracy of polygraph tests. *Journal of Applied Psychology, 79,* 252–259.

Vrij, A., Granhag, P., Mann, S., & Leal, S. (2011). Outsmarting the liars: Toward a cognitive lie detection approach. *Current Directions in Psychological Science, 20,* 28–32.

CHAPTER 3

Recognizing Objects

Demonstrations

3.1 Adelson's Brightness Illusion

The eyeball is sometimes compared to a camera: Both have a lens, both have a photosensitive surface, and so on. This comparison, however, is misleading, because a camera is largely a passive device, faithfully recording whatever is in view. It doesn't select; it doesn't supplement; it doesn't interpret. Our visual system, in contrast, is not at all passive. Instead, it actively shapes the input—altering some bits, emphasizing other bits, adding information where needed.

The active nature of vision is evident in many ways—including cases in which the visual system *distorts* the input in a fashion that leads to an illusion. For example, carefully examine the figure below (designed by Edward Adelson). Look at the color of the "middle square" (third row, third column) and also the color of the square marked with the arrow. See how different they are? Actually, the two are the exact same shade on the page. If you don't believe this, try blocking out the rest of the figure—with pieces of paper, perhaps, or your fingers—so that all you can see is these two squares. When they are isolated in this way, it becomes clear that these two squares are, in fact, the exact same brightness.

What produces this illusion? Two factors contribute. First, the "middle" square is surrounded by dark squares, and these, by contrast, make it look brighter. The square marked with the arrow, on the other hand, is surrounded by brighter regions, and these, by contrast, make it look darker. This contrast effect depends on mechanisms similar to the ones that produce the illusion in Demonstration 2.4 for Chapter 2 in this workbook.

In addition, the illusion on this page introduces a new factor. In this figure, the shadow cast by the cylinder falls on the middle square. It's a simple inference, therefore, that this square is receiving less illumination than squares *not* in this shadow. Once you've made this inference, though, you try to take the difference in illumination into account, in interpreting the scene: In essence, you say to yourself, "If it appears in this way with so little light shining on it, then what would it look like if it were brightly lit?" This leads you to adjust your perception of its brightness, causing it to seem brighter than it actually is.

The illusion here is powerful, and so it serves as a compelling reminder of how much *interpretive work* we do with visual input.

Demonstration adapted from Adelson, E. (2000). Lightness perception and lightness illusions. In M. Gazzaniga (Ed.), *The new cognitive neurosciences* (2nd ed., pp. 339–351). Cambridge, MA: MIT Press.

3.2   A Size Illusion and a Motion Illusion

In Demonstration 3.1, you made an inference about how strongly a target object was illuminated, and then you took this illumination into account in judging the *brightness* of the target: "If it appears as it does, even though it's illuminated only weakly, then its brightness must be great."

Other aspects of perception show the same pattern: In looking at the drawing on the next page you make an inference about *distance*, and you're likely to perceive that the top ghoul is farther from you than the bottom ghoul. You then take this distance into account in judging *size*. It's as if you were reasoning, "If the top ghoul appears as it does, even though it's far away, it must be quite large!" And thus you perceive the top ghoul as being larger than the bottom one, even though they're the exact same size on the page.

A related illusion requires a bit of work on your part—but the effect is worth it! Follow the directions shown on p. 29 to assemble the three-dimensional dragon. Then, once the dragon is assembled, set it on a desk, and watch the dragon carefully as you slowly move left or right. Odds are good that you will get a powerful motion illusion—so that the dragon moves as you move. To get a good sense of the illusion, you can also view a movie of the illusion online: http://www.grand-illusions.com/images/articles/opticalillusions/dragon_illusion/dragon_illusion.wmv. (You can also find the movie by doing a search for "dragon illusion movie.")

The dragon provides a clear case in which you, the perceiver, are *interpreting* (and, as it turns out, *misinterpreting*) the input. Your visual system (mistakenly) assumes the

dragon to be convex (bulging toward you) rather than concave, and this is an understandable error. (After all, how many hollow dragons have you seen in your lifetime? Or, more realistically, how many concave reptiles of any sort have you seen?) But then your visual system uses this faulty information to interpret the pattern of motion. Here your reasoning is along the lines of "The dragon is convex. I can see how my view of the dragon changes as I change my viewing position. How can I make sense of these two facts? The most likely explanation is that the dragon is moving as I move."

As it turns out, this interpretation is entirely consistent with the information that's reaching your eyes. If the dragon really were convex, and really were moving as you move, then the stimulation that would reach you would be virtually identical to what you're receiving from the concave stationary dragon actually in your view. In that sense, your perception of the figure is entirely reasonable. The problem, though, is the mistake you made at the start: registering the dragon as bulging outward when it's really hollow. Once you made that mistake, the perception of moving-as-you-move was, in truth, the only way to make sense of the input!

Indeed, what's in play here is a standard "recipe" for producing many perceptual illusions: When you're perceiving one aspect of a scene, you routinely need to take other aspects of the scene into account. Thus, when you perceive brightness, you first need to ask how strongly illuminated the surface is; you then take the illumination into account in judging the brightness. When you perceive size, you first need to ask how far away the object is; you then take distance into account. When you perceive motion, you first need to ask how the object is arranged in space (is it convex or concave?), and then you take that information into account. In each case, you can think of the sequence as a bit of "if . . . then . . ." reasoning: "If *that* is the illumination, then *this* must be the brightness"; "If *that* is the distance, then *this* must be the size." But, of course, if you make an error in the first step in this sequence—that is, if you get the "if" part wrong—then you're guaranteed to go off track in your perception. You will, in effect, be drawing a conclusion from a bad premise, and that usually means a bad conclusion. It's this simple logic that underlies many of the perceptual illusions, but this same logic also highlights the interpretive *activity* you engage in whenever you perceive.

3.3   Features and Feature Combinations

The chapter discusses the importance of *features* in your recognition of objects, and this priority of features is, in fact, easy to demonstrate. In each of the squares below, find the target.

Most people find the search in Square A (finding the *O*) to be extremely easy; the search in Square B (finding the *L*) is harder. Why is this? In Square A, all you need to do is search for the feature "curve" (or "roundness"). That single feature is enough to identify the target, and searching for a single feature is fast and easy. In contrast, the target in Square B is not defined in terms of a single feature. The target (the *L*) and the distractor items (the *T*'s) have the *same features* (one horizontal + one vertical); the target is distinguished from the distractors only in how the features are assembled. Therefore, you can't locate the target in B simply by hunting for a single feature; instead, you need to take an additional step: You need to think about how the features are put together, and that's a slower, more effortful process.

The data pattern becomes even clearer in Squares C and D. In Square C, the target (again, defined by a single feature) seems to "pop out" at you, and your search in C is just as fast as it was in A. In other words, when hunting for a single feature, you can hunt through eleven items (Square C) as quickly as you can hunt through four items (Square A).

In Square D, however, the target doesn't "pop out." Here you're searching for a feature *combination*, and so you need to examine the forms one by one. As a result, Square D (with eleven shapes to examine) takes more time than Square B (with just four).

Demonstration adapted from Thornton, T., & Gilden, D. (2007). Parallel and serial processes in visual search. *Psychological Review, 114,* 71–103.

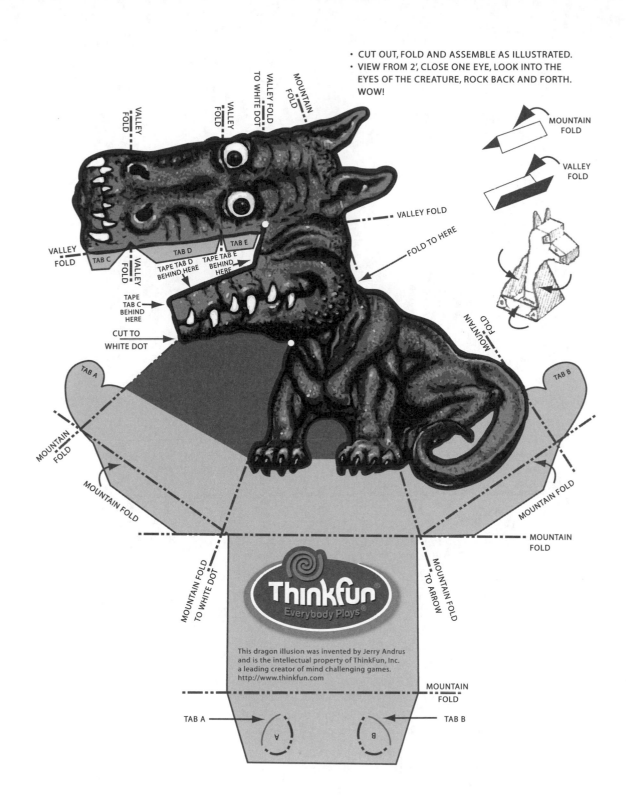

- CUT OUT, FOLD AND ASSEMBLE AS ILLUSTRATED.
- VIEW FROM 2', CLOSE ONE EYE, LOOK INTO THE EYES OF THE CREATURE, ROCK BACK AND FORTH. WOW!

MOUNTAIN FOLD

VALLEY FOLD

VALLEY FOLD

MOUNTAIN FOLD TO WHITE DOT

VALLEY FOLD

VALLEY FOLD

VALLEY FOLD

VALLEY FOLD

TAB C

TAB D

TAB E

TAPE TAB D BEHIND HERE

TAPE TAB E BEHIND HERE

TAPE TAB C BEHIND HERE

CUT TO WHITE DOT

VALLEY FOLD

FOLD TO HERE

MOUNTAIN FOLD

TAB A

TAB B

MOUNTAIN FOLD

MOUNTAIN FOLD

MOUNTAIN FOLD

MOUNTAIN FOLD

MOUNTAIN FOLD TO WHITE DOT

MOUNTAIN FOLD TO ARROW

MOUNTAIN FOLD

Thinkfun
Everybody Plays®

This dragon illusion was invented by Jerry Andrus and is the intellectual property of ThinkFun, Inc. a leading creator of mind challenging games.
http://www.thinkfun.com

MOUNTAIN FOLD

TAB A

TAB B

A

B

3.4   Inferences in Reading

The role of *inferences* within the normal process of reading is easy to demonstrate. Indeed, you make these inferences even when you don't want to—that is, even when you're trying to read carefully. To see this, count how many times the letter *F* appears in the following passage:

> FINISHED FILES ARE THE RESULT
>
> OF YEARS OF SCIENTIFIC STUDY
>
> COMBINED WITH THE EXPERIENCE
>
> OF YEARS.

The correct answer is *six*; did you find them all?

Many people miss one or two or even three of the *F*'s. Why is this?

In normal reading, you do not look at every letter, identifying it before you move on to the next. If you did, reading would be impossibly slow. (We can only move our eyes four or five times each second. If we looked at every letter, we'd only be able to read about five characters per second, or three hundred characters per minute. For most material, we actually read at a rate roughly 500% faster than this.)

How, then, do you read? You actually *skip* many of the characters on the page, letting your eyes hop along each line of print, relying on inference to fill in the information that your eyes are skipping over. As the text chapter describes, this process is made possible by the "inferential" character of your recognition network, and it is enormously efficient. However, the process also risks error—because your inferences sometimes are wrong, and because you can sometimes miss something (a specific word or letter) that you are hunting for—as in this demonstration.

The process of skipping and making inferences is especially likely when the words in the text are *predictable*. If (for example) a sentence uses the phrase "Birds of a feather flock together," you surely know what the last word in this sequence will be without looking at it carefully. As a result, this is a word you're likely to skip over as you read along. By the same logic, the word "of" is often quite predictable in many sentences, and so you probably missed one of the three *F*'s appearing in the word "of." (The *f* in "of" is also hard to spot for another reason: Many people search for the *f* by *sounding out* the sentence and listening for the [f] sound. Of course, "of" is pronounced as though it ended with a *v*, not an *f*, and so it doesn't contain the sound people are hunting for.)

Note in addition that this process of skipping and inferring is so well practiced and so routine that you cannot "turn off" the process, even when you want to. This is why proofreading is usually difficult, as you skip by (and so overlook) your own errors. It is also why this demonstration works—because you have a hard time forcing yourself into a letter-by-letter examination of the text, even when you want to.

Applying Cognitive Psychology

Research Methods: Dealing With Confounds

Imagine an experiment in which research participants are asked to recognize letter strings briefly presented on a computer screen—let's say for 30 milliseconds—followed by a mask. In the first 50 trials, the letter strings are random sequences ("okbo," "pmla," and so on). In the next 50 trials, the letter strings are all common four-letter words ("book," "lamp," "tree," and so on). Let's say that the participants are able, on average, to identify 30% of the random sequences and 65% of the words. This is a large difference; what should we conclude from it?

In fact, we can conclude nothing from this (fictional) experiment, because the procedure just described is flawed. The data tell us that participants did much better with the words, but why is this? One possibility is that words are, in fact, easier to recognize than nonwords. A different possibility, however, is that we are instead seeing an effect of *practice*: Maybe the participants did better with the word trials not because words are special, but simply because the words came later in the experiment, after the participants had gained some experience with the procedure. Conversely, perhaps the participants did worse with the nonwords not because they were hard to recognize, but because they were presented before any practice or warm-up.

To put this in technical terms, the experiment just described is *invalid*—that is, it does not measure what it is intended to measure—namely, the difference between words and nonwords. The experiment is invalid because a *confound* is present—an extra variable that could have caused the observed data pattern. The confound in this particular case is the *sequence*, and the confound makes the data ambiguous: Maybe words were better recognized because they're words, *or* maybe the words were better recognized simply because they came second. With no way in these data to choose between these interpretations, we cannot say which is the correct interpretation, and hence we can draw no conclusions from the experiment.

How should this experiment have been designed? One possibility is to *counterbalance* the sequence of trials: For half of the participants, we would show the words first, then the random letters. For the other half of the participants, we would use the reverse order—random letters, then words. This setup doesn't eliminate the effect of practice, but it ensures that practice has the same impact on both conditions. Specifically, with this setup, practice would favor one condition half the time and the other condition half the time. Thus, the contribution of practice would be the same for both conditions, and so it could not be the cause of a *difference* between the conditions.

If this point isn't perfectly clear, consider an analogy: Imagine a championship football game between the Rockets and the Bulldogs. As it turns out, there's a strong wind blowing across the field, and the wind is coming from *behind* the Rockets. The wind helps the Rockets throw and kick the ball farther, giving them an unfair advantage. The referees have no way to eliminate the wind. What they can do, though, is have the teams take turns in which direction they're moving. For one quarter of the game, the Rockets have their backs to the wind; then, in the next quarter, the direction of play is reversed, so it's the Bulldogs who have their backs to the wind, and so on. (This is, of course, how football games operate.) That way, the wind doesn't favor one team over the other, and so, when the Rockets win, we can't say it was because of the wind; in other words, the wind could not have caused the difference between the teams.

Returning to our word/nonword experiment, we know how it would turn out when properly done: Words are, in fact, easier to recognize. Our point here, though, lies in what it takes for the experiment to be "properly done." In this and in all experiments, we need to remove confounds so that we can be sure what lies beneath the data pattern. Several techniques are available for dealing with confounds; we've mentioned just one of them (counterbalancing) here. The key, however, is that the confounds must be removed; only then can we legitimately draw conclusions from the experiment.

FOR DISCUSSION

Imagine that your friend Peter is convinced that it's easier to read print written on *yellow* paper than it is to read print written on ordinary *white* paper. You think this is wrong, but you decide to put Peter's hypothesis to the test. You therefore print a newspaper editorial on white paper and a news article on yellow paper. You recruit ten friends, and first you have them read the editorial (on white paper), and then you test their comprehension of it. Next, you have them read the news article (on yellow paper), and you test their comprehension of it. You find that they have a better comprehension for the news article, and so you conclude (to your surprise!) that Peter is correct.

Is this conclusion justified? Or are there confounds here that make it impossible to draw any conclusions from this experiment? If there are confounds, how could you counterbalance the experiment so that the confounds are no longer a problem? (Be careful here, because there are *two* confounds in the experiment just described; how could you arrange the counterbalancing to make sure that *both* confounds are removed?)

We should also mention that the particular confounds you encounter can vary from one experiment to the next. However, some confounds come up over and over, and so it's good to be alert to them. One of these is *sequence*: which test comes first, and which comes later. Another common confound derives from *stimulus differences*, in which one condition involves easier materials, and one involves harder materials. A third common confound is the *participants' expectations*: they might come into one condition with a certain set of biases or a certain motivation, and they might come into another condition with a different perspective. A fourth is *gender*, or *intelligence level*, or *any other background factor* that shapes who the participants are; these factors should be matched in the experimental and control groups. Yet another is *manner of recruitment*: It is problematic if one group of participants is filled with volunteers and the other is filled with people who are forced to be in the experiment (e.g., as a course requirement). This could easily shape the attitudes and motivations that the participants bring to the study. Can you think of other common confounds?

Cognitive Psychology and Education: Speed-Reading

Students usually have many pages of reading to do each week, and they often wish they could read more quickly. Can we help them? Can we, in particular, help people to speed-read? In fact, it's easy to teach people this skill, and with just a little practice you can increase your reading speed by 50% or more. However, it's important to understand why speed-reading works, because this will help you see when speed-reading is a good idea—and when it is a disaster!

The text chapter emphasizes that people don't need to look at every letter when they're reading a word. This is because words follow predictable patterns, and so, having seen some of the letters, you can easily guess what the remaining letters have to be. Thus, you can speed up your word recognition by skipping over some letters, relying on inference to fill in what you've skipped.

In the chapter, we describe how these claims apply to the reading of single words—with the recognition network often able to "infer" letters that weren't clearly seen. Similar claims, however, apply to larger units of text—sentences, or paragraphs, or whole pages. These, too, follow predictable patterns, and so, having read a few words, you're often able to guess what the next words will be. Once again, this allows you to speed up your reading, by skipping along and relying on rapid inference to cover the skips.

This process is essential for normal reading. If you didn't make these skips, if—instead—you literally looked at every word (and, indeed, every letter) on the page, your reading would be much slower than it currently is. And the same process is central for speed-reading: Courses that teach you how to speed-read actually rely on simple strategies that help you to *skip more*, as you move down the page, and, with this, to increase your use of inference. As a result, speed-reading is not really "reading faster"; it is instead "reading *less* and inferring more."

How does this process work? First, before you speed-read some text, you need to lay the groundwork for the inference process—so that you'll make the inferences efficiently and accurately. Specifically, before you speed-read a text, you should flip through it quickly. Look at the figures and the figure captions. If there's a summary at the end, or a preview at the beginning, read that. If there are headings and subheadings scattered through the text, read those. Each of these steps will give you a broad sense of what the material is all about, and that broad sense will prepare you to make rapid—and more sensible—inferences about the material.

Second, make sure you do rely on inference; otherwise, you'll slide back into your habits of looking too carefully at the page and not relying enough on inference. To achieve this, read for a while holding an index card just under the line you are reading, or perhaps using your finger to slide along the lines of print to mark what you are reading at that moment. These procedures establish a physical marker of where you are on the page, a "pointer" that keeps track of where you are as you move from word to word. This use of a pointer will become easy and automatic after a few minutes of practice, and once it does, you're ready for the next (and key) step.

You've just practiced "following along" with the index card or your finger. What we're now going to do is reverse this, so that the marker isn't *following* your eye-position, it's instead *leading* your eye-position. Specifically, try moving the index card a bit more quickly than you have so far—or, if you've been sliding your finger along, try moving it a bit more quickly. In either case, try to move your eyes to "keep up" with this marker. This procedure will feel awkward at first, but it will become easier with just a bit of practice. Don't try to go too fast; you'll know if you are moving too swiftly if you suddenly realize that you don't have a clue what's on the page. Move quickly enough so that you feel you have to hustle along to keep up with your pointer, but don't move so quickly that you lose track of what you're reading.

You may want to practice this for a couple of days, and as you do, you'll learn to move the pointer faster and faster. As a result, you'll learn to increase your reading speed by 30%, or 40%, or more. But let's be clear about what's going on here: You are not learning (as ads sometimes claim) to "see more in a single glance." (That wouldn't be possible unless we rewire your eyeballs, and that's not going to happen.) Instead, you are simply shifting the balance between how much input you're taking in and how much you're filling in the gaps with sophisticated guesswork.

On this basis, you can easily see that speed-reading is a good bet if you are reading redundant or repetitive material; that's a situation in which your inferences about the skipped words are likely to be correct, and so you might as well use the faster process of making inferences, rather than the slower process of looking at individual words. By the same logic, though, speed-reading is a bad bet if the material is hard to understand; in that case, you won't be able to figure out the skipped words via inference, and then speed-reading will hurt you. Speed-reading is also a bad bet if you're trying to appreciate an author's style. Imagine, for example, that you speed-read Shakespeare's *Romeo and Juliet*. You probably will be able to speed-read and make inferences about the plot. (After all, the plot is simple: Romeo and Juliet are in love. Their families oppose the romance. In the end, everyone dies.) But you probably won't be able to make inferences about the specific words you're skipping over, and thus you won't be able to make inferences about the *language* that Shakespeare actually used (unless you happen to be just as good a writer as Shakespeare was). And, of course, if you miss the language of Shakespeare and miss the poetry, you've missed the point.

Do practice speed-reading, and do use it when text-guided inference will serve you well. This will allow you to zoom through many texts, and it will dramatically decrease the time you need for at least some of your reading. But do not speed-read material that is technical, filled with specific details that you'll need, or beautiful for its language. In those cases, what you want is to pay attention to the words on the page, and not rely on your own inferences.

FOR DISCUSSION

In speed-reading, you try to take in *less* information from the page and to rely on inference to fill in what you've skipped. In other settings, though, you want to do the opposite—to rely less on inference, and to carefully track what's on the page! Can you think of some circumstances in which you want this latter strategy—so that you're more attentive to what's actually in the print in front of your eyes? (An obvious hint comes from think-

ing through the circumstances in which speed-reading is a good idea and asking yourself what the "opposite" circumstances might involve.)

What strategies can you use when you do want to read more carefully—i.e., rely less on skipping and inference? One strategy is to read the passage out loud; can you figure out why this helps? Can you think of other strategies that would promote more careful reading?

Cognitive Psychology and the Law:
Cross-Race Identification

In Chapter 3, we argue that people use two different mechanisms for recognizing the stimuli they encounter. One mechanism is *feature based*, and it works by first identifying the input's parts. These parts are then assembled into larger and larger wholes until the entire input is identified. The other recognition mechanism is *configuration based*. It is less concerned with individual features, but it is exquisitely sensitive to the overall arrangement in the input.

The second of these mechanisms, relying on configurations, is crucial when we are recognizing faces, but we also use it in other settings: Expert bird-watchers, for example, seem to use this mechanism when making distinctions among different types of birds; expert dog-show judges rely on it to recognize individual dogs. Overall, it seems that people use the configuration-based mechanism whenever two factors are in place: First, this is the system people use when they are identifying specific individuals (Fred vs. Sam; this particular dog vs. that one); second, this system comes into play when people are making these identifications within an enormously familiar category. Thus, it's *expert* bird-watchers and expert dog-show judges who show this pattern; novices instead rely on features (and not configurations) when telling dogs or birds apart.

How is this pertinent to law enforcement? Imagine that you witness a crime. From the information you provide, the police develop a hypothesis about who the perpetrator might have been. They place the suspect's photo on a page together with five other photos and show you this "photospread." Will you recognize the perpetrator within this group? If so, this provides important evidence confirming the police officers' suspicions.

In this situation, your ability to identify the perpetrator depends on many factors, including the suspect's *race*. This is because people are much better at recognizing individuals from their own race than they are in recognizing individuals from other races. Indeed, if the criminal is present in the photospread, witnesses are roughly 50% more likely to miss the person if the identification is across races (e.g., a White person identifying an Asian person, or an Asian person identifying a Black person) than if it is within their race. Likewise, if the criminal is *not* present in the photospread, the risk of the witness falsely identifying someone who's actually innocent is roughly 50% higher in cross-race identification.

Why should this be? We have emphasized that the recognition system people use is configuration-based only when they're making an identification within an enormously familiar category—and the fact is that most people are extremely familiar with faces from their own race, but less so with faces from other races. As a result, people can rely on the configuration-based mechanism when making same-race identifications, and so they benefit from this system's sensitivity and sophistication. When making cross-race identifications, however, people are less sensitive to the face's configuration. They therefore have to base their identification on the face's features, and it turns out that this is an appreciably less effective means of identifying individual faces. As a result, cross-race identifications end up being less accurate. Apparently, then, courts need to be especially cautious in interpreting cross-race identifications.

But does every witness show this pattern? Or, perhaps, is the disadvantage with cross-race faces smaller for people who live in a racially integrated environment? Questions like these continue to be the subject of research, with some studies indicating that more contact between the races does, in fact, diminish the difference between same-race and cross-race identifications. However, the results of this research are uneven, making it unclear how (or whether) cross-race contact influences the effect. In the meantime, it's already clear that this issue may help the courts in deciding when to put full trust in a witness's identification and when to be wary of an identification's accuracy.

FOR DISCUSSION

Right after a crime, police officers usually ask witnesses to *describe* the perpetrator. Then, days later, the police show the witnesses a *photo* of the alleged perpetrator, together with five other photos, and ask the witnesses to select the perpetrator from this group. Of course, witnesses vary in how accurate their verbal descriptions are, but—perhaps surprisingly—there is little relationship between how accurate the description is and the probability, later on, that the witness will make an accurate identification. Sometimes the description is wrong on many points, but the witness recognizes the perpetrator's photo anyhow; sometimes the description is relatively accurate, but the witness does not recognize the photo.

Given what you know about feature-based and configuration-based recognition, can you explain this pattern? Why isn't there a closer correspondence between the accuracy of the description and the likelihood of recognizing the photo? In addition, what is your hypothesis about how this pattern might change in cross-race identifications? In other words, we can, for *same-race identifications*, examine the relationship between (1) accuracy of verbal description, and (2) likelihood of accurately recognizing a photo; then we can examine the same relationship for *cross-race identifications*. Would you expect a difference? (In fact, evidence suggests there is indeed a difference here; can you figure out what it is?)

For more on this topic

Bukach, C., Cottle, J., Ubiwa, J., & Miller, S. (2012). Individuation experience predicts other-race effects in holistic processing for both Caucasian and Black participants. *Cognition, 123,* 319–324.

Meissner, C. A., & Brigham, J. C. (2001). Thirty years of investigating the own-race bias in memory for faces: A meta-analytic review. *Psychology, Public Policy, and Law, 7,* 3–35.

Pezdek, K., Blandon-Gitlin, I., & Moore, C. (2003). Children's face recognition memory: More evidence for the cross-race effect. *Journal of Applied Psychology, 88,* 760–763.

Rhodes, M., & Anastasi, J. (2012). The own-age bias in face recognition: A meta-analytic and theoretical review. *Psychological Bulletin, 138,* 146–174.

CHAPTER 4

Paying Attention

Demonstrations

4.1   Shadowing

Many classic studies of attention involved a task called *shadowing*. The instructions for this task go like this:

> You are about to hear a voice reading some English text. Your job is to repeat what you hear, word for word, as you hear it. In other words, you'll turn yourself into an "echo box," following along with the message as it arrives and repeating it back, echoing as many of the words as you can.

As a first step, you should try this task. You can do this with a friend and have him or her read to you out of a book while you shadow what your friend is saying. If you don't have a cooperative friend, try shadowing a voice on a news broadcast, a podcast, or any other recording of a voice speaking in English.

Most people find this task relatively easy, but they also figure out rather quickly that there are steps they can take to make the task even easier. One obvious adjustment is to shadow *in a quiet voice*, because otherwise your own shadowing will drown out the voice you're trying to hear. Another adjustment is in the *rhythm* of the shadowing: People often settle into a pattern of listening to a phrase, rapidly spewing out that phrase, listening to the next phrase, rapidly spewing it out, and so on. This pattern of phrase-by-phrase shadowing has several advantages. Among them, your thinking about the input as a series of *phrases* (rather than as individual *words*) allows you to rely to some extent on *inferences* about what is being said—so that you can literally get away with listening less, and that makes the overall task of shadowing appreciably easier.

Of course, these inferences, and the whole strategy of phrase-by-phrase shadowing, depend on your being able to detect the *structure* within the incoming message—providing another example in which your perception doesn't just "receive" the input; it also *organizes* the input. How much does this matter? If you have a cooperative friend, you can try this variation on shadowing: Have your friend read to you from a book,

39

but ask your friend to read the material *backwards*. (So, for the previous sentence, your friend would literally say, "backwards material the read to friend your ask . . ."). Your friend will probably need a bit of practice to do this peculiar task, but, once he or she has mastered it, you can try shadowing this backwards English.

With backwards English, you'll find it difficult (if not impossible) to keep track of the structure of the material—and therefore much harder to locate the boundaries between phrases, and much harder to make inferences about what you're hearing. Is shadowing of this backwards material harder than shadowing of "normal" material?

Now that you're practiced at shadowing, you're ready for the third step. Have one friend read normally (not backwards!) to you, and have a second friend read *something else* to you. (Ask the second friend to choose the reading, so that you don't know in advance what it is.) Again, if you don't have cooperative friends nearby, you can do the same with any broadcast or recorded voices. (You can play one voice on your radio and another from your computer, possibly from a podcast. Or you can have your friend do one voice while the TV news provides another voice. Do whichever of these is most convenient for you.) Your job is to shadow the first friend for a minute or so. When you're done, here are some questions:

- What was the second voice saying? Odds are good that you don't know.
- Could you at least hear when the second voice started and stopped? If the second voice coughed, or giggled, or hesitated in the middle of reading, did you hear that? Odds are good that you did.

In general, people tend to be oblivious to the *content* of the unattended message, but they hear the physical attributes of this message perfectly well—and it's that pattern of results that we need to explain. The textbook chapter walks through the theories you'll need to explain these observations.

4.2   Color-Changing Card Trick

The phenomenon of "change blindness" is easily demonstrated in the laboratory, but it also has many parallels outside of the lab. For example, stage magicians often rely on (some version of) change blindness in their performances—with the audience amazed by objects seeming to materialize or dematerialize, or with an assistant mysteriously transformed into an entirely different person. In most of these cases, though, the "magic" involves little beyond the audience's failing to notice straightforward swaps that had, in truth, taken place right before their eyes.

A similar effect is demonstrated in a popular video on YouTube. You can find the video by using your search engine to find "color changing card trick," or you can try this address: www.youtube.com/watch?v=voAntzB7EwE. This demonstration was created by a wonderfully playful British psychologist named Richard Wiseman. Several of Wiseman's videos are available on YouTube, but you can find others on a website that Wiseman maintains: www.quirkology.com.

Watch the video carefully. Were you fooled? Did you show the standard change-blindness pattern: failing to notice large-scale changes in the visual input?

Notice also that you—like the audience at a magic performance—knew in advance that someone was trying to fool you with a switch that you would not notice. You were, therefore, presumably on your guard—extra-vigilant, trying not to be fooled. Even so, the odds are good that you were still fooled, and this is by itself an important fact. It tells us that being extra careful is no protection against change blindness, and neither is an effort toward being especially observant. These points are crucial for the stage magician, who is able to fool the people in the audience despite their best efforts toward detecting the tricks and penetrating the illusions.

These same points tell us something about the nature of *attention*: It is not especially useful, it seems, just to "try hard to pay attention." Likewise, *instructions* to "pay close attention" can, in many circumstances have no effect at all. In order to promote attention, people usually need some information about what exactly they should pay attention *to*. Indeed, if someone told you, before the video, to pay attention to the key (changing) elements, do you think you'd be fooled?

(And, by the way, for more videos showing related effects, search the Internet using the key words "invisible gorilla" and follow the links to the various demonstrations.)

4.3   The Control of Eye Movements

The chapter discusses movements of *spatial attention* and emphasizes that these movements are separate from the overt movements of your eyes. The main evidence for this lies in timing: You can shift attention much more rapidly than you can move your eyes.

Nonetheless, movements of the eyes are crucial for your pickup of information from the world. There are several reasons for this, including the fact (discussed in Chapter 2) that you can only see detail in a small portion of the visual world—namely: the portion that is currently falling on your foveas. You therefore have to move your eyes around in order to bring different bits of the visual world onto the fovea. Thus, by looking first *here* and then *there*, you gradually pick up detail from many positions in the world before you.

But how do you decide how to move your eyes? What guides these movements? Part of the answer lies in the (not-detailed) information you pick up from the edges of your vision; you use this information to decide where to look next.

To demonstrate this point, try reading the following three paragraphs. You can, if you wish, time yourself: How long do you need for the first paragraph? For the second? The third? Or, without timing, you can just get a sense of which paragraph is easier to read, and which is harder.

Paragraph 1:

This is how print normally appears, with a mix of lower- and upper-case letters, and spaces between the letters. As your eye moves along these lines, you can see, at the edge of your vision, the shapes and lengths of the upcoming words. This is fairly crude information, and certainly doesn't tell you what the upcoming words are. Nonetheless, this information is useful for you, because it helps you to plan your eye movements, as you decide where you're going to point your eyes after your next saccade.

Paragraph 2:

Here•we•have•removed•the•spaces•between•the•words.•We•haven't•blurred•everything•together•Instead,•we•have•inserted•a•character•in•between•the•words.•As•a•result,•it's•now•difficult•for•you•to•see,•in•your•peripheral•vision,•where•the•boundaries•between•words•are•located,•and•this•makes•it•difficult•for•you•to•see,•in•peripheral•vision,•whether•the•upcoming•words•are•long•or•short.•As•a•result,•you•can't•use•the•length•of•the•upcoming•words•as•a•guide•to•your•eye•movements.•Does•this•affect•your•reading?

Paragraph 3:

NOW, WE'VE LEFT THE SPACES BETWEEN THE WORDS, BUT HAVE SHIFTED ALL THE TYPE TO CAPITAL LETTERS. WITH LOWER-CASE LETTERS, WORDS OFTEN HAVE A DISTINCTIVE SHAPE, THANKS TO THE FACT THAT SOME LETTERS DANGLE DOWN BELOW THE LINE OF PRINT, WHILE OTHER STICK UP ABOVE THE LINE OF PRINT. ONCE THE WORDS ARE ALL CAPITALIZED, THESE DISTINCTIONS ARE ELIMINATED, AND ALL WORDS HAVE THE SAME RECTANGULAR SHAPE. HERE, THEREFORE, YOU CAN'T USE THE SHAPE OF THE UPCOMING WORDS AS A GUIDE TO YOUR EYE MOVEMENTS. DOES THIS MATTER?

Most people need more time to read Paragraphs 2 and 3, compared to Paragraph 1. There are actually several reasons for this, but part of the explanation lies in the fact that you use both the spaces between words *and* the "shape" of upcoming words to guide your eye movements. You might think about this the next time YOU CONSIDER HANDING IN A PAPER, OR USING HEADINGS IN A PAPER, ENTIRELY IN CAPS—YOU'RE ACTUALLY MAKING THOSE MATERIALS MORE DIFFICULT FOR YOUR READER!

4.4   Automaticity and the Stroop Effect

The chapter describes the classic version of the Stroop effect, in which you are looking at words but trying not to read them, and trying instead to name the color of ink in which the words are printed. However, there are many variations on this effect—cases in which your well-practiced (and therefore automatic) habits interfere with your intentions. For example, imagine a task in which you have to say out loud whether words are at the top or bottom of a computer screen, and you see the word "top" printed at the bottom of the screen. Or imagine a task in which you have to say whether a voice belongs to a male or a female, and you hear a woman's voice pronouncing the word "male." These setups are likely to cause interference, and your responses will be appreciably slower than they would have been if you were judging the position of some random letters on the computer screen, or if the woman's voice pronounced some irrelevant word.

Here's a different variation on the Stroop effect. If you like, you can collect some data with this demonstration by timing how long you need for the various conditions. Even without timing, though, you'll easily detect which conditions are easier, and which are harder.

Your task here is to count how many items there are in a row, and to say the count out loud. Therefore, if you see these two rows:

* * * *

\$ \$ \$

you would say out loud "four, three" (because there are four asterisks, and then three dollar signs).

How many items are in each row?	How about these rows?
# #	4 4
? ? ? ?	2 2 2 2
&	3
& &	3 3
/ / / /	1 1 1 1
#	4
? ?	2 2
/ / /	1 1 1
# # #	4 4 4
& & & &	3 3 3 3
?	2
/ /	1 1

Try this task, first, with the left column. How easy was this task? Were you able to go quickly? Did you make errors? Then try this with the right column. Again, how easy was it, and how quickly did you go? Did you make errors? You'll probably find the second task (with the right-hand column) much more difficult, because you have an automatic habit of *reading* the numerals rather than *counting* them—one more demonstration of the family of effects first documented in 1935 by Stroop.

Applying Cognitive Psychology

Research Methods: The Power of Random Assignment

Is it hazardous to talk on a cell phone while driving? Many people believe it is, and they point to evidence showing that people who use a cell phone while driving are more likely to be involved in accidents, compared to people who do not use a cell phone while driving. Perhaps surprisingly, this association—between increased accident risk and cell-phone use—stays in place even if we focus only on "hands-free" phones. The problem, it seems, is not that you take one hand off the steering wheel to hold the phone. Instead, the problem seems to be the phone conversation itself. But we need to ask: Is this evidence persuasive?

Actually, the accident statistics are ambiguous—open to more than one interpretation. Being alert to this sort of ambiguity is crucial for science, because if results can be interpreted in more than one way, then we can draw no conclusions from them. What is the ambiguity in this case? Perhaps talking on a cell phone while driving is, in fact, distracting and increases the likelihood of an accident. But, as an alternative, perhaps drivers who use cell phones while on the road are people who, from the start, are less cautious or more prone to take risks. This lack of caution is why these people talk on the phone while driving, and it's also the reason why they're more often involved in accidents. Thus, cell-phone use and accidents go together, but not because either one causes the other. Instead, both of these observations (cell-phone use and having accidents) are the by-products of a third factor: being a risk taker in the first place.

In technical terms, the problem here is that the people who drive while on the phone are a *self-selected group*. In other words, they decided for themselves whether they'd be in our "experimental group" (the cell-phone users) or our "control group" (people who don't use phones while they drive). Presumably, people make this choice for some reason—they have some tendency or attributes at the start that lead them to the behavior of using the phone while driving. And the problem, of course, is that it might be these initial attributes, not the cell-phone use itself, that caused the observed outcome—the increased accident rate.

If we really want to examine the effects of cell-phone use on driving, we need to make sure that our "phone group" and our "no-phone group" are equivalent to begin with, before cell phones enter the scene. If we then discover that cell-phone use is associated with more accidents, we'd know that the cell phones are indeed at fault, and not some preexisting difference between the groups.

Psychologists usually achieve this matching of groups by means of *random assignment*. In our example, rather than allowing research participants to sort themselves into a group of phone users and a group of nonusers, the experimenters would assign them to one group or the other on some random basis (perhaps a coin toss). This wouldn't change the fact that some drivers are careful and others are not, or that some are more attentive than others. But our coin toss would ensure that careless drivers have an equal chance of ending up in the phone or no-phone group, and likewise for careful drivers, or risky ones. As a result, our two groups would end up matched to each other, not because all of our participants were alike but instead because each group would contain the same mix of different driver types.

Random assignment is one of the most important tools in a psychologist's research kit, ensuring that groups are matched before an experiment begins. That way, if the groups differ at the *end* of the experiment, we can be sure it's because of our experimental manipulation, and not because of some preexisting difference.

With all of this said, what about cell-phone use? The evidence suggests that talking on a cell phone while driving *is* dangerous, because of the distraction. The evidence comes from laboratory studies because it would be unethical to require people to use phones while actually driving; this would put them in danger, so it is unacceptable as a research procedure! However, the studies use high-tech, extremely realistic driving simulators, and the data are clear: Phone conversations while driving do increase the risk of accidents. Hence there is an important message in these data—but it's not a message we can draw from the evidence mentioned at the start of this essay (the greater accident frequency among cell-phone users). That initial bit of evidence is ambiguous, for the reasons we've discussed here. The evidence we need for our conclusion comes instead from studies relying on random assignment, and these studies do tell us that even with other factors held constant, you shouldn't be conversing while you drive.

FOR DISCUSSION

Students who take Latin in high school usually get higher scores on the Scholastic Aptitude Test, and they usually get better grades in college. Many people conclude that students *should* take Latin in high school—that training in Latin improves academic performance. However, this conclusion is unwarranted, and the problem is a lack of random assignment. What exactly is the problem here? Why don't we have random assignment in this case? Finally, if we really wanted to find out if taking Latin improves academic performance, how could we use random assignment to develop a worthwhile experiment?

For more on this topic

Strayer, D. L., & Drews, F. A. (2007). Cell-phone-induced driver distraction. *Current Directions in Psychological Science, 16,* 128–131.

Cognitive Psychology and Education: ADHD

When students learn about *attention,* they often have questions about *failures of attention:* "Why can't I focus when I need to?" "Why am I so distracted by my roommate moving around the room when I'm studying?" "Why can some people listen to music while they're reading, but I can't?"

One question, however, comes up more than any other: "I" (or "my friend" or "my brother") "was diagnosed with attention-deficit disorder; what's that all about?" This question refers to a common diagnosis: attention-deficit/hyperactivity disorder, or ADHD. This disorder is often diagnosed in young children (e.g., before age 8), but it can also be diagnosed at later ages. The disorder is characterized by a number of behavioral problems, including impulsivity, constant fidgeting, and difficulty in keeping attention focused on a task. Children with ADHD have trouble organizing or completing projects, and they are usually perceived to be intrusive and immature. These problems generally become less intense as the child grows older, but some symptoms can persist throughout the life span.

The diagnosis of ADHD is controversial. There is no question that many children who receive this diagnosis have a genuine disorder, with genetic factors playing a large role in producing the symptoms. Some critics argue, though, that in other cases the diagnosis is just a handy label for children who are particularly active, or for children who don't easily adjust to a school routine or a crowded classroom. Indeed, some critics suggest that ADHD is often just a convenient categorization for physicians or school counselors who don't know how else to think about an unruly or especially energetic child.

In those cases in which the diagnosis is warranted, though, what does it involve? As we describe in the textbook chapter, there are many steps involved in "paying attention," and some of those steps involve *inhibition*—so that we don't follow every stray thought, or every cue in the environment, wherever it may lead. For most of us, this is no problem, and so we easily inhibit our responses to most distractors. We're thrown off track only by especially intrusive distractors—such as a particularly loud noise, a stimulus that has special meaning for us, or a completely unexpected input.

Some researchers propose, though, that people with ADHD have less effective inhibitory circuits in their brains, and so they are more vulnerable to momentary impulses and chance distractions. This is what leads to their scattered thoughts, their difficulty in schoolwork, and so on.

Setting aside these claims about what *causes* ADHD, what about the treatment? What can be done to help people with ADHD? One of the common treatments is *Ritalin*, a drug that is a powerful stimulant. It seems ironic that we'd give a stimulant to people who are already described as too active and too energetic, but the evidence suggests that Ritalin is effective in treating actual cases of ADHD—plausibly because the drug activates the inhibitory circuits within the brain, helping the child to guard against his or her wayward impulses.

However, we probably should not rely on Ritalin as our sole treatment for ADHD. One reason is the risk of overdiagnosis already mentioned; it is worrisome that this powerful drug may be routinely given to people—including young children—who don't actually have ADHD. In addition, there are concerns about the long-term effects and possible side effects of Ritalin, and this certainly motivates us to seek other forms of treatment. (Common side effects include weight loss, insomnia, anxiety, and slower growth in childhood.) Some of the promising alternatives involve restructuring of the environment: If children with ADHD are vulnerable to distraction, we can help them by the simple step of reducing the sources of distraction in their surroundings. Likewise, if people with ADHD are influenced by whatever cues they detect, we can perhaps surround them with *helpful* cues—reminders of what they're supposed to be doing and the tasks they're supposed to be working on. These simple interventions do seem to be helpful—especially with adults diagnosed with ADHD.

Overall, then, our description of ADHD requires multiple parts. The diagnosis may be used too often, which is troubling, especially if it leads to overuse of powerful medication. But the diagnosis is genuine in many cases, and the problems involved in ADHD are real and serious. The ADHD diagnosis has certainly been applied to more cases in recent years, but it is unclear whether this is overdiagnosis or better (and potentially helpful) early detection. Medication can help, but even here there is a concern about the side effects of the medication. Environmental interventions can also help and may, in fact, be our best bet for the long term, especially given the important fact that in most cases the symptoms of ADHD do diminish as the years go by.

FOR DISCUSSION

Some people need a quiet room, with no distractions, in order to do their best mental work. Other people, however, seem to work best when there's music playing in the background—although they might insist on a certain type of music (instrumental rather than vocal, or classical rather than modern). Likewise, some people sit still when they are working on an intellectual problem; others (including this textbook's author) pace when they're thinking about something difficult. Can you use the materials in the chapter to generate hypotheses about some of these patterns? Why might it be helpful (at least for some people) to have instrumental music playing while they read? Why might it be helpful (for some people) to pace while they work?

For more information on this topic

Barkley, R. A. (2004). Adolescents with ADHD: An overview of empirically based treatments. *Journal of Psychiatric Practice, 10,* 39–56.

Barkley, R. A. (2006). *Attention-deficit hyperactivity disorder: A handbook for diagnosis and treatment* (3rd ed.). New York: Guilford Press.

Halperin, J. M., & Schulz, K. P. (2006). Revisiting the role of the prefrontal cortex in the pathophysiology of attention-deficit/hyperactivity disorder. *Psychological Bulletin, 132,* 560–581.

Cognitive Psychology and the Law:
What Do Eyewitnesses Pay Attention To?

Throughout Chapter 4, we emphasized how little information people seem to gain about stimuli that are plainly visible (or plainly audible) *if they are not paying attention to these stimuli.* Thus, people fail to see a gorilla that's directly in front of their eyes (see the text's Figure 4.1), or a large-scale color change that's plainly in view (see Demonstration 4.2).

Think about what this means for law enforcement. Imagine, for example, a customer in a bank during a robbery. Perhaps the customer waited in line, directly behind the robber. Will the customer remember what the robber looked like? Will the customer remember the robber's clothing? There's no way to tell unless we have some indications of what the customer was paying attention to—even though the robber's appearance and clothing were salient stimuli in the customer's environment.

Of course, the factors governing a witness's attention are likely to vary from witness to witness and from crime to crime. One factor, though, is often important: the presence of a *weapon* during the crime. If a gun (for example) is in view, then of course witnesses will want to know whether the gun is pointed at them and whether the criminal's finger is on the trigger. After all, what else in the scene could be more important to the witness? But with this focus on the weapon, many other things in the scene will be unattended, so that the witness may fail to notice, and later on fail to remember, many bits of information crucial for law enforcement.

Consistent with these suggestions, witnesses to crimes involving weapons are sometimes said to show a pattern called *weapon focus*. They are able to report to the police many details about the weapon (e.g., its size, its color), and often many details about the hand that was holding the weapon (e.g., whether the person was wearing any rings or a bracelet). However, because of this focus, the witness may have a relatively poor memory for other aspects of the scene—including such forensically crucial information as what the perpetrator looked like. Indeed, studies suggest that eyewitness identifications of the perpetrator may be systematically *less accurate* in crimes involving weapons—presumably because the witness's attention was focused on the weapon, not on the perpetrator's face.

The weapon-focus pattern has been demonstrated in many studies, including those that literally track where participants are pointing their eyes during the event. Scientists have also used a statistical technique called meta-analysis, providing an overall summary of these data, to confirm the reliability of this pattern and, importantly, to show that the weapon-focus effect is stronger and more reliable in those studies that are closer to actual forensic settings. Thus, the weapon-focus effect seems not to be a peculiar by-product of the artificial situations created in the lab; indeed, the effect may be *underestimated* in laboratory studies.

Somewhat surprisingly, though, it is difficult to document weapon focus in actual crimes. I testified once in a case involving a bank robbery in which a witness to the crime offered a detailed description of the perpetrator's gun and the hand holding the gun. But the same witness said things that were plainly false about the perpetrator's face. (What she recalled was inconsistent with details that were visible on the videotape recorded by the bank's security system.) This certainly sounds like the pattern of weapon focus. But, even with this example in view, broader studies of actual police investigations usually show no evidence of weapon focus. In other words, studies have compared the likelihood that a witness will identify a criminal in crimes *with* a weapon and the likelihood of an I.D. in crimes *without* a weapon. These studies have often shown no difference—no indication of weapon focus.

Why is this? The answer is not clear. One plausible factor, though, is the *duration* of many crimes. A witness may focus initially on the weapon, but then, if the crime lasts long enough, the witness may have time to look at other aspects of the scene as well. This would, of course, decrease the overall impact of the weapon-focus effect.

Even with this complication, demonstrations of the weapon-focus effect are important for many reasons, including the fact that they can help the courts in their evaluation of eyewitness testimony. After all, we obviously want to know when we can trust an eyewitness's recollection and when we cannot. To make these assessments, we need to know what factors shape a witness's memory, and plainly some of those factors involve aspects of the crime that guided the witness's attention. It's on this basis that research on weapon focus can help us evaluate each case, with the aim of maximizing the quality of courtroom evidence.

FOR DISCUSSION

Can you generate other hypotheses about what people might pay attention to during a crime in addition to (or perhaps instead of) the weapon? Can you generate hypotheses about circumstances in which people are likely to focus their attention on details useful for the police and circumstances in which they're unable to focus their attention (perhaps because they are so anguished over the crime itself)? The more we can specify what witnesses focus on, during a crime, the better position we will be in to ask what the witnesses will remember—and which aspects of their recollection we can count on.

For more on this topic

Pickel, K. (2007). Remembering and identifying menacing perpetrators: Exposure to violence and the weapon focus effect. In R. Lindsay, D. Ross, J. Read, & M. Toglia (Eds.), *The handbook of eyewitness psychology: Vol. 2. Memory for people* (pp. 339–360). Hillsdale, NJ: Erlbaum.

Stanny, C. J., & Johnson, T. C. (2000). Effects of stress induced by a simulated shooting on recall by police and citizen witnesses. *American Journal of Psychology, 113,* 359–386.

Steblay, N. J. (1992). A meta-analytic review of the weapon focus effect. *Law and Human Behavior, 16,* 413–424.

Cognitive Psychology and the Law:
Guiding the Formulation of New Laws

In this workbook, we've been emphasizing cognitive psychology's role in guiding police investigations, or criminal prosecutions. But cognitive psychology is also relevant to a different aspect of the law: the step of choosing what the law should be.

For example, many jurisdictions now have laws prohibiting cell-phone use while driving, and the chapter describes evidence making it plain that these laws are sensible: Cell-phone use does interfere with driving. However, many jurisdictions allow drivers to use *hands-free* cell phones, and this is a mistake: The distraction from cell-phone use is the same whether the driver is using one hand to hold the phone or not; this point is clear in a number of studies. In this regard, therefore, the research should be helpful in formulating these laws, but the research has been ignored, and so the new laws provide less protection than we might wish!

Other jurisdictions (and many drivers) resist any laws limiting cell-phone use and offer a common-sense rebuttal to this research: Many drivers have spent many minutes on the phone without difficulty—without injuring themselves or others, without damaging their car or someone else's. They claim, therefore, that the studies exaggerate the risk here and that it's perfectly possible for a good driver to talk on the phone while moving down the road.

What's the response to this argument? A lot of driving is pretty much routine. You can adjust your steering to the road's curves without thinking much about what you're doing. You can rely on well-practiced habits in choosing a following distance for the car in front of you, or navigating the often-used route to the mall. Even so, situations do arise when your set of driving habits isn't enough: Perhaps you're looking for a highway exit you've never used before, or perhaps the traffic requires a tricky lane switch. In such cases, you'll need to choose the timing and sequence of your actions with care—and so you'll need the resource the chapter calls "executive control."

The same points can be made for conversations. Often these, too, can proceed without deep thought. You generally have an easy time formulating your ideas and choosing your words. And you've had years of practice in the step of "translating" your verbal intentions into muscle movements, and so you give little thought to the positioning of your tongue to make sure the right sounds come out of your mouth, or to the timing of your inhales and exhales. But what if the conversation becomes complex? What if you're asked a hard question, or want to choose your words with extra care? In these cases, you'll want to rise above habits—searching through memory, perhaps, to find the right example, or weighing your options in selecting the right phrase. Once again, you're stepping away from habit, and so need executive control.

And now we can put the pieces together: Ordinarily, driving while conversing is easy, because often neither driving nor the conversation requires much in the way of executive control. This is why, most of the time, you can use the cell phone while driving without any problems. But disaster can arise if, by chance, the driving and conversation both contain some unexpected element at roughly the same time. This is the setting in which you'll need executive control for both tasks—and executive control can only handle one task at a time. And, of course, there's no way to predict when this conflict will arise, and so the only safe plan is to make sure the conflict *can't* arise. This is why jurisdictions are being entirely sensible when they forbid cell phone use while driving.

By the way, we might mention that the debate over cell-phone use is certain to continue: In late 2011, the United States National Transportation Safety Board (NTSB) proposed a ban on all cell-phone use by drivers—whether they were talking or texting, whether the device was hand-held or hands-free. The NTSB was reacting in part to a Missouri crash that killed two people and injured 38 more; the accident also involved two school buses. Despite this disaster, the explicit NTSB recommendation, and the research data supporting this recommendation, most jurisdictions are resisting new controls. The situation, it seems, is one in which legislatures (and citizens) are choosing to overrule the data—in a fashion that, sadly, may continue to cost people their lives.

FOR DISCUSSION

The data are clear that it's dangerous to talk on a cell phone while driving, and the danger remains if the cell phone happens to be a "hands-free" model. The chapter explains, however, why things are different if you're talking to a *passenger* in the car; for sensible reasons, this turns out not to be dangerous. But this now invites some further questions: People do many things while driving, and we need to ask which of these activities are (like cell-phone use) dangerous, and which (like talking to a passenger) are benign. For example, what about listening to an "audio book" or podcast? What about listening to (and being guided by) GPS instructions? What about listening to your smartphone reading you your text messages? Using what's known about attention, can you figure out which of these activities are hazardous while driving, and which (again, like talking to a passenger in the car) seem to be safe?

CHAPTER 5

The Acquisition of Memories and the Working-Memory System

Demonstrations

5.1   Primacy and Recency Effects

The text describes a theoretical model in which working memory and long-term memory are distinct from each other, each governed by its own principles. But what's the evidence for this distinction? Much of the evidence comes from an easily demonstrated data pattern.

Read the following list of 25 words out loud, at a speed of roughly one second per word. (*Before you begin*, you might start tapping your foot at roughly one tap per second, and then keep tapping your foot as you read the list; that will help you keep up the right rhythm.)

1. tree	8. kitten	15. strap	22. bell
2. work	9. view	16. bed	23. view
3. face	10. light	17. wheel	24. seat
4. music	11. page	18. paper	25. rope
5. test	12. truck	19. candle	
6. nail	13. lunch	20. farm	
7. window	14. shirt	21. ankle	

Now turn to the next page so you can't see this list anymore, and write down as many words from the list as you can in the box provided, in any order that you can.

Write down as many of the words from the list on page 53 as you can recall here.

Compare your recall with the actual list. How many words did you remember? *Which* words did you remember?

- Chances are good that you remembered the first three or four words on the list. Did you? The textbook chapter explains why this is likely.
- Chances are also good that you remembered the *final* three or four words on the list. Did you? Again, the textbook chapter explains why this is likely.
- Even though you were free to write down the list in any order you chose, it's very likely that you started out by writing the words you'd just read—that is, the *first* words you wrote were probably the *last* words you read on the list. Is that correct?

The chapter doesn't explain this last point, but the reason is straightforward. At the end of the list, the last few words you'd read were still in your working memory, simply because you'd just been thinking about these words, and nothing else had come along yet to bump these items *out of* working memory. The minute you think about something else, though, that "something else" will occupy working memory and will displace these just-heard words.

With that base, imagine what would happen if, at the very start of your recall, you tried to remember, say, the first words on the list. This effort will likely bring those words into your thoughts, and so now these words are in working memory—

bumping out the words that were there, and potentially causing you to lose track of those now-displaced words. To avoid this problem, you probably started your recall by "dumping" working memory's current contents (the last few words you read) onto the recall sheet. Then, with the words preserved in this way, it didn't matter if you displaced them from working memory, and you were freed to go to work on the other words from the list.

- Finally, it's likely that one or two of the words on the list really "stuck" in your memory, even though the words were neither early in the list (and so didn't benefit from *primacy*) nor late on the list (and so didn't benefit from *recency*). Which words (if any) stuck in your memory in this way? Why do you think this is? Does this fit with the theory in the text?

5.2   Chunking

The text mentions the benefits of *chunking*, and these benefits are easy to demonstrate. First, let's measure your memory span in the normal way: A bit down on this page there is a list of letters; cover this list with your hand, or a piece of paper. Now, slide your hand or paper down, to reveal the first row of letters. Read the row silently, pausing briefly after you read each letter. Then close your eyes, and repeat the row aloud. Open your eyes. Did you get it right? If so, do the same with the next row, and keep going until you hit a row that is too long—that is, a row for which you make errors. Count the items in that row. This count is your digit span.

```
        C A

       G T Y

      R B O S

     P S Y R L

    R B D P N F

   Y H A R E I G

  R S O I U T C A

 E R S L J T E G F

S D O E U V M K V G
```

Now we'll do the exercise again, but this time, with rows containing *letter pairs*, not *letters*. Using the same procedure, at what row do you start to make errors?

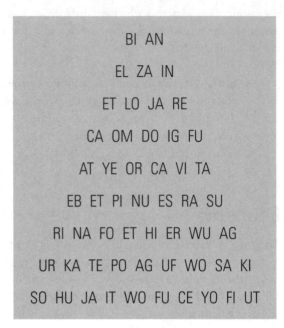

BI AN

EL ZA IN

ET LO JA RE

CA OM DO IG FU

AT YE OR CA VI TA

EB ET PI NU ES RA SU

RI NA FO ET HI ER WU AG

UR KA TE PO AG UF WO SA KI

SO HU JA IT WO FU CE YO FI UT

It's likely that your span measured with *single letters* was 6 or 7, or perhaps 8. It's likely that your span, measured with *letter pairs* was a tiny bit smaller, perhaps 5 or 6 pairs—but that means you're now remembering 10 or 12 letters. If we focus on the letter count, therefore, your memory span seems to have increased from the first test to the second. But that's the wrong way to think about this. Instead, your memory span is constant (or close to it). What's changing is how you *use* that span— that is, how many letters you cram into each "chunk."

Now, one more step: Read the next sentence to yourself, then close your eyes, and try repeating the sentence back.

The tyrant passed strict laws limiting the citizens' freedom.

Could you do this? Were you able to repeat the sentence? If so, notice that your memory now seems able to hold 51 letters. Again, if we focus on letter count, your memory span is growing at an astonishing speed! But, instead, let's count chunks. The phrase "The tyrant" is probably just one chunk, likewise "strict laws" and "the citizens'." Therefore, this sentence really just contains six chunks—and so is easily within your memory span!

5.3 The Effects of Unattended Exposure

How does information get entered into long-term storage? One idea is that mere exposure is enough—so that if an object is in front of your eyes over and over and over, you'll learn exactly what the object looks like. However, this claim is *false*. Memories are created through a process of active engagement with materials; mere exposure is insufficient.

This point is easy to demonstrate, but for the demonstration you'll need to ask one or two friends a few questions. (You can't just test yourself, because the textbook chapter gives away the answer, and so your memory is already altered by reading the chapter.)

Approach a friend who hasn't, as far as you know, read the *Cognition* text, and ask your friend these questions:

1. Which President is shown on the Lincoln penny? (It will be troubling if your friend gets this wrong!)
2. What portion of the President's anatomy is shown on the "heads" side of the coin? (It will be even more troubling if your friend gets this one wrong.)
3. Is the head facing forward, or is it visible only in profile? (This question, too, will likely be very easy.)
4. If the head is in profile, is it facing to the viewer's *right*, so that you can see the right ear and right cheek, or is it facing to the viewer's *left*, so that you can see the left ear and left cheek?

(For Canadian or British readers, you can ask the same questions about your nation's penny—assuming that pennies are still around when you run the test. Of course, your penny shows, on the "heads" side, the profile of the monarch who was reigning when the penny was issued. But the memory questions—and the likely outcome—are otherwise the same.)

Odds are good that half of the people you ask will say "facing right" and half will say "facing left." In other words, people trying to remember this fact about the penny are no more accurate than they would be if they answered at random.

Now, a few more questions. Is your friend wearing a watch? If so, reach out and put your hand on his or her wrist, so that you hide the watch from view. Now ask your friend:

5. Does your watch have all the numbers, from 1 through 12, on it? Or is it missing some of the numbers? If so, which numbers does it have?
6. What style of numbers is used? Ordinary numerals or Roman numerals?
7. What style of print is used for the numbers? An italic? A "normal" vertical font? A font that is elaborate in some way, or one that's relatively plain?

How accurate are your friends? Chances are excellent that many of your friends will answer these questions incorrectly—even though they've probably looked at their watches over and over and over during the years in which they've owned the watch.

By the way, this demonstration may yield different results if you test *women* than if you test *men*. Women are often encouraged to think of wristwatches as jewelry and so are more likely to think about what the watch looks like. Men are encouraged to take a more pragmatic view of their watches—and so they often regard them as timepieces, not jewelry. As a result, women are more likely than men to notice, and think about, the watch's appearance, and thus to remember exactly what their watches look like!

Even with this last complication, the explanation for all of these findings is straightforward. Information is not recorded in your memory simply because the information has been in front of your eyes at some point. Instead, information is recorded into memory only if you pay attention to that information and think about it in some way. People have seen pennies thousands of times, but they've not had any reason to think about Lincoln's position. Likewise, they've looked at their watches many, many times but probably haven't had a reason to think about the details of the numbers. As a result, and despite an enormous number of "learning opportunities," these unattended details are simply not recorded into memory.

Demonstration adapted from Nickerson, R., & Adams, M. (1979). Long-term memory for a common object. *Cognitive Psychology, 11,* 287–307.

5.4   Depth of Processing

Many experiments show that "deep processing"—paying attention to an input's meaning, or its implications—helps memory. In contrast, materials that receive only shallow processing tend not to be well remembered. This contrast is reliable and powerful, and also easily demonstrated.

On the next page is a list of questions followed by single words. Some of the questions concern categories. For example, the question might ask: "Is a type of vehicle? Truck." For this question, the answer would be yes.

Some of the questions involve rhyme. For example, the question might ask: "Rhymes with chair? Horse." Here the answer is no.

Still other questions concern spelling patterns—in particular, the number of vowels in the word. For example, if asked "Has three vowels? Chair," the answer would again be no.

Go through the list of questions at a comfortable speed, and say "yes" or "no" aloud in response to each question.

Rhymes with angle?	Speech	Rhymes with coffee?	Chapel
Is a type of silverware?	Brush	Has one vowel?	Sonnet
Has two vowels?	Cheek	Rhymes with rich?	Witch
Is a thing found in a garden?	Fence	Is a type of insect?	Roach
Rhymes with claim?	Flame	Has two vowels?	Brake
Has two vowels?	Flour	Has one vowel?	Twig
Is a rigid object?	Honey	Rhymes with bin?	Grin
Rhymes with elder?	Knife	Rhymes with fill?	Drill
Has three vowels?	Sheep	Is a human sound?	Moan
Rhymes with merit?	Copper	Has two vowels?	Claw
Rhymes with shove?	Glove	Is a type of entertainer?	Singer
Is a boundary dispute?	Monk	Rhymes with candy?	Bear
Rhymes with star?	Jar	Has four vowels?	Cherry
Has two vowels?	Cart	Is a type of plant?	Tree
Is a container for liquid?	Clove	Rhymes with pearl?	Earl
Is something sold on street corners?	Robber	Has two vowels?	Pool
Is a part of a ship?	Mast	Is a part of an airplane?	Week
Has four vowels?	Fiddle	Has one vowel?	Pail

This list contained twelve of each type of question—twelve rhyme questions, twelve spelling questions, and twelve questions concerned with meaning. Was this task easy or hard? Most people have no trouble at all with this task, and they give correct answers to every one of the questions.

Each of these questions had a word provided with it, and you needed that word to answer the question. *How many of these "answer words" do you remember?* Turn to the next page, and write down as many of the answer words as you can.

Now, go back and check your answers. First, put a checkmark alongside the word if it did in fact occur in the earlier list—so that your recall is correct.

Second, for each of the words you remembered, do the following:

Put an *S* next to the word you recalled *if* that word appeared in a spelling question (i.e., asking about number of vowels).

Put an *R* next to the word you recalled *if* that word appeared in one of the rhyming questions.

Put an *M* next to the word you recalled *if* that word appeared in one of the questions concerned with meaning.

How many *S* words did you recall? How many *R* words? How many *M* words?

It's close to certain that you remembered relatively few *S* words, more of the *R* words, and even more of the *M* words. In fact, you may have recalled most of the twelve *M* words. Is this the pattern of your recall? If so, then you just reproduced the standard level-of-processing effect, with deeper processing (attention to *meaning*) reliably producing better recall, for the reasons described in the textbook chapter.

Demonstration adapted from Craik, F., & Tulving, E. (1975). Depth of processing and the retention of words in episodic memory. *Journal of Experimental Psychology: General, 104,* 269–294.

Applying Cognitive Psychology

Research Methods: Replication

In the Research Methods essays so far, we've talked about some of the steps needed to make sure the results of an experiment are unambiguous. We've talked, for example, about the need for a precise hypothesis, so that there's no question about whether the results fit with the hypothesis. We've talked about the advantages of random assignment, to make certain that the results couldn't be the product of preexisting differences in our comparison groups. We've discussed the need to remove confounds so that, within the experiment, there is no ambiguity about what caused the differences we observe.

Notice, though, that all of these points concern the interpretation of individual experiments, so that each study yields clear and unambiguous findings. It's important to add, however, that researchers rarely draw conclusions from individual experiments, no matter how well designed the experiment is. One reason is statistical: A successful *replication*—a reproduction of the result in a new experiment—provides assurance that the original result wasn't just a fluke or a weird accident. Another reason is methodological: If we can replicate a result with a new experimenter, new participants, and new stimuli, this tells us there was nothing peculiar about these factors in the first experiment. This is our guarantee that the result was produced by the factors deliberately varied in the experiment and was not the chance by-product of some unnoticed factor in the procedure or the context.

In addition, researchers generally don't repeat experiments exactly as they were run the first time. Instead, replications usually introduce new factors into the design, to ask how these new factors alter the results. (In fact, many scientific journals are hesitant to publish straight replications, largely because space is limited in the journals; however, they routinely publish studies that include a replication as part of a larger design that also introduces some new variation in the procedure.)

This broad pattern of "replication + variation" allows researchers to refine their hypotheses and to test new hypotheses about a result. We gave one example of this approach in the textbook chapter: Specifically, if people are asked to recall as many words as they can from a list they just heard, the results show a characteristic U-shaped serial-position curve (see textbook, p. 168, Figure 5.2). This result is easily replicated, so we know it doesn't depend on idiosyncratic features of the experimental context—it doesn't depend on the specific words that are used in the procedure, or the particular group of participants we recruit, or the time of day in which we run the experiment. This allows us to move forward, asking the next question: What produces this reliable pattern? One proposal, of course, is provided by the *modal model*, a theoretical account of memory's basic architecture. But is this model correct?

To address this question, researchers have varied a number of factors in the basic list-learning experiment—factors that should, if the hypothesis is correct, alter the results. One factor is speed of list presentation: According to our hypothesis, if we slow down the presentation, this should increase recall for all but the last few words on the list. A different factor is distraction right after the list's end: Our hypothesis predicts that this will decrease the recency effect but will have no other effects. These predictions both turn out to be right.

Notice, then, that our claims about the modal model rest on many results, and not just one, and this is the typical pattern in any science. Single results, on their own, are often open to more than one interpretation. Broad *patterns* of results, in contrast, usually allow just one interpretation—and that is what we want. Within the broad data pattern, some of the results show the replicability of the basic findings (e.g., the U-shaped data pattern). Other results provide tests of specific predictions derived from our model. In the end, though, it's the full fabric of results that tells us our explanation is correct, and it's this full fabric that tells us the explanation is powerful—able to explain a wide range of experimental data.

FOR DISCUSSION

As the textbook chapter describes, many studies show that someone's memory is improved if the person is led to do *deep and elaborate processing* of the material to be remembered. However, many of these studies test how well someone can memorize a list of words, and in our day-to-day lives we usually want to remember more complex, more interesting materials—such as complicated arguments or rich, many-part events. It's therefore important to test this hypothesis: "Instructions to do deep and elaborate processing also improve memory for complex materials, such as memory for an event."

Testing this hypothesis would, first of all, allow us to replicate the benefits of deeper processing; in this way, we could show that these benefits really are reliable. Testing this hypothesis would, in addition, allow us to extend our claims about deeper processing into a new arena. Can you design a study that would test this hypothesis?

Cognitive Psychology and Education: "How Should I Study?"

Throughout our lives, we often encounter new information that we hope to remember later. For instance, when a friend recommends a new restaurant, we want to remember the restaurant's name; when we're heading to the store, we want to remember the list of ingredients needed for dinner. The effort toward placing information in memory is particularly intense, though, for students in college courses or workers getting trained for a new job. These groups spend hours trying to master new information and new skills. If you're in one of these groups, what lessons can be drawn from the material in Chapter 5 that might help you?

For a start, you shouldn't spend much effort worrying about whether you'll remember the material. This is because the available evidence suggests the *intention to memorize* contributes little. Instead, you should focus your efforts on making sure you *understand* the material, because if you do, you're likely to remember it.

As one way of working toward this understanding, you'll be well served by asking yourself, for each of the facts you learn: "Does this fact fit with other things I know? Does this fact make sense? Do I know why this fact is as it is?" Seeking answers to these questions will promote understanding, which will in turn promote memory. In the same spirit, it's often useful to rephrase what is in your reading, or in your notes, in your own words—doing so will force you to think about what the words mean, which is a good thing for memory.

It's also useful to study with a friend—so that he or she can explain topics to you, and you can do the same in return. This step has several advantages: In explaining things, you're forced into an active role, in contrast to the more passive role you might take in reading or listening, and this activity seems itself to promote memory. Working with a friend is also likely to enhance your understanding, because each of you can help the other to understand bits you're having trouble with. You'll also benefit from hearing your friend's insights and perspective on the materials being learned. This additional perspective offers the possibility of creating new connections among ideas, and therefore new retrieval paths, making the information easier to recall later on.

Memory will also be best if you spread your studying out across multiple occasions—using what's called *spaced learning* (essentially, taking breaks between study sessions) rather than *massed learning* (essentially, "cramming" all at once). There are several reasons for this, including the fact that spaced learning makes it likely that you'll bring a slightly different perspective to the material each time you turn to it. This new perspective will allow you to see connections you didn't see before, and—again—the new connections create new links among ideas, which will provide retrieval paths that promote recall.

What about mnemonic strategies, such as a peg-word system? These are enormously helpful—but only in some circumstances, and often at a cost. As the chapter mentions, focusing on the mnemonic may divert your time and attention away from efforts at understanding the material, and so you'll end up understanding the material less well. You will also be left with only the one or two retrieval paths that the mnemonic provides, and not the multiple paths created by comprehension. There are circumstances in which these drawbacks are not serious, and so mnemonics are often useful for remembering specific dates or place names, or particular bits of terminology. But for richer, more meaningful material, mnemonics may hurt you more than they help.

Finally, let's emphasize that there's much more to say about these issues, largely because our discussion in this essay (like Chapter 5 itself) focuses only on the "input" side of memory—getting information into storage, so that it's available for use later on. We'll therefore return to the broad question of how psychology can help you study in the workbook's coverage of Chapters 6 and 7, when we consider how to get information out of memory, when you need it!

Before we're done, though, we will have offered a lengthy catalog of activities and strategies that can dramatically improve your memory in classroom settings and beyond.

FOR DISCUSSION

Cognitive psychology provides some important general messages about how you should study: Do not agonize over whether you're memorizing the material or not; incidental learning is just as good as intentional! And by all means *do* make sure you understand, and know how to organize, the material; that will surely help you to remember.

However, these general messages simply invite a new round of questioning: What exactly should you do to promote understanding and organization? What are the best ways to achieve these goals? This essay provides some suggestions, but you may have your own ideas, and you might also benefit from hearing your friends' ideas. Therefore, it's worth discussing: If your goals are understanding and organization (with the clear expectation that these steps will virtually guarantee good memory), what strategies seem a good bet for achieving these goals? What strategies seem less likely to succeed? Minutes spent on these questions will likely pay off later on, in improved academic performance!

For more on this topic

Graesser, A. (2011). Improving learning. *Monitor on Psychology, 42*(7), 58–64.

Cognitive Psychology and the Law: The Video-Recorder View

One popular conception of memory is sometimes dubbed the "video-recorder view." According to this commonsense view, everything in front of your eyes gets recorded into memory, much as a video camera records everything in front of the lens. This view seems to be widely held, but it is simply *wrong*. As Chapter 5 discusses, information gets established in memory only if you pay attention to it and think about it in some fashion. Mere exposure is not enough.

Wrong or not, the video-recorder view influences how many people think about memory—including eyewitness memory. For example, many people believe that it is possible to hypnotize an eyewitness and then "return" the (hypnotized) witness to the scene of the crime. The idea is that the witness will then be able to recall minute details—the exact words spoken, precisely how things appeared, and more. All of this would make sense if memory were like a video recorder. In that case, hypnosis would be akin to rewinding the tape and playing it again, with the prospect of noting things on the "playback" that had been overlooked during the initial event. However, none of this is correct. There is no evidence that hypnosis improves memory. Details that were overlooked the first time are simply not recorded in memory, and neither hypnosis nor any other technique can bring those details back.

Similarly, consider a technique often used in trials to raise questions about an eyewitness's recall. The attorney will ask the eyewitness question after question about an event and will quickly discover that the witness recalls some facts but not others. Thus (for example) the witness might remember the suspect's words but not his clothing, or might recall the clothing but be uncertain where people in the crime scene were standing. Later, the attorney is likely to ask the jury, "How can we trust this witness's recall? With so many gaps in the witness's recollection, it's clear that the witness was not paying attention or has a poor memory. We therefore cannot rely on what the witness says!"

However, the attorney's argument assumes the video-recorder view. If memory were like a video recorder, then we *should* worry if the playback has gaps or errors in it. (If your actual video recorder, or your DVD player, has gaps in its playback, skipping every other second or missing half the image, that surely does sound like a malfunction.) But this is not how memory works. Instead, memory is selective. People recall what they paid attention to, and if a witness cannot recall some aspects of a crime, this merely tells us that the witness wasn't paying attention to everything. And, given what we know about the limits of attention, the witness *couldn't* pay attention to everything. Hence, it is inevitable that the witness's memory will be incomplete (i.e., not recording every single detail within a scene), and we certainly should not use that incompleteness as a basis for distrusting the witness.

Related examples are easy to find, with many popular ideas about memory resting on the (incorrect) video-recorder view. Once we understand how memory works, therefore, we gain more realistic expectations about what eyewitnesses will or will not be able to remember. With these realistic expectations, we are in a much better position to evaluate and understand eyewitness evidence.

FOR DISCUSSION

If hypnosis is *not* the way to improve witnesses' memory, then what *is* the way? Are there steps we can take to help witnesses remember more? Alternatively, if we can't improve memory, can we at least find ways to *evaluate* witnesses to decide which ones are likely to have correct and complete memories, and which ones are likely to have partial or inaccurate memories? We will have more to say about these topics in upcoming textbook chapters, but several ideas about these points are already suggested by our discussion in Chapter 5. In thinking this through, you might reflect on your own experiences: What do you think has helped you, in some circumstances, to remember more? You might also consider what *steps* or *activities* are helpful in encoding information into memory, and then think about how these steps or activities might be relevant to the circumstances of an eyewitness.

For more on this topic

Brewer, N., Potter, R., Fisher, P., Bond, N., & Luszcz, M. (1999). Beliefs and data on the relationship between consistency and accuracy of eyewitness testimony. *Applied Cognitive Psychology, 13*, 297–313.

Dywan, J., & Bowers, K. (1983). The use of hypnosis to enhance recall. *Science, 222*, 184–185.

Newman, A., & Thompson, J. (2001). The rise and fall of forensic hypnosis in criminal investigation. *Journal of the American Academic of Psychiatry and the Law, 29*, 75–84.

Steblay, N. M., & Bothwell, R. (1994). Evidence for hypnotically refreshed testimony: The view from the laboratory. *Law and Human Behavior, 19*, 635–651.

CHAPTER 6

Interconnections Between Acquisition and Retrieval

Demonstrations

6.1   Retrieval Paths and Connections

Often the information you seek in memory is instantly available: If you try to remember your father's name, or the capital of France, the information springs immediately into your mind. Other times, however, the retrieval of information is more difficult.

How well do you remember your childhood? For example, think back to the sixth grade: How many of your sixth-grade classmates do you remember? Try writing a list of all their names in the box below. Do it now, before you read any farther.

Now read the questions below.

- What house did you live in when you were in the sixth grade? Think about times that friends came over to your house. Does that help you remember more names?
- Were you involved in any sports in the sixth grade? Think about who played on the teams with you. Does that help you remember more names?
- Where did you sit in the classroom in sixth grade? Who sat at the desk on your left? Who sat at the desk on your right? In front of you? Behind? Does that help you remember more names?
- Did you ride the bus to school, or carpool, or walk? Were there classmates you often saw on your way to or from school? Does that help you remember more names?
- Was there anyone in the class who was always getting in trouble? Anyone who was a fabulous athlete? Anyone who was incredibly funny? Do these questions help you remember more names?

Chances are good that at least one of these strategies, helping you "work your way back" to the names, did enable you to come up with some classmates you'd forgotten—and perhaps helped you to recall some names you hadn't thought about for years!

Apparently, these "extra" names were in your memory, even though you couldn't come up with them at first. Instead, you needed to locate the right *retrieval path* leading to the memory, the right *connection*. Once that connection was in your mind—once you were at the right "starting point" for the path—it led you quickly to the target memory. This is just what we would expect, based on the claims in the chapter.

6.2   Encoding Specificity

The textbook argues that the material in your memory is not just a reflection of the sights and sounds you have experienced. Instead, the material in your memory preserves a record of how you *thought about* these sights and sounds, how you interpreted and understood them. This demonstration, illustrating this point, is a little complicated because it has three separate parts. First, you'll read a list of words (on p. 69). Next, you should leave the demonstration and go do something else for 15 to 20 minutes—run some errands, perhaps, or do a bit of your reading for next week's class. Then your memory will be tested.

Here is the list of words to be remembered. For each word, a short phrase or cue is provided to help you focus on what the word means. Read the phrase or cue out loud, then pause for a second, then read the word, then pause for another second, to make sure you've really thought about the word. Then move on to the next. Ready? Begin.

A day of the week:	Thursday	A large city:	Tokyo
A government leader:	King	A sign of happiness:	Smile
A type of bird:	Cardinal	A student:	Pupil
A famous psychologist:	Freud	A long word:	Notwithstanding
A menu item:	Wine	Has four wheels:	Toyota
A personality trait:	Charm	A part of a bird:	Bill
A vegetable:	Cabbage	A member of the family:	Grandfather
Associated with heat:	Stove	A happy time of year:	Birthday
A round object:	Ball	A part of a word:	Letter
Found in the jungle:	Leopard	A tool:	Wrench
A crime:	Robbery	Found next to a highway:	Motel
A baseball position:	Pitcher	A type of sports equipment:	Racket
Associated with cold:	North	Part of a building:	Chimney
Song accompaniment:	Banjo	Made of leather:	Saddle
Taken to a birthday party:	Present	A tropical plant:	Palm
A girl's name:	Susan	A synonym for "big":	Colossal
A type of footgear:	Boots	Associated with lunch:	Noon
A manmade structure:	Bridge	Part of the intestine:	Colon
A weapon:	Cannon		
A sweet food:	Banana		
An assertion of possession:	Mine		

Now, what time is it? Go away and do something else for 15 minutes, then come back for the next part of this demonstration.

Next, we're going to test your memory for the words you learned earlier. To guide your efforts at recall, a cue will be provided for each of the words. Sometimes the cue will be exactly the same as the cue you saw before, and sometimes it will be different. In all cases, though, the cue will be closely related to the target word. There are no misleading cues.

Here are the cues; next to each cue, write down the word from the previous list that is related to the cue. Do not look at the previous list. If you can't recall some of the words, leave those items blank.

A facial expression: _____

A large city: _____

Associated with coal: _____

A fruit: _____

A weapon: _____

A card game: _____

Needed in snow: _____

A girl's name: _____

A grammatical tense: _____

A musical instrument: _____

Associated with cold: _____

An article of pottery: _____

A type of illegal activity: _____

Found in the jungle: _____

A social event: _____

A kitchen appliance: _____

A vegetable: _____

A small trinket: _____

An alcoholic beverage: _____

A famous psychologist: _____

A clergyman: _____

A member of royalty: _____

A day of the week: _____

A punctuation mark: _____

A time of day: _____

A synonym for "big": _____

Part of the hand: _____

Associated with horse: _____

Part of a building: _____

A type of noise: _____

A vacation rest-stop: _____

A tool: _____

A form of communication: _____

A special day: _____

A member of the family: _____

A month reminder: _____

A type of car: _____

A long word: _____

Found in the eye: _____

Here are the *answers*. Check which ones you got right.

A facial expression:	Smile		A member of royalty:	King
A large city:	Tokyo		A day of the week:	Thursday
Associated with coal:	Mine		A punctuation mark:	Colon
A fruit:	Banana		A time of day:	Noon
A weapon:	Cannon		A synonym for "big":	Colossal
A card game:	Bridge		Part of the hand:	Palm
Needed in snow:	Boots		Associated with horse:	Saddle
A girl's name:	Susan		Part of a building:	Chimney
A grammatical tense:	Present		A type of noise:	Racket
A musical instrument:	Banjo		A vacation rest-stop:	Motel
Associated with cold:	North		A tool:	Wrench
An article of pottery:	Pitcher		A form of communication:	Letter
A type of illegal activity:	Robbery		A special day:	Birthday
Found in the jungle:	Leopard		A member of the family:	Grandfather
A social event:	Ball		A request for money:	Bill
A kitchen appliance:	Stove		A type of car:	Toyota
A vegetable:	Cabbage		A long word:	Notwithstanding
A small trinket:	Charm		Found in the eye:	Pupil
An alcoholic beverage:	Wine			
A famous psychologist:	Freud			
A clergyman:	Cardinal			

These words are obviously in groups of three. For the *second* word in each group ("Tokyo," "Cannon," etc.), the cue is *identical* to the cue you saw on the very first list. How many of these (out of 13) did you get right?

For the *first* word in each group ("Smile," "Banana," etc.), the cue is *closely linked* to the one you saw at first ("A sign of happiness" was replaced with "A facial expression," and so on). How many of these (out of 13) did you get right?

For the *third* word in each group ("Mine," "Bridge," etc.), the cue actually *changed the meaning* of the target word. (On the first list, "Bridge" was "A manmade structure," not "A card game"; "Racket" was "A type of sports equipment," not "A type of noise.") How many of these (out of 13) did you get right?

Most people do best with the *identical* cues and a little worse with the *closely linked* cues. Most people recall the fewest words with the *changed-the-meaning* cues.

Is this the pattern of your results? If so, your data fit with what the chapter describes as *encoding specificity*. This term reflects the fact that what goes into your memory is not just the words; it is more specific than that—the words *plus* some record of what you thought about each word. Thus, what's in your memory is not (for example) the word "bridge." If that were your memory, a cue like "card game" might do the trick. Instead, what's in your memory is something like "structure used to get across a river," and, to trigger that idea, you need a different cue.

Demonstration adapted from Thieman, T. J. (1984). Table 1, A classroom demonstration of encoding specificity. *Teaching of Psychology, 11* (2), 102. Copyright © 1984 Routledge. Reprinted by permission from the publisher (Taylor & Francis Group, http://www.informaworld.com).

6.3   Spreading Activation in Memory Search

On a piece of paper, list all of the *men's first names* you can think of that are also *verbs*. For example, you can *Mark* something on paper; you shouldn't *Rob* a bank. If you're willing to ignore the spelling, you can *Neil* before the queen and *Phil* a bucket. How many other men's names are also verbs? Spend a few minutes generating the list.

How do you search your memory to come up with these names? One possibility is that you first think of all the men's names that you know, and then from this list you select the names that work as verbs. A different possibility reverses this sequence: You first think of all the verbs that you know, and from this list you select the words that are also names. One last possibility is that you *combine* these steps, so that your two searches go on in parallel: In essence, you let activation spread out in your memory network from the MEN'S NAMES nodes, and at the same time you let activation spread out from the VERBS nodes. Then you can just wait and see which nodes receive activation from both of these sources simultaneously.

In fact, the evidence suggests that the third option (simultaneous activation from two sources) is the one you use. We can document this by asking a different group of people just to list all the verbs they know. When we do this, we find that some verbs come to mind only after a long delay—if at all. For example, if you're just thinking of verbs, the verb "rustle" may not pop into your thoughts. If, therefore, you were trying to think of verbs-that-are-also-names by *first* thinking about verbs and then screening them, you're unlikely to come up with "rustle" in your initial step (i.e., generating a list of verbs). Therefore, you won't think about "rustle" in this setting, and so you won't spot the fact that it's also a man's name ("Russell"). On this basis, this name won't be one of the names on your list.

The reverse is also true: If you're just thinking about men's names, the name "Russell" may not spring to mind, and so, if *this* is the first step in your memory search (i.e., first generate a list of names; then screen it, looking for verbs), you won't come up with this name in the first place. Therefore, you won't consider this name, won't see that it's also a verb, and won't put it on your list.

It turns out, though, that relatively rare names and rare verbs *are* often part of your final output. This makes no sense if you're using a "two-step" procedure (first generate names, then screen them; or first generate verbs, then screen them) because the key words would never show up in the first step of this process. But the result does make sense if your memory search combines the two steps. In that case, even though these rare items are only weakly activated by the MEN'S NAMES nodes, and only weakly activated by the VERBS nodes, they are activated perfectly well if they can receive energy from *both sources at the same time*—and that is why these rare items come easily to mind.

And, by the way, there are at least 50 men's names that are also verbs, so keep hunting for them! It may help to remember that Americans *Bob* for apples at Halloween. Yesterday, I *Drew* a picture and decided to *Stu* the beef for dinner. I can *Don* a suit, *Mike* a speaker, *Rush* to an appointment, *Flip* a pancake, or *Jimmy* a locked door. These are just some of the names that could be on your list!

6.4 Semantic Priming

As Chapter 6 describes, searching through long-term memory relies heavily on a process of spreading activation, with currently activated nodes sending activation outward to their neighbors. If this spread brings enough activation to the neighbors, then those nodes will themselves become activated. However, even if these nodes do not receive enough activation to become activated themselves, the "subthreshold activation" still has important effects.

Here is a list of anagrams (words for which we've scrambled up the letters). Can you unscramble them to figure out what each of the words is?

MOUNNTIA	HRTIS
AES	VWAE
PLOTI	CORVIT
DLISNA	NOCAE

Did you get them all? Turn the page to see the answers.

The answers, in no particular order, are "sea," "shirt," "victor," "island," "mountain," "wave," "pilot," and . . . what? The last anagram in the list actually has two solutions: It could be an anagram for the boat used in North America to explore lakes and streams, or it could be an anagram for the body of water that sharks and whales and sea turtles live in.

Which of these two solutions came to your mind? If you happen to be a devoted canoeist, then "canoe" may have come rapidly into your thoughts. But the odds are good that "ocean" is the word that came to mind for you. Why is this? Several of the other words in this series ("sea," "island," "mountain," "wave") are semantically associated with "ocean." Therefore, when you solved these earlier anagrams, you activated nodes for these words, and the activation spread outward from there to the neighboring nodes—including, probably, OCEAN. As a result, the word "ocean" was already primed when you turned to the last anagram, making it likely that this word, and not the legitimate alternative, would come to your thoughts as you unscrambled NOCAE.

6.5   Priming From Implicit Memory

Imagine that yesterday you read a particular word—"couch," for example. This encounter with the word can change how you react to the word when you see it today. This will be true even if your memory contains no explicit record of yesterday's event, so that you have no conscious memory of having read that particular word. Even without an explicit record, your unconscious memory can lead you to interpret the word differently the next time you meet it, or it can lead you to recognize the word more quickly. Implicit memories can also change your *emotional* response to a word. The emotional effect probably won't be enough to make you laugh out loud or shed a tear when you see the word, but it may be enough to make the word seem more attractive to you than it would have been without the priming.

These implicit memory effects are, however, difficult to translate into quick demonstrations, because a classroom (or do-at-home) demonstration is likely to leave you with both an implicit *and* an explicit memory of the stimulus materials, and the explicit memory will overshadow the implicit memory. In other words, if an experience does leave you with an explicit memory, this record might lead you to overrule the implicit memory. Thus, your implicit memory might pull you toward a particular response, but your explicit memory might allow you to refuse that response and lead you to a different one instead—perhaps a response that's not even close to the one favored by the implicit memory.

We can, however, demonstrate something close to these effects. For example, write a short sentence using each of the following words.

Wind	Bottle	Close
Read	Record	Refuse
Dove	Foot	Desert
Pet	Tear	Lead

It turns out that several of these words can be used in more than one way or have more than one meaning. (Think about how the "wind" blows and also how you "wind" up some types of toys.) How did you use these items in your sentences? It turns out that this use is guided by your memory: If you recently read a sentence like "He dove into the pool," you're more likely to use "dove" to indicate the activity rather than the bird. This effect will work even if you didn't especially notice the word when you first saw it, and even if, now, you have no conscious recollection of recently seeing the word. In other words, these priming effects depend on implicit memory, not explicit.

It turns out that the opening paragraphs of this demonstration used the word "read" in the past tense, priming you to use the word in the past tense. Did you, in your sentence? The paragraphs also primed you to use "record" as a noun, not a verb; "tear" as the name for the thing that comes out of your eye, not an action; "close" as an adjective, not a noun or a verb; and "refuse" as a verb, not a noun. You were also primed by the opening paragraphs to think of "lead" as a verb, not a noun.

Did the priming work for you, guiding how you used the test words in the sentences you composed? Did you notice the primes? Did you remember them?

Let's be clear, though, that these priming effects don't work every time, simply because a number of other factors, in addition to priming, also influence how you use these words. Even so, the probability of your using the word a certain way is often changed by the prime, and so most people do show these priming effects.

Applying Cognitive Psychology

Research Methods: Chronometric Studies

Our mental processes are usually quite fast, but even so, they do take a measurable amount of time, and, by scrutiny of these times, we can learn a great deal about the mind. This is why *chronometric* (time-measuring) studies play a key role in our science. In these studies, participants are asked a specific question in each trial, and we measure how long they need to respond; hence our data take the form of *response times* (RTs). However, we need to be clear about what response-time data really tell us.

Let's take as an example a lexical-decision task. In each trial of this task, a sequence of letters is presented, and the participant must decide whether the sequence forms a word or not. If it does, the participant presses one button; if not, then a different button. In this situation, the trials we're interested in are the trials in which the sequence does form a word; those trials tell us how rapidly the participants can "look up" the word in their "mental dictionary." Trials in which the letter sequences *aren't* words are not helpful for this question. Nonetheless, we need to include these nonword trials as *catch trials*. If we didn't, then the correct answer would be "Yes, this sequence is a word" on every trial. Participants would quickly figure this out and would shift to a strategy of hitting the "yes" button every time without even looking at the stimulus. To avoid this problem, we include nonwords as catch trials to make sure that participants take the task seriously.

But let's focus on the trials that do involve words; those are the trials that provide our data. For these trials, we can, if we wish, think about this task as including several steps: On each trial, the participants first have to perceive the letters on the screen; then they have to look up this letter sequence in memory. Then, when they locate the relevant information in storage, they must draw the conclusion that, yes, the sequence does form a word. Finally, they must make the physical movement of pressing the appropriate button to indicate their decision.

As it turns out, though, we're only interested in a part of this sequence—namely, the time needed to locate the word in memory. In other words, the *total* response time isn't useful for us, because it includes many elements that we really don't care about. How, then, can we isolate just that bit of the process that is of interest? The key, quite simply, is *subtraction*. Specifically, let's imagine a comparison between trials in which the target word has been primed and trials with no priming. Both types of trials include letter reading; both include a decision that, yes, the stimulus is a word; both include the physical movement of a button press. Therefore, if we find *differences* between these two types of trials, the differences cannot be the result of these elements, because these elements are the same in both types. Any differences, then, must be the result of the one stage that *is* different between the two types of trials—a memory look-up in the presence of priming, as opposed to a memory look-up without priming. By examining that difference, we can ask what the effect of priming is—and that, in general, is the key to chronometric studies. We are usually interested in the differences in response times between conditions, and not the absolute times themselves; these differences allow us to isolate (and thus to measure) the processes we want to study.

Clearly, then, some craft is involved in the design of chronometric experiments. We must arrange for the proper comparisons so that we can isolate just the processes that we're interested in. But with the appropriate steps taken, chronometric studies can provide enormously useful information about memory, perception, imagery, and many other mental processes.

FOR DISCUSSION

Social psychologists argue that people are often influenced by *implicit associations*. For example, in our memories the representation for "secretary" is associated with the representation for "female," and so the moment we hear about a secretary, we are automatically primed to think about females—and thus to assume that a secretary will be a woman, rather than a man. Similar associations guide our thinking about other professions (e.g., the moment we hear about a doctor, we are primed to think about males) and about different racial or ethnic groups.

Can you design an experiment that might test this proposal? You probably want to rely on chronometric methods, and you might rely on the procedures used for lexical-decision tasks. Bear in mind that these procedures show us that activating, let's say, the nodes for BREAD causes activation to spread to the neighboring nodes, including the nodes for BUTTER. These procedures then provide a direct way of detecting this priming of the nodes for BUTTER. Can you adapt these procedures to study implicit associations?

You might also think about how these implicit associations influence us. If people start thinking "female" every time they hear about secretaries, or if they start thinking "violence" every time they hear about members of certain racial or ethnic groups, how will this influence their judgments or their behavior? And if these associations are part of the automatic (thus, inevitable) spread of activation within memory, people may be guided by these associations whether they want to be or not.

Research Methods: Double Dissociations

The textbook chapter describes a number of results showing that *implicit* memories are different from *explicit* ones. Thus, certain forms of brain damage affect explicit memory but leave implicit memory intact. Likewise, explicit memory is strongly influenced by level of processing during encoding, whereas implicit memory may not be. And so on.

It turns out, though, that the results just mentioned are ambiguous, and that ambiguity leads us to an important methodological issue. On the one side, we can read these results as suggesting that implicit memory is fundamentally different from explicit memory—governed by its own principles and served by separate portions of the brain. But on the other side, perhaps implicit and explicit memory are not different types at all. Perhaps they are fundamentally the same, obeying the same rules and principles. In that case, the memories we call "explicit" might simply be a more fragile version of this single type of memory, and hence they are more easily influenced by external factors such as brain damage or level of processing.

The issue at stake here is one that often arises in science: What is being asked, in essence, is whether the difference between the memory types is qualitative or quantitative, and it's important to get this straight. Claiming a *qualitative* difference is equivalent to claiming that the two are different "species" of memory. In that case, we will need different theories for implicit and explicit memory, and we'll confuse ourselves by classing the two types of memory together, seeking principles that apply to both. In contrast, claiming a *quantitative* difference is equivalent to saying the two are fundamentally similar, differing only in some "adjustment" or "parameter." In this case, we'd be wasting our time if we search for separate governing principles, because the same principles apply to both.

How can we resolve this ambiguity? The key lies in realizing that the facts we have mentioned so far (the effects of brain damage or of level of processing) are concerned with ways we can influence explicit memory with no effect on implicit. To demonstrate a qualitative difference, we also need the reverse result—cases in which we can influence implicit memory but not explicit. The moment we find such a result, we know that explicit memory is not just more fragile, or more easily influenced, than implicit memory—because sometimes, with some manipulations, it's implicit memory that's more easily influenced. As a consequence, we could no longer claim that either type of memory is weaker or more fragile than the other: Each type seems, in some experiments, to be the "stronger" memory (resistant to manipulations) and seems, in other experiments, to be the "weaker." The only possible conclusion in this setting is that we can't talk about the two types in terms of which is stronger or weaker, more fragile or less; instead, we need to acknowledge that the two types are simply different from each other, each open to its own set of influences—and that is precisely the conclusion we are after.

This overall pattern of evidence—with some factors influencing one sort of memory but not the other, and some factors doing the reverse—provides what is called a *double dissociation*, and it allows us to rule out the possibility that explicit memories are simply more fragile than implicit (and hence more readily influenced by any manipulation). This in turn allows us to conclude that the difference is not just a quantitative one.

As it turns out, we do have a double dissociation for implicit and explicit memory: Certain factors (including forms of brain damage) influence explicit memory but not implicit. (Those factors provide a *dissociation*.) Other factors (and other forms of brain damage) influence implicit memory but not explicit (and so now we have a *dissociation* in the opposite direction, and hence a *double* dissociation).

With all these data in view, it's clear that neither type of memory is, in general, easier to influence than the other. Thus, we can set aside the hypothesis that one of these types of memory is just a more fragile version of the other. Instead, the evidence tells us that each type of memory is indeed affected by its own set of factors. That tells us a lot about these forms of memory, but it also illustrates the power of a double dissociation.

FOR DISCUSSION

In Chapter 5, we discussed the difference between *working memory* and *long-term memory*. These are two different types of storage, we argued, each with its own characteristics. Imagine, though, that someone offered an alternative view: "There's really just one type of memory. What we call 'working memory' is merely the information that's just arrived in memory, so that it's weaker, more easily disrupted, more likely to be forgotten, than memory that's been in storage for a longer time." This view suggests that the difference between (so-called) working memory and long-term memory is *not* a difference between types of memory; it is instead just a quantitative difference—a difference of "how much" (how strong, how long lasting) rather than a difference of "which type."

What evidence can you think of that speaks against this alternative view? Can we use the logic of a *double dissociation* here to show that working memory is not just weaker, shorter lasting, or more fragile but is instead truly different from long-term memory?

If you get stuck, think back to the basic logic of a dou-ble dissociation: Are there factors that influence working memory but not long-term memory? Are there are also factors that influence long-term memory but not working memory? If you can come up with factors of both sorts, this indicates that we can't just argue that one type of memory is "weaker" or "more easily disrupted" than the other—and that's the point.

Cognitive Psychology and Education:
The Importance of Multiple Retrieval Paths

The chapter discusses evidence for the idea that memory performance is generally better if there's a "match" between your perspective and circumstances at the time of *learning* and your perspective and circumstances at the time of *test*. Hence, if you learn materials in a particular room, you'll have an advantage if the test is given in that same room. If you focus on the *sounds* within the materials at the time of learning, you'll be well served if you again focus on sounds at the time of the test.

These observations have three pragmatic implications: First, if you can predict in advance when, where, and how you'll be retrieving material, you might want to "tune" your study efforts accordingly, so that your learning will be properly aligned with the subsequent context of memory retrieval. That way, you'll ensure from the start that there will be a "match" between your learning and test circumstances. Thus, if you know in advance that your instructor will be providing German words and asking for the English translation, you should study with the vocabulary items in that same format. Likewise, if you know that your instructor will be naming organic molecules and asking for their pKa values, again you should structure your studying in the same way.

Second, you can often improve your memory by means of *context reinstatement*—doing what you can, at the time of memory retrieval, to re-create the circumstances of learning. Let's emphasize, though, that what matters here is the *mental context*, and not the physical context. Thus, if you studied in your dorm room or apartment, context reinstatement doesn't require you to take the test in that same location. Instead, all you need to do is spend a moment, early in the exam, thinking back to how you felt while in your dorm room, and how the world around you looked, and perhaps what other thoughts were in your mind. Likewise, if, during the exam, you're having trouble recalling what you heard in the professor's lecture, it will help to spend a moment "resetting the stage." Think about where you were in the room on the day that lecture was given. Think about who was next to you. Think about what others issues in the lecture might have caught your attention. By creating this mental perspective, you'll often help yourself recall bits you otherwise would miss!

The third implication, though, is the most important: You know in advance that you'll be well served by a "match" between your learning perspective and your perspective at the time of memory retrieval. But you often have no way of predicting what your perspective will be later on. Will you need the information you're studying when, later, you take an exam? Or will you need it as a useful illustration in a class discussion, or as a good fact to use in an argument with your mother? Usually, there's no way to forecast these things.

How, therefore, should you proceed? The answer is obvious: If you establish many retrieval paths, all leading to the target information, you'll be able to reach that information from many different starting points. In that case, you're ready for anything! But how can you establish that variety of paths? The answer returns us to a theme we've met several times before: When you *understand* an explanation (or a diagram, or a story), you see how the elements of the explanation are linked to each other, and how they're linked to other things you know. And the deeper your understanding, the more links you see.

Understanding, in other words, creates multiple connections—and hence multiple retrieval paths, so that well-understood materials can be retrieved from many directions. In studying, then, you shouldn't worry about *memorizing*, and you probably shouldn't worry about setting up the right retrieval paths. Instead, make sure you understand the material. Can you explain the material in your own words? Can you answer a friend's questions about the material? Can you trace out some of the implications of the material? If you can do these things, the retrieval paths are in place, and good memory is assured.

FOR DISCUSSION

We've now argued that it's useful for students to establish *multiple retrieval paths*, all leading to the target materials. That way, you'll be able to reach the target materials from many different starting points. But what exactly should you do to follow this advice? The essay lists several steps that can be helpful (explaining the material in your own words, answering a friend's questions, tracing out some implications), but are there others? What else can you do to create lots of links so that you have many retrieval paths available?

Cognitive Psychology and Education: Familiarity Is Potentially Treacherous

Sometimes you see a picture of someone and immediately say, "Gee—she looks familiar!" This seems a simple and direct reaction to the picture, but the chapter describes just how complicated "familiarity" really is. Indeed, the chapter makes it clear that we can't think of familiarity just as a "feeling" somehow triggered by a stimulus. Instead, familiarity seems more like a *conclusion* that you draw, at the end of a many-step process. As a result of these complexities, *errors* about familiarity are possible: cases in which a stimulus feels familiar even though it's not, or cases in which you correctly realize that the stimulus is familiar but then make a mistake about *why* it's familiar.

These points highlight the dangers, for students, of relying on familiarity. As one illustration, consider the advice that people sometimes give for taking a multiple-choice test. They tell you, "Go with your first inclination" or "Choose the answer that feels familiar." In some cases these strategies will help, because sometimes the correct answer will indeed feel familiar. But in other cases these strategies can lead you astray, because the answer you're considering may seem familiar *for a bad reason*: What if your professor once said, "One of the common mistakes people make is to believe . . ." and then talked about the claim summarized in the answer you're now considering? Alternatively, what if the answer seems familiar because it *resembles* the correct answer but is, in some crucial way, different from the correct answer (and therefore mistaken)? In either of these cases your sense of familiarity might lead you directly to a wrong answer.

To make this even worse, one study familiarized people with phrases like "the record for tallest pine tree." Thanks to this exposure, these people were later *more likely to accept as true* a longer phrase, such as "the record for tallest pine tree is 350 feet." Why? They realized that (at least) part of the sentence was familiar and therefore drew the reasonable inference that they must have encountered the entire sentence at some previous point. The danger here for students should be obvious: On a multiple choice test, *part* of an incorrect option may be an exact duplicate of some phrase in your reading; if so, relying on familiarity will get you into trouble! (And, by the way, this particular claim about pines is false; the tallest pine tree, documented in early 2011, is a mere 268 feet tall.)

As a different concern, imagine the following scenario. You're talking with a friend, brainstorming about possible topics for a term paper you need to write. Your friend makes a suggestion, but you scoff at it because the idea seems too complicated. A few days later, you're again trying to think of topics for the paper, and the same idea pops into your thoughts. By then, you may have forgotten your conversation with your friend, and so you might have forgotten that your friend offered this very idea. But on this new consideration, the idea seems far more promising—perhaps because the earlier exposure gave you some "warm-up" in thinking through the idea, and so it doesn't seem so complicated the second time around (even though, again, you don't realize that this is "the second time around"!). As a result, you might now endorse the idea, and since you've forgotten your friend's suggestion, you might claim the idea as your own.

In fact, several studies have shown that this sort of *unconscious plagiarism* is relatively common. In this situation, the idea you're presenting as your own is, objectively speaking, familiar to you, thanks to your earlier conversation with your friend. However, the idea may not *feel* familiar. Thanks to the earlier encounter, you're now a bit more fluent in your thinking about the idea, and this does make the idea feel special and distinctive. But (mistakenly) you don't interpret this specialness as familiarity; instead, you interpret it as an indication that the idea is especially clever. As a result—with no explicit memory of the earlier conversation with your friend, and with no sense of familiarity—you sincerely (but falsely) claim that the idea is yours.

What can you do to avoid these dangers—to avoid (in the multiple-choice case) the error of being misled by familiarity, and to avoid (in the unconscious plagiarism case) the problem of *not detecting* an idea's familiarity? Perhaps the best answer is just to be alert to the complexities associated with familiarity. After all, you don't want to ignore familiarity, because sometimes it is helpful: Sometimes an option on a multiple-choice test seems familiar because it *is* the (correct) idea discussed in class. But given the difficulties we've mentioned here, it may be best to regard familiarity just as a clue about the past and not as an iron-clad indicator. That attitude may encourage the sort of caution that will allow you to use familiarity without being betrayed by it.

FOR DISCUSSION

We've just noted that students don't want to *ignore* familiarity, because sometimes it is helpful. Perhaps the key, then, is to seek some means of *distinguishing* cases in which familiarity is helpful from cases in which familiarity might mislead you. That leads us to ask: Are there steps you can take to make sure your familiarity comes from the "right source"? Is there some way to check on whether an idea (or name, or vocabulary item) feels familiar because you met that idea within the course materials?

A plausible path forward here focuses on the learning process: Are there steps you can take during learning that will help you to "anchor" ideas to an appropriate context, so that, later you'll remember when, where, and in what setting you met the idea?

For more on this topic

Jacoby, L., & Hollingshead, A. (1990). Reading student essays may be hazardous to your spelling: Effects of reading incorrectly and correctly spelled words. *Canadian Journal of Psychology, 44*, 345–358.

Kahneman, D. (2011). Thinking, fast and slow. New York, NY: Farrar, Straus and Giroux.

Preston, J., & Wegner, D. M. (2007). The Eureka error: Inadvertent plagiarism by misattributions of effort. *Journal of Personality and Social Psychology, 92*, 575–584.

Stark, L.-J., Perfect, T., & Newstead, S. (2008). The effects of repeated idea elaboration on unconscious plagiarism. *Memory & Cognition, 36*, 65–73.

Cognitive Psychology and the Law:
Unconscious Transference

Imagine that you witness a crime. The police suspect that Robby Robber was the perpetrator, and so they place Robby's picture onto a page together with five other photos, and they show you this "photospread." You point to Robby's photo and say, "I think that's the guy, but I'm not at all sure." The police can't count this as a positive identification, but, based on other evidence they become convinced that Robby is guilty, and so he's arrested and brought to trial.

During the trial, you're asked to testify, and, when you're on the stand, the prosecutor asks, "Do you see the perpetrator in the courtroom?" You answer "yes," and so the prosecutor asks you to indicate who the robber is. You point to Robby and say, "That's the guy—the man at the defense table."

In-court identifications, like the one just described, are powerful events and are enormously persuasive for juries. But, in truth, in-court ID's are problematic for *four* reasons. First, research tells us that people are often better at realizing *that* a face is familiar than they are in recalling *why* the face is familiar. In the imaginary case just described, therefore, you might (correctly) realize that Robby's face is familiar and sensibly conclude that you've seen his face before. But then you might make an error about *where* you'd seen his face before, perhaps mistakenly concluding that Robby looks familiar because you saw him during the crime, when in actuality he looks familiar only because you'd seen his picture in the photospread! This error is sometimes referred to as *unconscious transference*, because the face is, in your memory, unconsciously "transferred" from one setting to another. (You actually saw him in the photospread, but in your memory you "transfer" him into the original crime—memory's version of a "cut-and-paste" operation.)

Second, notice that in our hypothetical case you had made a tentative identification from the photospread. You had, in effect, made a commitment to a particular selection, and, once done, it's often difficult to set aside your initial choice in order to get a fresh start in a later identification procedure. Thus, your in-court ID of Robby is likely to be influenced by your initial selection from the photospread—even if you made your initial selection with little confidence.

Third, in-court identifications are inevitably suggestive. In the courtroom, it's obvious from the seating arrangement who the defendant is. The witness also knows that the police and prosecution believe the defendant is guilty. These facts, by themselves, put some pressure on the witness to make an identification of the defendant—especially if the defendant looks in any way familiar.

Fourth, the speed of the justice system is less than any of us would wish, and so trials often take place many months (or years) after a crime. Therefore, there has been ample opportunity for a witness's memory of the crime to *fade*. As a result, the witness doesn't have much of an "internal anchor" (a good and clear memory) to guide the identification, making the witness all the more vulnerable to the effects of suggestion or the effect of the earlier commitment.

How worried should we be about these various problems—the risk of unconscious transference, the effects of commitment, the impact of a suggestive identification procedure, the effect of passing time? Research suggests that each of these can have a powerful effect on eyewitness identifications, potentially compromising in-court identifications. Indeed, some researchers would argue that even though in-court identifications are very dramatic, they are—because of the concerns discussed here—of little value as evidence.

In addition, note that some of these concerns also apply to out-of-court identifications. I testified in one trial in which the victim claimed that the defendant looked "familiar," and she was "almost certain" that he was the man who had robbed her. It turned out, though, that the man had an excellent alibi. What, therefore, was the basis for the victim's (apparently incorrect) identification? For years, the defendant had, for his morning run, used a jogging path that went right by the victim's house. It seems likely, therefore, that the defendant looked familiar to the victim because she had seen him during his run—and that she had then unconsciously (and mistakenly) transferred his face into her memory of the crime.

It's crucial, therefore, that the courts and police investigators do all that they can to avoid these various concerns. Specifically, if a witness thinks that the defendant "looks familiar," it's important to ask whether there might be some basis for the familiarity other than the crime itself. With steps like these, we can use what we know about memory to improve the accuracy of eyewitness identifications—and, in that way, improve the accuracy and the efficiency of the criminal justice system.

FOR DISCUSSION

Can you think of examples from your own life in which you've experienced unconscious transference? This would include situations in which you were sure that you knew someone from one setting, when in fact you really had met the person in a completely different setting.

Likewise, can you think of examples in which you realized that someone looked familiar, but you couldn't figure out *why* the person looked familiar? Is there some way we can communicate these examples to a jury, so that the jurors will make better use of identification evidence?

For more on this topic

Brown, E., Deffenbacher, K., & Sturgill, W. (1977). Memory for faces and the circumstances of encounter. *Journal of Applied Psychology, 62,* 311–318.

Davis, D., Loftus, E. F., Vanous, S., & Cucciare, M. (2008). "Unconscious transferrence" can be an instance of "change blindness." *Applied Cognitive Psychology, 22,* 605–623.

Dysart, J. E., Lindsay, R. C. L., Hammond, R., & Dupuis, P. (2001). Mug shot exposure prior to lineup identification: Interference, transference, and commitment effects. *Journal of Applied Psychology, 86,* 1280–1284.

Cognitive Psychology and the Law:
The Cognitive Interview

Police investigations often depend on eyewitness reports: Who was present at the scene of the crime? What words did they say? How were they dressed? Questions like these can provide valuable clues—but what can we do if eyewitnesses can't recall the event, and so can't answer these questions? Are there steps we can take to help witnesses remember?

A number of exotic procedures have been proposed to promote witness recollection, including hypnosis and memory-enhancing medications. Evidence suggests, however, that these procedures provide little benefit (and may, in some settings, actually harm memory). Indeed, "hypnotically enhanced memory" is inadmissible as trial evidence in most jurisdictions. A much more promising approach is the *cognitive interview,* a technique developed by psychologists with the specific aim of improving eyewitness memory. Many studies suggest that this procedure does help witnesses remember more about an event; especially important, it does so without encouraging memory errors. It is gratifying, then, that the cognitive interview has been adopted by a number of police departments as their preferred interview technique.

How does the cognitive interview work? Let's start with the fact that sometimes you cannot remember things simply because you didn't notice them in the first place, and so no record of the desired information was ever placed in long-term storage. In this situation, no procedure—whether it's the cognitive interview, or hypnosis, or simply trying really really hard to recall—can locate information that isn't there to be located. You cannot get water out of an empty bottle, and you cannot read words off a blank page. In the same fashion, you cannot recall information that was never placed in memory to begin with.

In other cases, though, the gaps in your recollection have a different source: The desired information *is* in memory, but you're unable to find it. (We'll have more to say about this point in Chapter 7, when we discuss theories of forgetting.) To overcome this problem, the cognitive interview relies on context reinstatement: The police investigator urges the witness to think back to the setting of the target event: How did the witness feel at the time of the crime? What was the physical setting? What was the weather? As Chapter 6 discusses, these steps are likely to put the witness back into the same mental state, the same frame of mind, that he or she had at the time of the crime—and, in many cases, these steps will promote recall.

In addition, the chapter's discussion of retrieval paths leads to the idea that sometimes you'll recall a memory only if you approach the memory from the right angle—using the proper retrieval path. But how do you choose the proper path? The cognitive interview builds on the simple notion that you don't have to choose! Instead, you can try recalling the events from lots of different angles (via lots of different paths), in order to maximize your chances of finding a path that leads to the desired information.

Thus, for example, the cognitive interview encourages witnesses first to recount the event from its start to its end, and then recount it in reverse sequence from the end back to the beginning. Sometimes, witnesses are also encouraged to take a different *spatial* perspective: "You just told me what you saw; try to remember what Joe would have seen, from where he was standing."

As you can see, then, the cognitive interview builds on principles well established in research—the role of context reinstatement, for example, or the importance of retrieval paths. It's no surprise, therefore, that the cognitive interview is effective; the procedure capitalizes on mechanisms that we know to be helpful. More important, the cognitive interview provides a clear example of how we can use what we know about memory to aid anyone—including law enforcement professionals—who needs to draw as much information from memory as possible.

FOR DISCUSSION

Based on the material in the chapter, are there other steps police officers should take to maximize what someone can recall? Are there steps that police officers should *avoid* taking to make sure they don't lead the witness in any way? In addition, can we carry these insights into other arenas? Imagine a physician trying to learn as much as possible about a patient's medical history; will the same procedures work there? Will the procedures need to be modified in any way? How about a newspaper reporter trying to write a story and needing information from witnesses to some newsworthy event? Will the procedures work in that case? Are any modifications needed?

For more on this topic

Davis, M. R., McMahon, M., & Greenwood, K. M. (2005). The efficacy of mnemonic components of the cognitive interview: Towards a shortened variant for time-critical investigations. *Applied Cognitive Psychology, 19*, 75–93.

Fisher, R., Milne, R., & Bull, R. (2011). Interviewing cooperative witnesses. *Current Directions in Psychological Science, 20*, 16–19.

Fisher, R., & Schreiber, N. (2007). Interview protocols to improve eyewitness memory. In R. Lindsay, D. Ross, J. Read, & M. Toglia (Eds.), *Handbook of eyewitness psychology; Vol. 1. Memory for events* (pp. 53–80). Hillsdale, NJ: Erlbaum.

Holliday, R. E., & Albon, A. J. (2004). Minimising misinformation effects in young children with cognitive interview mnemonics. *Applied Cognitive Psychology, 18*, 263–281.

Koehnken, G., Milne, R., Memon, A., & Bull, R. (1999). The cognitive interview: A meta-analysis. *Psychology, Crime & Law, 5*, 3–27.

Milne, R., & Bull, R. (2002). Back to basics: A componental analysis of the original cognitive interview mnemonics with three age groups. *Applied Cognitive Psychology, 16*, 743–753.

CHAPTER 7

Remembering Complex Events

Demonstrations

7.1   Associations and Memory Error

This is a test of immediate memory. Read List 1; then turn the page over and try to write down in the box, from memory, as many words as you can from the list. Then come back to this page, read List 2, turn the page over, and try to write down as many of its words as you can. Then do the same for List 3. When you're all done, read the material that follows.

List 1	List 2	List 3
Door	Nose	Sour
Glass	Breathe	Candy
Pane	Sniff	Sugar
Shade	Aroma	Bitter
Ledge	Hear	Good
Sill	See	Taste
House	Nostril	Tooth
Open	Whiff	Nice
Curtain	Scent	Honey
Frame	Reek	Soda
View	Stench	Chocolate
Breeze	Fragrance	Heart
Sash	Perfume	Cake
Screen	Salts	Tart
Shutter	Rose	Pie

List 1	List 2	List 3

Don't read beyond this point until you've tried to recall each of the three lists!

Each of these lists is organized around a theme, but the word that best captures that theme is not included in the list. All of the words in List 1, for example, are strongly associated with the word "window," but that word is not in the list. All of the words for List 2 are strongly associated with "smell," and all in List 3 are strongly associated with "sweet," but again, these theme words are not in the lists.

In your recall of the lists, did you include seeing "window" in List 1? "Smell" in List 2? "Sweet" in List 3?

This procedure is called the "DRM procedure," in honor of the researchers who have developed this paradigm (Deese, Roediger, and McDermott). In this situation, often half of the people tested do make these specific errors—and with considerable confidence. Of course, the theme words are associated with the list in your memory, and it is this association that leads many people into a memory error.

Demonstration adapted from McDermott, K., & Roediger, H. (1998). False recognition of associates can be resistant to an explicit warning to subjects and an immediate recognition probe. *Journal of Memory and Language, 39,* 508–520. Also, Roediger, H., & McDermott, K. (1995). Creating false memories: Remembering words not presented in lists. *Journal of Experimental Psychology: Learning, Memory and Cognition, 21*(4), 803–814.

7.2   Memory Accuracy and Confidence

As you have seen, a large part of Chapter 7 is concerned with the errors people make when they're trying to recall the past. But how powerful are the errors? Here is one way to find out. In this demonstration, you will read a series of sentences. Be warned: The sentences are designed to be tricky and are similar to each other. Several of the sentences describe one scene; several describe other scenes. To make this challenging, though, the scenes are interwoven (and so you might get a sentence about Scene 1, then a sentence about Scene 2, then another about Scene 1, then one about Scene 3, and so on).

Try to remember the sentences—including their wording—as accurately as you can. Try this demonstration in a quiet setting, so that you can really focus on the sentences. Can you avoid making any mistakes?

To help you just a little, the memory test will come immediately after the sentences, so that there's no problem created by a long delay. To help you even more, the memory test will be a *recognition* test, so that the sentences will be supplied for you, with no demand that you come up with the sentences on your own.

Finally, to allow you to do your best, the memory test won't force you into a yes-or-no format. Instead, it will allow you to express degrees of certainty. Specifically, in the memory test you'll judge, first, whether each test sentence was included in the original list or not. Second, you'll indicate how confident you are, using 0% to indicate "I'm really just guessing" and 100% to indicate "I'm totally certain." Of course, you can use values between 0% and 100% to indicate intermediate levels of certainty.

In short, this is a demonstration designed to ask *how good* memory can be—with many factors in place to support performance: concrete, meaningful materials; ample warning about the nature of the materials; encouragement for you to give your best effort; immediate testing; recognition testing (not recall); and the option for you to "hedge your bets" by expressing your degree of certainty. Can we, in these ways, document nearly perfect memory?

Here are the sentences to memorize. Read them with care, because—as we already said—they are tricky to remember.

1. The girl broke the window on the porch.
2. The tree in the front yard shaded the man who was smoking his pipe.
3. The hill was steep.
4. The cat, running from the barking dog, jumped on the table.
5. The tree was tall.
6. The old car climbed the hill.
7. The cat running from the dog jumped on the table.
8. The girl who lives next door broke the window on the porch.
9. The car pulled the trailer.
10. The scared cat was running from the barking dog.
11. The girl lives next door.
12. The tree shaded the man who was smoking his pipe.
13. The scared cat jumped on the table.
14. The girl who lives next door broke the large window.
15. The man was smoking his pipe.
16. The old car climbed the steep hill.
17. The large window was on the porch.
18. The tall tree was in the front yard.
19. The car pulling the trailer climbed the steep hill.
20. The cat jumped on the table.
21. The tall tree in the front yard shaded the man.
22. The car pulling the trailer climbed the hill.
23. The dog was barking.
24. The window was large.

Now, immediately go to the next page for the memory test.

For each of the sentences below, was the sentence on the previous list? If so, mark "Old." Or is this a new sentence? If so, mark "New." Also, for each one mark how confident you are, with 0% meaning "just guessing" and 100% indicating "totally certain." Remember, you can also use values between 0% and 100% to indicate intermediate levels of certainty.

Old ___ New ___ Confidence _____	The car climbed the hill.
Old ___ New ___ Confidence _____	The girl who lives next door broke the window.
Old ___ New ___ Confidence _____	The old man who was smoking his pipe climbed the steep hill.
Old ___ New ___ Confidence _____	The tree was in the front yard.
Old ___ New ___ Confidence _____	The scared cat, running from the barking dog, jumped on the table.
Old ___ New ___ Confidence _____	The window was on the porch.
Old ___ New ___ Confidence _____	The barking dog jumped on the old car in the front yard.
Old ___ New ___ Confidence _____	The tree in the front yard shaded the man.
Old ___ New ___ Confidence _____	The cat was running from the dog.
Old ___ New ___ Confidence _____	The old car pulled the trailer.
Old ___ New ___ Confidence _____	The tall tree in the front yard shaded the old car.
Old ___ New ___ Confidence _____	The tall tree shaded the man who was smoking his pipe.
Old ___ New ___ Confidence _____	The scared cat was running from the dog.
Old ___ New ___ Confidence _____	The old car, pulling the trailer, climbed the hill.
Old ___ New ___ Confidence _____	The girl who lives next door broke the large window on the porch.

How well did you do? This is the moment at which we confess that there is a trick here: *Every one of the test sentences was new*. None of the test sentences were identical to the sentences used in the original presentation.

For many of the test sentences, you probably (correctly) said "New" and were quite confident in your response. Which test sentences were these? Odds are good that you gave a high-confidence "New" response to a test sentence that *mixed together elements from the different scenes*. For example, you were probably confident and correct in rejecting "The old man who was smoking his pipe climbed the steep hill," because the man with the pipe came from one scene (he was by the tree) and the steep hill came from a different scene (with the car climbing the hill). For these sentences, you could rely on your memory for the overall gist of the memory materials, and memory for gist tends to be quite good. On this basis, you easily (and accurately) rejected sentences that didn't fit with that gist.

But for other test sentences, you probably said "Old" and may even have indicated 90% or 100% confidence that the sentences were familiar. But, no matter how certain you were, you were wrong. Let's be clear, therefore, that we cannot count on *confidence* as an indication of accurate memories. Even high-confidence recollection can be wrong.

As a separate implication, notice how hard it is to remember a sentence's phrasing even in circumstances that are designed to *help* your memory. (Again, the testing was immediate. Recognition testing meant that you didn't have to come up with sentences on your own. You were warned that the test would be difficult. You were trying to do well.) Even in this setting, errors (including high-confidence errors) can occur.

Of course, one might argue that this is an acceptable pattern. After all, what you typically *want* to remember is the gist of a message, not the exact wording. Do you care whether you recall the exact phrasing of this paragraph? Or is it more important that you remember the point being made here? Nonetheless, there are situations in which you *do* want to remember the wording, and for that reason the results of this demonstration are troubling. There are also situations in which you might have misunderstood what you experienced, or your understanding might be incomplete. Those situations make it worrisome that what you remember seems to be dominated by your understanding, and not by the "raw materials" of your experience.

Demonstration adapted from Bransford, J. (1979). *Human cognition: Learning, understanding and remembering,* 1E. Belmont, CA: Wadsworth. © 1979 Wadsworth, a part of Cengage Learning, Inc. Reproduced by permission. www.cengage.com/permissions

7.3 The Tip-of-the-Tongue Effect

Your memory usually serves you well, quickly and easily providing all the information you need. But your memory can also let you down. Sometimes, you'll fail to remember something because you paid insufficient attention to the information when you first met it. As a result, the information was never *recorded* in memory, and so of course you can't remember it later. In other settings, the information was recorded in memory but has now been lost—perhaps through decay, or perhaps through interference. In still other cases, the information was recorded in memory *and* remains there, but you can't find the information when you want it. This last pattern is what we call "retrieval failure"—an inability to locate information that is, in fact, still in storage.

Retrieval failure is our best explanation for cases in which you fail to remember something but later (when provided with a proper hint, or suitable context) *can* recall the target information. The fact that your recall eventually succeeds tells us that the information *was* recorded and *wasn't* lost. The initial failure to remember, therefore, has to be understood as a problem in retrieval.

Retrieval failure is often complete: You utterly forget that you were supposed to stop at the bank on the way home (but then remember, when you later reach into your empty pocket). You completely forget about a concert you attended years ago (but then remember, when you hear that band on the radio). Sometimes, however, retrieval failure is *partial*: you can recall part of the information you're after, but not all.

Consider, for example, the common (but maddening) state in which you're trying to think of a word, but you just can't come up with it. You're sure you know the word, but, no matter how hard you try, you can't recall it, and so the word remains, people say, "on the tip of your tongue". Following this lead, psychologists refer to this as the "TOT" effect. In this situation, you may eventually come up with the word—and so it plainly *was* in your memory. Your initial inability to recall the word, therefore, is another instance of retrieval failure—an inability to locate information in storage.

In case you've never experienced the frustration of the TOT state, consider the following definitions. In each case, is the word or name in your vocabulary? If it is, can you think of the word? If the word is in your vocabulary but you can't think of it right now, can you recall what letter the word starts with? Can you remember how many syllables it has?

You may not know some of these terms at all; other terms will immediately spring to mind. But in at least some cases, you're likely to end up in the frustrating state of having the word at the tip of your tongue but not being able to think of it.

1. The aromatic substance found in the gut of some whales, valued in earlier years for the manufacture of perfumes.

2. A tube-shaped instrument that is rotated to produce complex, symmetrical designs, created by light shining through mirrors inside the instrument.

3. A structure of open latticework, usually made of wood, used as a support for vines or other climbing plants.

4. The legendary Roman slave who was spared in the arena when the lion recognized him as the man who had removed a thorn from its paw.

5. An infectious, often fatal disease, often transmitted through contaminated animal substances and sometimes transmitted, in powder form, as an agent in germ warfare.

6. The scholarly study of word origins and word histories.

7. The American magician who died in 1926, famous for his escapes from chains, handcuffs, straitjackets, and padlocked boxes.

8. People who explore caves as a hobby or sport.

9. An instance of making a discovery by lucky accident.

10. An instrument for measuring wind velocity.

11. An Oriental art form involving complex paper folding.

12. The formal term for the collection and study of postage stamps and related material.

13. A word or phrase that reads the same way backward or forward (e.g., "Madam I'm Adam").

14. A building, usually stone, housing a large tomb or several tombs.

15. The verb meaning *to give up the throne*.

16. The sense of resentment, often felt in response to an imagined insult.

17. The term for the three-dots used to indicate a pause or an omission . . .

18. The length of leather used in older times for sharpening a razor.

19. The accumulation of stones carried along, and eventually dropped, by a glacier.

20. Someone who makes maps.

21. Lasting only a very brief time.

Turn to the next page to find out what the words are.

Here are the words.

1. Ambergris	8. Spelunkers	15. Abdicate
2. Kaleidoscope	9. Serendipity	16. Umbrage
3. Trellis	10. Anemometer	17. Ellipsis
4. Androcles	11. Origami	18. Strop
5. Anthrax	12. Philately	19. Moraine
6. Etymology	13. Palindrome	20. Cartographer
7. Houdini	14. Mausoleum	21. Ephemeral

Demonstration adapted from Brown, R., & McNeill, D. (1966). The "tip of the tongue" phenomenon. *Journal of Verbal Learning and Verbal Behavior, 5,* 325–337. Also: James, L., & Burke, D. (2000). Phonological priming effects on word retrieval and tip-of-the-tongue experiences in young and older adults. *Journal of Experimental Psychology: Learning, Memory and Cognition, 26,* 1378–1391.

7.4   Childhood Amnesia

Each of us remembers many things about our lives, so that, overall, our memories are rich and detailed. There is, however, one well-documented limit on the memories we have: Think back to something that happened when you were 10 years old. (It will probably help to think about what grade you were in and who your teacher was. Can you remember anything about that year?) How about when you were 9 years old? When you were 8? When you were 7? What is the *earliest event in your life* that you can remember?

Many people have trouble remembering events that took place before they were 4 years old. Very few people can remember events that took place before they were 3. This pattern is so common that it often gets a name—*childhood amnesia,* or sometimes *infantile amnesia.* Do you fit this pattern? Can you remember any events from the first three years of your life? If you can, is it possible that you're not remembering the event itself, but instead remembering family discussions about the event? Or remembering some photograph of the event?

Several explanations have been offered for childhood amnesia, and probably each of them captures part of the truth. One important consideration, though, hinges on the young child's understanding of the world. As the textbook chapter discusses, we typically remember events by associating them with other knowledge that we have. But, of course, this requires that you *have* that other knowledge, so that you can link the new information to it. Young children lack this other knowledge—they lack a scaffold to which they can attach new information, and this makes it difficult for them to establish new information in memory.

As a further exploration, ask some of your friends about the earliest events in their lives that they can remember. Several lines of evidence suggest that women can recall earlier life events than men, and that children who were quite verbal at an early age can recall earlier life events than children who were less verbal. Do these claims fit with your observations?

Applying Cognitive Psychology

Research Methods: External Validity

How accurately do eyewitnesses to crimes remember what they have seen? To find out, many researchers have run "crime-simulation studies" in which they show their participants brief videos depicting a crime and then test the participants' memories for the video. But can we trust this research?

In these studies, we can set things up in just the way we like. We can design the video so that it allows the comparisons crucial for our hypotheses. We can take steps to remove confounds from the procedure and use random assignment to make sure our groups are matched at the experiment's start. Steps like these guarantee that our results will be unambiguous and informative.

But one thing about these studies is worrisome: The laboratory is in many ways an artificial setting, and it's possible that people behave differently in the lab than they do in other environments. In that case, the crime-simulation studies may lack *external validity*—that is, they may not reflect the real-world phenomena that ultimately we wish to understand. As a consequence, we cannot *generalize* the lab results to situations outside of the lab.

How do we decide whether a laboratory result is generalizable or not? This is an issue to be settled by *research*, not by argument. As one option, we can draw on the "replication + variation" strategy we discussed in the Research Methods essay for Chapter 5. Specifically, we can see whether we get the same result with different participant groups, different stimuli, different instructions, and so on. If the result keeps emerging despite these changes in procedural detail, we can conclude that the result *does not depend on* these details in any way. This conclusion, in turn, would strengthen the claim that we can extrapolate from the results to new settings and new groups of people, including settings outside of the carefully designed research environment.

Another important strategy involves the effort toward making our controlled studies as realistic as possible—for example, using "live" (staged) crimes, rather than videos depicting crimes, or conducting our studies in natural settings, rather than in university laboratories. These steps, on their own, diminish the concern about external validity. In addition, these steps allow us to make some crucial comparisons: Does the effect we're interested in grow weaker and weaker as our studies become more and more realistic? If so, this is an argument *against* extrapolating the result to real-world settings. Or does the effect we're interested in hold steady, or perhaps even grow stronger, as our studies become more and more realistic? This pattern, when we observe it, is an argument *supporting* the extrapolation from our current data.

Yet another option is quite powerful, but not always available: Sometimes we can collect data from field studies—for example, studies of actual witnesses to actual crimes—and then compare these new data to our controlled experiments. The field studies by themselves are often difficult to interpret. (We obviously can't arrange a crime to remove confounds from our comparisons, nor can we randomly assign witnesses to one condition or another. This means that the field studies by themselves often suffer from the ambiguities described in earlier Research Methods essays in this workbook.) Nonetheless, we can ask whether the field data are as we would expect, based on the laboratory findings. If so, this increases our confidence that the lab findings must be taken seriously.

How do all of these efforts work out? Are our data, in the end, externally valid? There's no single answer here, because the pattern of the evidence varies, case by case: Some of our claims, based on lab findings, *can* be generalized to real-world settings; for other claims, the answer is less clear. Above all, though, let's emphasize that the broad issue here—and the question about external validity—needs to be taken seriously, and has to be addressed through research. Only then do we know whether each of our claims, initially rooted in controlled studies, can be applied to the real-world phenomena we eventually want to explain.

FOR DISCUSSION

A witness to a crime is likely to be afraid, or perhaps angry, as the crime unfolds. Participants in a research study, in contrast, are likely to stay calm, and they know they are observing an artificial event that will probably have no consequences for their lives. Using the logic of this essay, what evidence should we gather to find out how—or whether—these differences matter? Are these considerations a reason *not* to extrapolate from our controlled studies to the circumstances of an actual eye witness?

Cognitive Psychology and Education:
Overconfidence

Students are given a lot of new material to learn, but they generally have a limited amount of study time (especially if they want to include other activities in their lives, in addition to studying!). Students therefore need to use their study time efficiently, and, for this purpose, students often need to assess their own learning: "Have I mastered this material? Will I recall these facts later on?" If the answer to these questions is "yes," the student can move on to other materials, or perhaps end the studying session. If the answer is "no," the student should probably devote more time to these materials.

A student who's making these self-assessments is relying on *meta-memory*—judgments, by a person, about the status of his or her own memory—and one aspect of meta-memory involves *confidence*. Said differently, whenever someone says, "I'm confident my memory is right," or "I'm confident I'll recall this later," they're making a meta-memorial judgment. But, as we saw in Chapter 7, this type of judgment can be mistaken: People are often confident in their recall, but we then discover their recall is wrong (or perhaps just incomplete). And sometimes people *lack* confidence in their recall, even though their memories are accurate and detailed!

In fact, students often engage in practices that lead them to be *overconfident* in their own memories. Consider, for example, the common practice of studying material by re-reading it (that is, re-reading your notes, or re-reading the textbook). This re-reading does promote memory, but the benefit is small (and so this study strategy is plainly inferior to other strategies that we've discussed in earlier workbook essays). In contrast, though, this re-reading can have a large impact on memory confidence. As a result, re-reading can produce a substantial "disconnect" between accuracy and confidence—boosting your confidence in a fashion that's out of step with what you'll actually be able to remember.

The real bottom line, therefore, is that students shouldn't rely on their meta-memories and shouldn't, in particular, rely on confidence in structuring their study time. What should students do instead? The answer is straightforward: Rather than relying on your confidence in recall, you can *check* on your recall: Make up quizzes for yourself. Or—far better—get together with a friend, and quiz each other. (This approach is better because the quizzes you make up for yourself might leave out the material you've already forgotten, and might give too little emphasis to materials that you mistakenly thought were unimportant. Working with a friend can diminish these risks.) These simple steps are much more informative than subjective self-assessments, and so lead to better school performance.

In addition, let's pause to highlight the problems inherent in re-reading. This strategy can encourage fairly passive interactions with the material you're studying. You'll be far better off if you can, in reading your assignments, find more active ways to engage the material—by seeking paraphrases, or trying to explain *why* the information you're reading makes sense. These procedures will lead you to better memory and better performance in the classroom.

FOR DISCUSSION

One of the best ways to clarify your thinking about a topic, and also one of the best ways to check on your understanding of the topic, is to try *explaining* the topic to someone else. Said differently, one of the best ways to learn is by teaching—that is, presenting and explaining the material to someone new. In this fashion, learning can be—and perhaps should be—a social activity.

This essay, with its emphasis on *testing yourself*, adds another reason that learning can be a social activity:

In many settings, you'll be better off testing a friend's understanding, and having him or her test yours. Other essays, for other chapters, have also suggested social dimensions to learning. Can you recall these points? Put differently, can you catalogue the full set of gains from treating the learning process as a social process? Are there *costs* or *concerns* about the social aspects of learning? Thinking this through may help you decide how you want to structure your own studying!

For more on this topic

Hartwig, M., & Dunlosky, J. (2012). Study strategies of college students: Are self-testing and scheduling related to achievement? *Psychonomics Bulletin & Review, 19*, 126–134.

Cognitive Psychology and Education:
Remembering for the Long Term

Sometimes you need to recall things after a short delay: A friend tells you her address, and you drive to her house an hour later. You study for a quiz that you'll take tomorrow morning. Sometimes, however, you want to remember things over a much longer time span, and so you might want to recall things that you learned weeks ago—or months or even years ago. This longer-term retention is certainly important, for example, in educational settings: Facts that you learn as an undergraduate may be crucial for your professional work later in life. Likewise, facts that you learned in your first year at your university may be crucial in your third or fourth year. How, therefore, can we help people to remember things for the very long term?

The answer turns out to be straightforward: The key is simply to revisit what you've learned periodically, and even a very brief refresher can help enormously. In one study, for example, students were quizzed on little factoids they had learned at some prior point in their lives. ("Who was the first astronaut to walk on the moon?" "Who wrote the fable about the fox and the grapes?") In many cases, the students couldn't remember these little facts, and so they were given a quick reminder. The correct answer was shown to them for 5 seconds, with the simple instruction that the students should look at the answer because they'd need it later on.

Without this reminder, participants couldn't recall these answers at all. But nine days after this quick reminder, they were able to remember roughly half the answers. This isn't perfect performance, but it's surely an enormous return from a very small investment. And it's likely that a *second* reminder a few days later, again lasting just 5 seconds, would have lifted their performance still further and allowed them to recall the items after an even longer delay.

One suggestion, then, is that testing yourself (perhaps with flashcards—with a cue on one side, and an answer on the other) can be quite useful. Flashcards are often a poor way to *learn* material, because (as we've seen) learning requires thoughtful and meaningful engagement with the materials you're trying to memorize, and running through a stack of flash cards probably won't promote that thoughtful engagement. But using flashcards may be an excellent way to review material that is already learned, and thus to avoid forgetting this material.

Other forms of testing can also be valuable. Think about what happens each time you take a vocabulary quiz in your Spanish class. A question like "What's the Spanish word for 'bed'?" gives you practice in retrieving the word, and that practice promotes fluency in retrieval. In addition, seeing the word (*cama*) can itself refresh the memory, promoting retention.

Consistent with these ideas, several studies have shown that students who have taken a test will have better retention later on, in comparison to students who didn't take the initial test. This pattern has been documented with students of various ages (including high school students and college students) and has been documented with different sorts of material.

The implications for students should be clear. It really does pay to go back periodically and review what you've learned—including material you've learned earlier this academic year and also the material you learned in previous years. The review does not have to be lengthy or intense; in the first study described here, just a 5-second exposure was enough to decrease forgetting dramatically.

In addition, you shouldn't complain if a teacher insists on frequent quizzes. These quizzes can, of course, be a nuisance, but apparently they serve two functions: They help you assess your learning (and so provide another way to overcome overconfidence—see the previous essay), and they can actually help you to hold onto what you've learned—for days, and probably months, and perhaps even decades after you've learned it.

FOR DISCUSSION

Many students would find it burdensome and anxiety-provoking if their instructors gave them quiz after quiz after quiz. Yet, as this essay describes, these quizzes can have a powerful educational effect—helping students to learn, and helping them retain what they've learned.

You might spend some time thinking about, and discussing, the trade-offs here. On the one side, repeated testing does offer important benefits. On the other side, we don't want to add to students' workload, or their levels of anxiety or stress. Can we find a balance between these considerations? This seems worth discussing—perhaps with the goal of students instructing their instructors on what the proper "schedule of testing" might be?

For more on this topic

Berger, S. A., Hall, L. K., & Bahrick, H. P. (1999). Stabilizing access to marginal and sub-marginal knowledge. *Journal of Experimental Psychology: Applied, 5,* 438–447.

Butler, A., & Roediger, H. L. (2008). Feedback enhances the positive effects and reduces the negative effects of multiple-choice testing. *Memory & Cognition, 36,* 604–616.

Carpenter, S., Pashler, H., & Vul, E. (2007). What types of learning are enhanced by a cued recall test? *Psychonomic Bulletin & Review, 13,* 826–830.

Carpenter, S., Pashler, H., Wixted, J., & Vul, E. (2008). The effects of tests on learning and forgetting. *Memory & Cognition, 36,* 438–448.

Linton, M. (1982). Transformations of memory in everyday life. In U. Neisser (Ed.), *Memory observed: Remembering in natural contexts* (pp. 77–92). San Francisco: Freeman.

Cognitive Psychology and the Law: Jurors' Memory

Chapter 7 of the textbook covers many topics directly relevant to the question of what eyewitnesses to crimes—or crime *victims*—can or cannot remember. But memory is also relevant to the courts for another reason: Members of a jury sit and listen to hours (and, sometimes, many days) of courtroom testimony. Then they move into the jury room, where, on the basis of their recollection of the testimony, they must evaluate the facts of the case and reach a verdict. But what if the jurors don't remember the testimony they have heard? In some courtrooms, members of the jury are allowed to take notes during the trial, but in many jurisdictions, they are not. Perhaps we should worry, therefore, about *jurors'* memories just as much as we worry about *witnesses'* memories.

Jurors' memories are, of course, influenced by the same factors as any other memories. For example, we know in general that people try to fit complex events into a mental framework, or schema. Aspects of the event that fit well with this framework are likely to be remembered. Aspects that do not fit with the framework may be forgotten or remembered in a distorted form, so that the recollection, now with its distorted content, *does* fit with the framework. This pattern has been documented in many settings, and so it's not surprising that it can also be demonstrated in jurors.

To see how this plays out, bear in mind that, in the opening phase of a trial, lawyers from each side have a chance to address the jury, and they use this opportunity to describe the case-to-come, foreshadowing what their arguments will be, and what the evidence will show. Often, these presentations take the form of a "story," describing in narrative form the sequence of events that is central for the trial. These stories can have a large impact on jurors, so that, for example, jurors generally remember more of the trial evidence if they have one of these stories in mind from the trial's start. The reason, simply, is that jurors, listening to the trial testimony, can fit each new fact into the framework provided by the story, and this link to the framework supports memory. For similar reasons, it's unsurprising that jurors will remember more of the trial evidence if we make it easier for them to fit the evidence into a story. Concretely, they'll remember more if the testimony presents the trial evidence in "story sequence"—first, the earliest events in the story; then, later events; and so on.

But there's also a downside: Once jurors have adopted a story about the trial, evidence that's consistent with the story is more likely to be remembered; evidence inconsistent with the story is often forgotten. In addition, jurors can sometimes "remember" evidence that actually wasn't presented during the trial but that is consistent with the story!

These findings are just what we'd expect, based on what we know about memory in other settings. But these facts are also troubling, because we would obviously prefer that jurors remember all the evidence—and remember it accurately. Perhaps, therefore, we should seek changes in courtroom procedures so that, in the end, the jurors' verdict will be based on an unbiased and complete recollection of the trial evidence.

In addition, it's important to bear in mind that jurors work together, as a group, to reach their verdict. Perhaps, therefore, jury members can remind each other, during their deliberations, about points that some of them may have forgotten, and can correct each other's memory errors when they retire to the jury room to discuss the case. This happens to some extent, and so deliberation does seem to improve jurors' memory—but only to a small extent. Why small? In the jury room, the people most likely to speak up about the evidence are the people who are most confident that they recall the trial well. However, the textbook chapter discusses the fact that *confidence* in one's memory is not always an indication that the memory is accurate. Therefore, the people who speak up may not always be the ones who remember the evidence correctly!

Overall, then, it seems that memory research highlights juror memory as yet another arena in which errors are possible, and the research points to another topic on which efforts at improving the legal system might be possible, and are surely desirable.

FOR DISCUSSION

In some jurisdictions, jurors are allowed to *take notes* during a trial to help them remember the trial evidence. In other jurisdictions, jurors are allowed to *ask questions* of the witness. (The jurors submit their questions to the judge, who screens them to make certain the questions are legally permissible; if they are, the judge reads the questions to the witness, who then answers.) In still other jurisdictions, the judge *gives the jury instructions*, before the trial even begins, about the legal issues that are in play and how the key legal terms are defined. (In most jurisdictions, though, these instructions come only at the trial's end, just before the jury begins its deliberation.)

Based on what we know about memory, which of these variations in procedure are likely to improve jurors' ability to remember the trial evidence? Based on what we know about memory, are there other steps we can (or should) take that would help jurors to remember the evidence?

For more on this topic

Pennington, N., & Hastie, R. (1992). Explaining the evidence: Tests of the story model for juror decision making. *Journal of Personality and Social Psychology, 62,* 189–206.
Pritchard, M., & Keenan, J. (2002). Does jury deliberation really improve jurors' memories? *Applied Cognitive Psychology, 16,* 589–601.

CHAPTER 8

Concepts and Generic Knowledge

Demonstrations

8.1 The Search for Definitions

The textbook chapter argues that people are typically unable to define their concepts—including concepts that they use all the time. Some concepts, though, do seem to have a firm definition. For example, what is a "bachelor"? According to most people, a bachelor is an *unmarried adult human male*. But does this definition really reflect the way people think about bachelors? For example, imagine that you were running an Internet matchmaking service, and you've decided to advertise your service to "bachelors." Which of the following men should receive your advertising?

- Alfred is an unmarried adult male, but he has been living with his girlfriend for the last 8 years. Their relationship is happy and stable. Should you send advertising to Alfred?
- Bernard is an unmarried adult male who does not have a partner. But Bernard is a monk, living in a monastery. Should you send advertising to Bernard?
- Charles is a married adult male, but he has not seen his wife for many years. Charles is earnestly dating, hoping to find a new partner. Should you send advertising to Charles?
- Donald is a married adult male, but he lives in a culture that encourages males to take two wives. Donald is earnestly dating, hoping to find a new partner. Should you send advertising to Donald?

Now, let's try a different perspective. Imagine that you work for the government, and you are trying to design a new set of tax laws. You believe that to make the law fair, people who are living with a partner, and perhaps supporting children, should be taxed differently from those who are only paying for their own expenses. For this reason, you want to define the term "bachelor" within the tax code, with the key idea being that a "bachelor" does not have a life-partner and (in most cases) does not have children. *For purposes of the tax law*, which of the four men described earlier should be counted as a "bachelor"?

As you read through the four examples, think about what it is that guides your judgments. The "guide" will, in part, involve your expectations about marriage and also society's rules for eligibility for marriage. You'll also want to think about the cultural setting (how common is it in our culture for bachelors to have children?). In light of these points, do you think that the term "bachelor" can be adequately represented in the mind by a clear definition? Can it be represented in the mind via a prototype or by some set of exemplars (with variation, from one occasion to another, in which exemplar you choose when you think about bachelors)? Or, perhaps, does this concept need to be represented by means of a network of beliefs, linking your idea of bachelor to your idea of marriage, family structure, and so on?

Demonstration adapted from Fillmore, C. (1982). Towards a descriptive framework for spatial deixis. In R. J. Jarvella & W. Klein (Eds.), *Speech, place and action: Studies in deixis and related topics* (pp. 31–60). Chichester, England: Wiley.

8.2   Assessing Typicality

Many of the claims in Chapter 8 rest on the influence of *typicality*. But how do we assess typicality? In many experiments, participants have been given an instruction like this:

> Some items of clothing are more typical of the category *clothing* than others. Rate each of the items below for how typical it is, using a "4" to indicate that the item is a highly typical item of clothing, and a "1" to indicate that the item is not at all typical. Use values in between to indicate intermediate levels of typicality.
>   For each item, how typical is it?

Now, go ahead and rate the following items:

Shoes	Grass skirt	Gym shorts	Sari
T-shirt	Fedora	Socks	Top hat
Blue jeans	Pajamas	Sweatshirt	Stockings
Bathing suit	Belt	Leather pants	Miniskirt
Necktie	Ski boots	Mittens	Hawaiian shirt
Vest	Parka	Stole	Sweater
Underwear	Bra	Bathrobe	Dress shirt

Next, read the list to a friend and collect your friend's ratings of typicality. How much do you and your friend agree in your ratings? As you'll see, you and friend probably agree to an impressive extent. Apparently, therefore, typicality judgments aren't random or idiosyncratic. Instead, these judgments are a systematic reflection of the world in which we live—sometimes reflecting *frequency of encounter* (thus, clothing items that you often think about are counted as typical), and sometimes reflecting *beliefs* about what's central or important for the category.

Of course, you and your friend may disagree on some items. Can you find any pattern to the disagreement? If there is a pattern, will it lead us to alter our notion of what typicality is?

8.3 Basic-Level Categories

It is possible to categorize almost any object in several ways. Right now, are you looking at a book? Or a college book? Or a cognitive psychology college book? Or is it just an "information source," or even a "physical object"? All of these labels are sensible, but which is the preferred label?

Spend a minute or so listing all of the traits you can think of that are *shared by all cars*.

Next, spend a minute or so listing all of the traits you can think of that are shared *by all moving vehicles* (including normal cars but also dogsleds, jets, and the U.S. space shuttle).

Next, spend a minute or so listing all of the traits you can think of that are *shared by all Japanese cars.*

Most people find the first task (*cars*) easier than the second (*moving vehicles*). For cars, you could list "has an engine," "has wheels," "has a steering wheel," and many other traits as well. For moving vehicles, your list surely included "can move," and "can carry people or freight," but perhaps few traits beyond these.

This pattern fits with Rosch's claim that there is a level of categorization—she calls it the "basic level"—that seems most natural. Members of a basic-level category (such as the category "car") really do seem to have a lot in common. "Moving vehicles," in contrast, is an example of a superordinate category—one that includes several basic-level categories. Superordinate categories strike people as providing less-natural groupings of objects, and the specific items within such a category often seem rather different from each other (space shuttle versus dogsled). This is why it is harder to come up with traits that are shared by all vehicles.

The category *Japanese cars* is a subordinate category—just a part of the basic-level category *cars*. Subordinate categories are narrower (i.e., they contain fewer things), but despite this greater precision, a categorization at the subordinate level provides you with little new information that you didn't already have from the basic-level category. For the category *cars*, you probably were able to list many attributes. For the category *Japanese cars*, were you able to add any attributes other than "made by a Japanese company" and, perhaps "reputation for reliability"?

It seems, then, that we lose information if our categorization is too general (i.e., if it focuses on a superordinate category). But it's not the case that the best categorization is the one that's most specific. That's because we gain a lot of information (i.e., we can identify many common attributes) when we shift from a superordinate category (like *vehicle*) to a basic-level category (like *car*), but then we gain very little information if we try to use more specific categorizations.

Demonstration adapted from Rosch, E., Mervis, C., Gray, W., Johnson, D., & Boyes-Braem, P. (1976). Basic objects in natural categories. *Cognitive Psychology, 3,* 382–439.

Applying Cognitive Psychology

Research Methods: Converging Operations

How should we study conceptual knowledge? How can we find out what your concept of "dog" includes, or your concept of "ideal Presidential candidate," or your concept of "worst date ever"? As we've seen in this chapter, our research often begins with a simple task: We can show you various pictures, and ask whether each is a dog or not. We can describe various dates and ask which comes closest to your worst-case scenario.

The problem, though, is that results from this task are ambiguous: It's possible that your judgments in this task reflect the pattern of your broad underlying knowledge. But it's also possible that your judgments merely reflect your approach *to this specific task*, a task in which we're explicitly asking you to use your concept to categorize new, unfamiliar cases. Perhaps, therefore, we'd get a different pattern if we give you some other task—for example, one that had you thinking about familiar cases. If so, then our first data set is providing only a partial portrait of your conceptual knowledge, and might not tell us much about how you use this knowledge in other settings.

To address this ambiguity, the path forward should be obvious: We can ask what happens if we give you a new concept task, perhaps one that involves familiar cases, or perhaps a task that doesn't explicitly require categorization. If the data pattern changes, we know that the first data set was shaped by the task itself. If the data pattern holds steady, we draw the opposite conclusion—namely, that we'd succeeded in revealing the general character of your conceptual knowledge, a profile that would show up no matter how, on a particular occasion, you were using that knowledge.

This sort of issue arises throughout cognitive psychology. Of course, in some cases, we do want to know how people perform a specific task—how they solve a particular type of problem, or retrieve a certain type of information from memory. In many other cases, though, we're interested in someone's underlying knowledge pattern, independent of how they've accessed the knowledge in a specific setting. Likewise, we're often interested in strategies that (we believe) are used in a wide variety of tasks, and not just for the task we've set for our participants in a particular experiment.

These questions are especially prominent, however, in the study of concepts. Here we're trying to develop theories about conceptual knowledge itself, rather than theories about how this knowledge happens to be used on some special occasion, or in some specialized context. It's crucial, therefore, that we test our claims with a diverse set of paradigms and a diverse set of stimuli. What we're hoping for, of course, is that we'll get similar patterns despite this variation in procedures. Technically speaking, we're hoping for *converging operations*: a variety of studies that all point toward (and so "converge on") the same theoretical claims.

Let's put all of this in concrete terms. We know that people rely on typicality when deciding whether newly encountered objects are in a specified category or not—whether a particular animal is a "dog," or a particular utensil is a "spoon," and so on. Is this simply the way people approach *this task*? If so, we might see a smaller role (or no role at all) for typicality in other tasks. Or is the typicality result a reflection of the basic nature of your category knowledge? If so, we would expect a converging pattern of data—with evidence for typicality coming from a wide range of tasks.

As the chapter makes clear, though, the actual data lie somewhere between these two poles. People do rely on typicality in a range of tasks, and so the data from many tasks do converge on the idea that prototypes are a crucial part of your conceptual knowledge. However, people do not rely on typicality in all tasks. And, when they *do* rely on typicality, they need to supplement this knowledge with other knowledge. (We made this point in the chapter by arguing that judgments about typicality have to rely on an assessment of *resemblance*—usually, the resemblance between a candidate object and the category prototype. Resemblance, in turn, depends on other knowledge—knowledge about which features *matter* for judging resemblance, and which features can be ignored.)

It seems, therefore, that we do find a pattern of convergence from a variety of tasks: a data pattern, across different procedures, consistently pointing toward a single conclusion (namely, the centrality of typicality). This is of enormous importance for us, but no less important is the *limit* on the convergence. This limit tells us that typicality is important, but is not the whole story.

Putting these points into a larger context, perhaps the most important message here is the role of *multiple experiments*, and also *diverse* experiments, in testing our various claims. Indeed, we've mentioned in other essays that it's extremely rare in science that a claim rests on a single study, no matter how compelling that study is. Instead, science relies on a fabric of interwoven studies—drawing insights from the agreements and convergence across studies, but also (as in this case) drawing insights from the disagreements.

FOR DISCUSSION

The textbook chapter argues that prototypes are an important part of conceptual knowledge, but only *part*. That broad point implies that you sometimes rely on prototypes and sometimes don't, and so you sometimes are influenced by typicality (resemblance to the prototype) and sometimes you're not. Can you generate a hypothesis about *when* people are likely to rely on prototypes, and when not? Do you think that *fast-paced reasoning* might be the key? Do you think that *motivation to be careful* might be the key? How about *familiarity with the concept*, so that prototype use is more common with less familiar concepts?

Once you've developed your hypothesis, design a test for it. According to your hypothesis, what sorts of tasks (or what sorts of concepts) should show a typicality effect, and what sorts should not?

Cognitive Psychology and Education:
Learning New Concepts

In your studies, you encounter many new terms. In your textbooks, for example, you'll find **boldfaced terms**, introducing new concepts, and often the book provides a helpful definition, perhaps in the page's margin. As the chapter argues, though, this mode of presentation doesn't line up all that well with the structure of human knowledge. The reason, in brief, is that you don't have (or need) a definition for most of the concepts in your repertoire; in fact, a definition may not even exist. And even when you do know a definition, your use of the concept often relies on other information—including a prototype for that term, as well as a set of exemplars. In addition, your use of conceptual information routinely depends on a broader fabric of knowledge, linking this concept to other things you know. This broader knowledge encompasses what the text calls your "theory" about that concept, a theory that (among other things) explains why the concept's attributes are as they are.

You use your theory about a concept in many ways. For example, we've argued that whenever you rely on a prototype, you're drawing conclusions based on the *resemblance* between the prototype and the new case you're thinking about, and resemblance depends on your theory: It's your theory that tells you which attributes to pay attention to, in judging the resemblance, and which to ignore. (Thus, if you're thinking about computers, your "theory" about computers tells you that the *color* of the machine's case is irrelevant. If, in contrast, you're identifying types of birds, your knowledge tells you that color is an important attribute.)

You also draw on your theory for classifying new, unexpected cases (in the chapter, we used the example of recognizing someone as "drunk" when they jumped into a swimming pool fully clothed). Likewise, you use your theory to guide your *inferences* about a concept (allowing you to decide, for example, that an illness carried by fleas is likely to affect your dog, but probably not your goldfish).

Let's be clear, then, that learning a definition for some new concept is a good place to start, but you shouldn't be fooled into thinking that knowing the definition is the same as understanding the concept, or that knowing the definition is the same as mastery of the concept. Indeed, if you *only* know the definition, you may end up using your concept foolishly. ("That couldn't be a computer; it's the wrong color!")

What other information do you need, in addition to the definition? At the least, you should seek out some *examples* of the new concept, because you'll often be able to draw analogies based on these examples. You also want to think about what these examples have in common; that will help you develop a *prototype* for the category. Above all, though, you want to think about what makes these count as examples—what is it about them that puts them into the category? How are the examples different, and why are they all in the same category despite these differences? Why are other candidates, apparently similar to these examples, *not* in the category? Are some of the qualities of the examples predictable from other qualities? What caused these qualities to be as they are?

These questions (and other questions like them) will help you to start building the network of beliefs that provide your theory about this concept. These beliefs will help you to understand and use the concept. But, as the chapter discusses, these beliefs are also *part of* the concept—providing the knowledge base that specifies, in your thoughts, what the concept is all about.

These various points put an extra burden on you and your teachers. It would be easier if the teacher could simply provide a crisp definition for you to memorize, and then you could go ahead and commit that definition to memory. But that's not what it means to learn a concept, and strict attention just to a definition will leave you with a conceptual representation that's not very useful, and certainly far less rich than you want.

FOR DISCUSSION

We all rely on conceptual knowledge for many aspects of our day-to-day lives. However, some people rely on a specific type of categorization in their *professional* work. After all, think about what a *diagnosis* is—whether we're considering a dermatologist announcing that a rash is poison ivy, a radiologist deciding that a shadow on an X-ray is not a tumor, or a psychotherapist concluding that a client suffers from borderline personality disorder. In each of these cases, an experienced professional is categorizing a particular case, and (often) choosing a treatment based on this categorization.

Based on the chapter's content, what advice would you offer to someone who's *training* dermatologists, radiologists, or psychotherapists? What steps should be included in the training? Is there an effective way to decide when the training has been sufficient, so that the person is now ready to go out and diagnose real cases?

For more on this topic

Dorek, K., Brooks, L., Weaver, B., & Norman, G. (2012). Influence of familiar features on diagnosis: Instantiated features in an applied setting. *Journal of Experimental Psychology: Applied, 18*, 109–125.

Cognitive Psychology and the Law:
Defining Legal Concepts

In court cases, there's often disagreement about what the defendant did: Was he in the bank the day of the crime? Did he set the fire? Did he lie to the police? But then, once the jury figures out these points, they still have another job to do: The law requires that the jury "categorize" those actions. They might need to decide, for example, whether the defendant's actions can truly be categorized as "sexual harassment," and the jury's decision on this categorization will determine their verdict. (If the defendant was offensive in some awful way, but his actions don't fit into the category of "harassment," then he isn't guilty of harassment.) Alternatively, the jury might be certain that the defendant caused someone's death, but they still need to decide whether the crime should be categorized as "first-degree murder" or "second-degree." In this case, the categorization has huge implications for the likely punishment.

To help juries make these categorizations, the laws define each crime in precise terms, so that there is a careful definition of "robbery," a clear definition of "trespassing," and so on. Even with these definitions, though, juries regularly encounter ambiguous cases in which it's just not clear how to categorize someone's actions, and—crucially—not clear whether the person's actions satisfy the definition of the crime the person is charged with. At the least, this reminds us how difficult it is to find adequately detailed, broadly useful definitions for concepts, a point that was important throughout the textbook chapter. But, in addition, we need to ask: How do jurors proceed when they encounter one of these ambiguous cases?

The chapter makes it clear that people often have *prototypes* in mind for their various concepts, and they assess a new case by asking how closely it resembles that prototype. It turns out that jurors do the same in making legal judgments; thus, they're appreciably more likely to convict someone if the trial facts resemble their prototype for the crime—if these facts fit their notion of, say, a "typical bank robbery" or a "typical hit and run violation." Put differently, a "typical" crime with weak evidence is more likely to lead to a conviction than an unusual crime with similarly weak evidence. Of course, this is legally nonsensical: Convictions should depend on the quantity and quality of the evidence, and not the typicality of the crime. Indeed, juries' prototypes should have no bearing whatsoever on their decisions, especially when we acknowledge that the prototypes are probably shaped more by TV crime shows than by the official statutes. Nonetheless, the prototypes do influence the jury, and so legal judgments, like concept use in general, are plainly influenced by typicality.

In addition, we argued in the chapter that concept users often seem to have a theory in mind about why a concept is as it is, and they use the theory in reasoning about the concept. For example, the textbook used the example of someone jumping into a pool fully clothed. You're likely to categorize this person as a "drunk," not because the person fits your definition for being drunk or even fits your prototype, but because you have a set of beliefs about why people act the way they do and how drunks are likely to act. Based on those beliefs (i.e., based on your theory), you decide that drunkenness is the most plausible explanation for the behavior you just observed, and you categorize accordingly.

Again, it seems that people carry these categorization habits into the courtroom. For example, consider the crime of *stalking*. This crime is difficult to define in a crisp way, and it is defined in different ways in different states. Often, though, the definition includes the notion that the stalker *intended to force some sort of relationship* with the victim—perhaps a relationship involving intimacy, or a relationship in which the victim feels fear. It's often the case, though, that there's no direct evidence of this intention, so the jury needs to *infer* the intention from the defendant's behaviors, or from the context. For example, juries are sometimes influenced by the fact that the defendant was a former intimate of the person being stalked, with the jurors apparently guided by the idea that former (but now *rejected*) lovers will sometimes respond to the rejection by stalking their previous partner.

Notice, though, that in these cases, the jurors seem to rely on a broad set of beliefs about stalking—including what it is that motivates one person to stalk another, and what kinds of people are more likely to be stalkers. In this way, stalking seems to rely on an implicit theory, just as other concepts do.

FOR DISCUSSION

Imagine that you're working for the Judicial Committee for your community. Try to write a definition of stalking that could be used in deciding whether someone is guilty of this crime or not. Make sure to "test" your definition by trying to imagine cases that, in your view, *should* count as stalking; do they fall within your definition? Also try to imagine cases that, in your view, *should not* count as stalking, even if they have some of the elements often associated with this crime. Are they (correctly) excluded by your definition?

For more on this topic

Dennison, S., & Thomson, D. (2002). Identifying stalking: The relevance of intent in commonsense reasoning. *Law and Human Behavior, 26,* 543–561.

Huntley, J., & Costanzo, M. (2003). Sexual harassment stories: Testing a story-mediated model of juror decision-making in civil litigation. *Law and Human Behavior, 27,* 29–51.

Smith, V. L., & Studebaker, C. A. (1996). What do you expect? The influence of people's prior knowledge of crime categories on fact-finding. *Law and Human Behavior, 20,* 517–532.

CHAPTER 9

Language

Demonstrations

9.1 Phonemes and Subphonemes

A *phoneme* is the smallest unit of sound that can distinguish words within a language. The difference between "bus" and "fuss," therefore, lies in the initial phoneme, and the difference between "bus" and "butt" lies in the words' last phoneme. However, not all sound differences are phonemic differences. For example, the word "bus" can be pronounced with a slightly longer [s] sound at the end, or with a slightly shorter [s]. Even with this difference, both of these pronunciations refer to the motor vehicle used to transport groups of people. The difference between the long [s] and the short [s], in other words, is a *subphonemic* difference—one that does not distinguish words within the language.

What counts as a subphonemic difference, however, depends on the language. To see this, imagine that you were going to say the word "key" out loud. Get your tongue and teeth in position so that you're ready in an instant to say this word—but then freeze in that position, as if you were waiting for a "go" signal before making any noise. Now, imagine that you were going to say "cool" out loud. Again, get your tongue and teeth in position so that you're ready to say this word. Now, go back to being ready, in an instant, to say "key." Now, go back to being ready, in an instant, to say "cool."

Can you feel that your tongue is moving into different positions for these two words? That's because, in English, the [k] sound used in the word "key" is different from the [k] sound used in "cool," and so, to make the different sounds, you need to move your tongue into different positions.

The difference between the two [k] sounds is, however, subphonemic in English (so it doesn't matter for meaning). In other words, there *is* an acoustic difference between the two sounds, but this difference is inconsequential for English speakers. This difference does matter, though, in other languages, including several Arabic languages. In these languages, there are two distinct [k] sounds, and changing from one to the other will alter the identity of the word being spoken, even if nothing else in the word changes. In other words, the difference between the two [k] sounds is phonemic in Arabic, not subphonemic.

These differences between languages actually lead to changes in how we *perceive* sounds. Most English speakers, for example, cannot hear the difference between the two [k] sounds; for Arabic speakers, the difference is obvious. A related example is the difference between the starting sound in "led" and the starting sound in "red." This difference is phonemic in English, so that (for example) "led" and "red" are different words, and English speakers easily hear the difference. The same acoustic difference, however, is subphonemic in many Asian languages, and speakers of these languages have trouble hearing the difference between words like "led" and "red" or between "load" and "road." It seems, then, that speakers of different languages literally hear the world differently.

Can you learn to control which [k] sound you produce? Once again, get your mouth ready to say "key" out loud, but freeze in place before you make any sound. Now, without changing your tongue position at all, say "cool" out loud. If you do this carefully, you will end up producing the [k] sound that's normally the start for "key," but you'll pronounce it with the "oo" vowel. If you practice a little, you will get better at this; and if you listen very carefully, you can learn to hear the difference between "cool" pronounced with this [k], and "cool" pronounced with its usual [k]. If so, you've mastered one (tiny) element of speaking Arabic!

In this exercise, you've received instruction in how to produce (and perhaps perceive) these distinct sounds. Most people, however, receive no such instruction, leading us to ask: How do they learn to hear these different sounds, and to produce them, as required by the language they ordinarily speak? The answer, oddly enough, is that they *don't* learn. Instead, young infants just a couple of months old seem perfectly capable of hearing the difference between the two [k] sounds, whether they live in an English-speaking community or an Arabic-speaking community. Likewise, young infants a few months old seem perfectly capable of hearing the difference between "led" and "red," whether they are born in an English-speaking environment or in Tokyo. However, if a distinction is not phonemic in their language, the infants lose the ability to hear these differences. This is, in other words, a clear case of "use it or lose it," and so, in a sense, infants at (say) 3 months of age can hear and make more distinctions than infants at 10 or 11 months of age.

9.2   The *Speed* of Speech

Humans are incredibly skilled in most aspects of language use, including the "decoding" of the complex acoustic signals that reach our ears whenever we're listening to someone speaking. There are many ways to document this skill, including some observations about how well we can understand *fast speech*.

The "normal" rate of speaking is hard to define. People from New York, for example, have a reputation for speaking quickly (although most New Yorkers are convinced that they speak at a "normal" speed and everyone else speaks slowly!). Likewise, people from America's South have a reputation for speaking slowly (although, again, they're convinced that *theirs* is the normal rate, and everyone else is in too much of a hurry). Across this variation, though, the rate of 180 words per minute (roughly: 15 phonemes per second) is often mentioned as a normal rate for spoken English.

Languages also differ in their speed. According to one recent estimate, Japanese speakers typically fire off speech at a pace of 7.84 syllables per second; Spanish is a bit slower, at 7.82 syllables per second. English is slower still (6.19 syllables per second) but not as slow as Mandarin Chinese (5.18). We need to be clear, though, that languages also differ in how much information they pack into a single syllable. Chinese speakers, for example, provide further information via the "tone" with which the syllable is pronounced, so even if they produce fewer syllables per second, they may provide more information per syllable!

In any language, though, what happens with faster speech? Some "fast talkers" are hard to understand because they slur their speech or blur their pronunciation; this is true, for example, of many auctioneers, who may be blurring their speech deliberately to create a sense of excitement in the auction (with the aim of encouraging more bids!). Related, visit You Tube (www.youtube.com) and search for "fastest talker." You'll find videos of individuals who hold the Guinness Record for fast talking (about 600 words per minute), and you'll see that, at this speed, these people are almost impossible to understand. However, the problem here is not the speed itself. Instead, these super-fast speakers use various shortcuts to achieve their speed, and the shortcuts create difficulties for the listener. For example, these fast talkers don't change their pitch as much as other people do, so they end up speaking in a monotone. This is a concern for listeners, who ordinarily use prosody as one of the cues marking phrase boundaries, and also as a cue highlighting key words. (Hearing these key words helps the listener to understand the gist of what's being said, which in turn helps the listener to "decode" the speech.) In addition, ordinary speakers use *variations* in speed as a further cue, slowing down (for example) to put emphasis on a word, or to mark the end of a phrase. Fast talkers, in contrast, don't just talk at a high speed; they also talk at a *uniform* speed, and this impedes the listener.

If we set all these shortcuts to the side, what is the fastest speech we can understand? Again, the answer varies, and some of us seem to be "faster listeners," just as some of us are "faster talkers." As a rough estimate, though, most English-speakers can follow speech at 250 words per minute (40% faster than "normal"). But this estimate may be conservative. Again, visit You Tube, and search for some of the classic TV commercials for FedEx starring John Moschitta. (Or search for Moschitta's appearance on Sesame Street.) You'll need to pay close attention to follow his speech, but you probably can!

For more on this topic

Pellegrino, F., Coupé, C., & Marsico, E. (2011). Across-language perspective on speech information rate. *Language*, 87, 539–558.

9.3   Coarticulation

Speech perception is made more challenging by the fact of *coarticulation*—the fact that, as you pronounce each phoneme, you're already getting ready for the next phoneme. Coarticulation guarantees variation in the actual sounds associated with each phoneme—because the pronunciation (and hence the sound) is shaped by the phoneme *before* and the phoneme *after* the one you're uttering right now.

We've already encountered coarticulation in an earlier demonstration, focused on the contrast between phonemic and subphonemic differences (see Demonstration 9.1). But the variations caused by coarticulation are quite widespread. As a further example, therefore, let's consider the shape of your mouth when you pronounce the "s" in "seat" and the shape of your mouth when you pronounce the "s" in "suit." You're producing the same phoneme (the [s]) in both cases, but your mouth shapes (and hence the sounds) are quite different because as you pronounce the "s" sound, you're already getting ready to produce the vowel—and that alters how you pronounce the "s" itself.

In fact, if you focus your attention in the right way, you can hear the difference between these two sounds. Get your mouth ready to say "seat," and, with your mouth "frozen" in that position, hiss the "s" sound. Now get your mouth ready to say "suit," and, with your mouth again frozen in place, hiss this "s" sound. You may have to alternate back and forth once or twice to hear the difference. But, in truth, the difference is large, if we measure the sound using the appropriate instruments, and, with a tiny bit of effort, you can hear the difference.

9.4   The Most Common Words

The text describes several complexities in speech perception, but there are also factors that make speech perception *easier*. One important factor lies in the observation that, even though there are tens of thousands of words in our language, most of what we hear, minute by minute or day by day, relies on a tiny vocabulary. Indeed, George Miller estimated, many years ago, that the 50 most commonly used words make up roughly half of what we hear.

So what are these commonly used words? You can probably guess most of them. Take a blank piece of paper, and write down your nominees for English's most commonly used words. Then, once you've finished, you can check your list against the list compiled by the people who publish the Oxford English Dictionary. Their list of the 100 most commonly used words appears at the end of the workbook entry for this chapter (p. 127). How many of the (actual) top 10 appeared on your list? How many of the (actual) top 20?

9.5 Patterns in Language

Chapter 9 argues that in many ways our language is *generative* but also *patterned*. The *generativity* is evident in the fact that new forms can always be developed—and so you can create new words and new phrases that no one has ever uttered before. The *patterns*, though, are evident in the observation that some sequences of words (or morphemes, or phonemes) seem acceptable and some do not—as if the generativity was governed by rules of some sort. Thus, the rules allow you to create novel sentences like "Comical cartons cruise carefully," but not the sequence "Cruise cartons carefully comical." Likewise, you might say, "The leprechaun envied the cow's artichoke," but not "artichoke cow's the envied leprechaun the."

But what is the nature of the "rules" apparently governing these sequences? As one way to explore this issue, ask the following questions to a couple of friends:

- Imagine that a beaver has been gnawing on a tree. If you later should see the tree, you'll see the marks the beaver has left behind. Are these *tooth-marks* or *teeth-marks*?

- Imagine that a hundred field mice are living in a farm house. Is the house *mouse-infested* or *mice-infested*?

- Now, imagine that 50 rats have also moved into the farm house. Is the house now *rat-infested* or *rats-infested*?

- Or, if 4-year-old Connor has written on the wall with three pens, did he leave behind *pen-marks* or *pens-marks*?

For the first two questions, most people feel like they could go either way—*tooth-marks* or *teeth-marks*; *mouse-infested* or *mice-infested*. They may have a preference for one form or the other, but the preference is usually weak, and they regard the other form as acceptable. For the next two questions, though, people reliably reject one of the options and insist that the house is *rat-infested* and that Connor left *pen-marks*. Is this consistent with how your friends answered?

What's going on here? It turns out that these combinations follow a rule—one that governs how morphemes combine. In essence, the rules says that if a noun has an *irregular plural*, then it can be combined with other morphemes in either its plural form or its singular form. But if a noun has a regular plural, it can be combined with other morphemes *only* in the singular form.

Our point here, though, is not to explore this particular rule. (In fact, this rule is derived from other rules governing how morphemes combine.) Our point instead is that this regular pattern exists within English, even though most people have never been trained on this pattern, have never thought about the pattern, and may not even realize the pattern is in place. In following this rule, therefore, people are surely not consciously aware of the rule. Nonetheless, it's a rule they have been following since they were 3 or 4 years old. This by itself makes it clear that language is in fact heavily patterned, and that a large part of what it means to "know a language" is to learn (and to respect) these patterns.

Demonstration adapted from Gordon, P. (1986). Level-ordering in lexical development. *Cognition, 21,* 73–93.

9.6 Ambiguity

Language is a remarkable tool for conveying ideas from one person to another. Sometimes, however, the transmission of ideas doesn't work quite the way it should. In some cases, the sentences you hear (or read) are unclear or misleading. In other cases, the sentences you encounter are ambiguous, so the meaning you draw from them may be different from the meaning that the speaker (or writer) intended.

Sometimes the ambiguity you encounter concerns just one word: If you hear "Sam is looking for the bank," do you think Sam is looking for the river's edge or a financial institution? Sometimes the ambiguity is tied to the sentence's structure: If you hear "I saw a man on a horse wearing armor," then who is wearing the armor? Is it the man or the horse?

Remarkably, though, ambiguity in language is often overlooked. That's because we are all so skilled at picking up the intended meaning of the speaker that we don't even realize that there's another way we might have interpreted the words. This failure to detect ambiguity is usually a good thing, because, if we're oblivious to the alternative meaning, we won't be distracted or misled by it. But the failure to detect ambiguity can sometimes be a problem. In many cases, for example, newspapers have printed headlines without realizing that there was more than one way to interpret what they'd printed—leading to considerable embarrassment. In fact, all of the following are actual headlines that were printed in real newspapers. In each case, can you find both ways to interpret each headline?

> EYE DROPS OFF SHELF
>
> KIDS MAKE NUTRITIOUS SNACKS
>
> STOLEN PAINTING FOUND BY TREE
>
> DEALERS WILL HEAR CAR TALK AT NOON
>
> MINERS REFUSE TO WORK AFTER DEATH
>
> MILK DRINKERS ARE TURNING TO POWDER
>
> COMPLAINTS ABOUT NBA REFEREES GROWING UGLY
>
> POLICE BEGIN CAMPAIGN TO RUN DOWN JAYWALKERS
>
> GRANDMOTHER OF EIGHT MAKES HOLE IN ONE
>
> HOSPITALS ARE SUED BY 7 FOOT DOCTORS
>
> ENRAGED COW INJURES FARMER WITH AX
>
> SQUAD HELPS DOG BITE VICTIM
>
> HERSHEY BARS PROTEST

Applying Cognitive Psychology

Research Methods: Metalinguistic Judgments

In most psychological research, we don't ask our research participants to reflect on, and tell us about, their mental processes. The reason (as we discussed in Chapter 1) is that self-report is often an unreliable research tool. However, sometimes we do care how people feel about, and talk about, the workings of their own minds. This was, for example, an issue for us in the workbook coverage of Chapter 7, where we mentioned the importance of "meta-memory"—the assessments each of us makes about the status of our own memories. Self-assessment was also relevant for Chapter 6, where we discussed the ways people notice, and respond to, the *fluency* of their own mental processes, and we'll return to the issue of fluency in Chapter 13.

Self-assessments also play an important role in language research—with participants often asked to make **metalinguistic judgments.** In these cases, we are asking people, not to *use* language as they ordinarily would but instead to *reflect* on and comment on language. Why are these judgments important? Let's start with the fact that, for many purposes, researchers certainly want to know what is said and what is not said in ordinary language use. However, data of this sort are limited in one important regard, because it's not clear what we should conclude if a word or phrase is *absent* from ordinary usage. If, for example, Leo never uses the word "boustrephedon," is it because he doesn't know the word or because he simply has no interest in talking about boustrephedon? If Miriam never uses the word "unmicrowavable," is it because she regards the word as illegitimate or merely because she's in the habit of using some other term to convey this idea?

In addition, spontaneous speech is filled with performance errors. Sometimes you start a sentence with one idea in mind, but then you change your idea as you're speaking, perhaps realizing your words need clarification, or even realizing you want to say something altogether different. Thus, you might end up saying something like, "He went my father went yesterday," even though you realize, as you are uttering these words, that the sentence contains an error. On other occasions, you slip in your production and end up saying something different from what you had intended. You might say, "They were I mean weren't fine," even though you notice (and regret) the slip the moment you produce it.

These speech errors are of considerable importance if we are studying the ways in which speech is actually produced. However, these slips are a nuisance if we are trying to study the content of your linguistic knowledge. The reason is that, in most cases, you would agree that you had, in these utterances, made an error. In many cases, you know how to repair the error in order to produce a "correct" sentence. Clearly, therefore, your original performance, with its errors, doesn't reflect the full extent of your knowledge about how English sentences are constructed.

Because of considerations like these, we sometimes need to examine language **competence** rather than language **performance**, with "competence" defined as the pattern of skills and knowledge that might be revealed under optimal circumstances (Chomsky, 1957, 1975). One way to reveal this competence is via metalinguistic judgments: People are asked to reflect on one structure or another (a particular word, phrase, or sentence) and to tell us whether they find the structure acceptable or not. Note that we are not asking people whether they find the structure to be clumsy, or pleasing to the ear, or useful. Instead, we are asking them whether the structure is something that one could say, if one wished. Thus, "There's the big blue house" seems fine, but "There's house blue big the" does not. Or, to return to an earlier example, you might slip and say, "He went my father went yesterday," but you certainly know there is something wrong with this sequence. It's these "acceptability judgments" that reveal linguistic competence.

Let's emphasize that these judgments about language are not our only research tool. Indeed, the chapter covers evidence drawn from a rich set of other measures, and other procedures. Nonetheless, these metalinguistic judgments are an important source of evidence for us—and are, in particular, of enormous value when we are trying to understand what's involved in language competence.

FOR DISCUSSION

Imagine that we present some word sequence to participants and then ask them: "Is this a grammatical sentence?" We might, for example, present them with *Colorless green ideas sleep furiously,* and then ask, "Is this grammatical?" In this setting, we're asking participants whether the word sequence *follows the rules of syntax,* but there's no guarantee that participants will understand the question in the way we intend. Their answers, therefore, may instead focus on whether the word sequence is meaningful, or something you might say in ordinary conversation, and that's not what we want!

To address these concerns, what instructions might we give participants before collecting metalinguistic data? What can we do to maximize the likelihood that they will understand the question the way we intend?

In addition, perhaps we should collect some other data, as a means of checking on participants' judgments of grammaticality. For example, we might ask whether sequences judged to be grammatical are easier to remember, or can be read more quickly. In this way, we would be comparing metalinguistic judgments to some other (objective, behavioral) measure. If we find a relationship between these two types of data, that would move us forward in two ways: It would provide some assurance that the grammaticality judgments we are collecting are sensible, *and* it would give us some indications of how (or whether) grammaticality matters for other aspects of language use. Can you design an experiment that would provide this sort of objective "check" on grammaticality judgments?

For more on this topic

Chomsky, N. (1957). *Syntactic structures.* The Hague, Netherlands: Mouton.
Chomsky, N. (1975). *Reflections on language.* London: Temple-Smith.

Cognitive Psychology and Education: Writing

Students are often called on to do a lot of writing—for example, in an essay exam or a term paper. Can cognitive psychology provide any help in this activity—specifically, helping you to write more clearly and more persuasively?

Some bits of advice are mentioned in the Cognitive Psychology and the Law essay for this chapter. Research tells us, for example, that people usually have an easier time with active sentences than passive, and so (all things being equal) active sentences are preferable. We also know that people approach a sentence with certain strategies (e.g., minimal attachment), and so sentences are easiest to understand if they are compatible with those strategies. Related, we know that people can understand material more readily if they can fit the material into a framework or schema that's already in place. That's part of the reason that sentences are clearer if the structure of the sentence is laid out early, with the details following, rather than the other way around. (Some guidelines refer to this as an advantage for "right-branching sentences" rather than "left-branching sentences." The idea here is that the "branches" represent the syntactic and semantic complexity, and you want that complexity to arrive late, after the base structure is established.) By the same logic, lists are easier to understand if they arrive late in the sentence ("I went to the store with Sam, Fred, George, Sue, and Judy"), so that they can be fit into the structure, rather than arriving early ("Sam, Fred, George, Sue, Judy, and I went to the store") *before* the structure.

Readers are also helped by occasional words or phrases that help them grasp the "flow" of ideas in the material they're reading. Sentences that begin "In contrast," or "Similarly," or "However," provide the reader with some advanced warning about what's coming up, and how it's related to the ideas covered so far. This warning, in turn, makes it easier for the reader to see how the new material fits into the framework established up to that point. The warning also requires the *writer* to think about these relationships and often that encourages the writer to do some fine-tuning of the sequence of sentences!

In addition, it's important to remember that many people *speak* more clearly than they *write*, and it is interesting to ask why this is so. One reason is *prosody*—the pattern of pitch changes, and pauses, that we use in speaking. These cannot be reproduced in writing—although prosodic cues can sometimes be mimicked by the use of commas (to indicate pauses) or italics (to indicate emphasis). These aspects of print can certainly be overused, but they are in all cases important, and writers should probably pay more attention to them than they do, in order to gain in print some of the benefits that (in spoken language) are provided by prosody. But how should you use these cues correctly? One option is to rely on the fact that as listeners and speakers we all know how to use prosodic cues, and when we write we can exploit that knowledge by means of a simple trick: reading your prose out loud. If you encounter a comma on the page but you're not inclined, as a speaker, to pause at that moment, then the comma is probably superfluous. Conversely, if you find yourself pausing as you read aloud but there's no comma, then you may need one.

Another advantage of spoken communication, as opposed to written, is the prospect of immediate feedback. If you say something that isn't clear, your conversation partner may frown, or look confused, or say something to indicate misunderstanding. What can take the place of this feedback when you're writing? As one option, it's almost always useful to have someone (a friend, perhaps) read over your drafts; this peer editing can often catch ambiguities, absence of clarity, or absence of flow that you might have missed on your own. Even without a peer editor, you can gain some of the same benefits from, once again, reading your own prose out loud. Some studies suggest that reading your own prose out loud helps you to gain some distance from the prose that you might not have with ordinary (silent) reading, so that you can, at least in a rough way, provide your own peer editing. Related, we know that people routinely *skip* words when they are reading (this was important for us in the Chapter 3 discussion of speed-reading). This skipping helps when you're reading, but it's a problem when you're editing your own prose (how can you edit words that you didn't even see?). It's important, therefore, that the skipping is less likely when you read the prose out loud—another advantage of reading aloud when you're checking on your own writing.

Finally, many people shift into a different style of expressing themselves when they are writing. Perhaps they are convinced that they need some degree of formality in their written expression. Perhaps they are anxious while writing, and this stiffens their prose. Or perhaps they are trying to impress the reader, so they deliberately reach for more complex constructions and more obscure vocabulary. Whatever the reason for these shifts, they are often counterproductive and make your writing less clear, wordier, and stiffer than your ordinary (spoken) expression. Part of the cure here is to abandon the idea that complex and formal prose is better prose. And part of the cure—once more—lies in either peer editing or reading aloud. In either case, the question to ask is this: Would you express these ideas more clearly, more simply, if you were *speaking* them rather than writing them? Often this, too, will lead you to better writing.

Will these simple suggestions improve every writer? Probably not. Will these suggestions take obscure, fractured prose and lift it to a level that makes you eligible for a Pulitzer Prize? Surely not. Even so, the suggestions offered here may well help you in some ways, and for anyone's writing, any source of improvement should be welcome!

FOR DISCUSSION

Many people (and probably most students) create their prose by typing their words directly into a word processing program. In other words, they write using a computer, and they see their words on the computer screen. When it comes time to *edit* their prose, however, many people have the intuition that it's best to *print* what they've written, and to edit the prose from a printed page. (Of course, many people don't have the opportunity to do this print-and-read, even if they believe it to be a good strategy.)

Do you share this intuition? Or do you believe you can edit as easily from the computer screen as from a printed page? In a survey I have run with my own students, the huge majority believe they can edit more effectively from a printout. What is your hypothesis, first, about whether this is a justified belief or a mere superstition? Second, if editing from a printout is better, why might this be? (As far as I know, there are no data available that would allow firm answers to these questions, so you might think about designing a study that would provide those answers!)

For more on this topic

Oppenheimer, D. M. (2006). Consequences of erudite vernacular utilized irrespective of necessity: Problems with using long words needlessly. *Applied Cognitive Psychology, 20,* 139–156.

Cognitive Psychology and the Law: Jury Instructions

In some countries—including the United States—court cases are often decided by juries, and of course most jurors are not lawyers, so they need to be instructed in the law. This is usually accomplished by the judge providing *jury instructions* as the last step of the trial—just before the jury begins its deliberation. The instructions in a typical case might include a reminder of the jury's overall task, the exact definition of the crime being considered, the elements that must be proved in order to count a person as guilty of that crime, and so on.

These instructions obviously need to be accurate, and so they must capture the precision and exact definitions involved in the law. But the instructions also need to be clear—so that ordinary jurors (often people with just a high school education) can understand and remember the instructions and thus be guided by the law in their deliberation. It turns out, however, that these two requirements are often in conflict with each other, and sometimes *perfectly precise language* is not the same as *clear and comprehensible language*. As a result, the judges' instructions are often difficult to understand.

In fact, some studies suggest that over half of judges' instructions are misunderstood by jurors; in some cases, less than 10% of the instructions are still remembered by the jurors after a brief delay. The failure to understand instructions can be documented in college students who are given the instructions as part of an experiment, and in actual jurors who hear the instructions as part of a real trial. In some cases the misunderstandings concern subtle details, but in other cases jurors seem to misunderstand fundamental points about the law. For example, American law rests on the idea that someone is innocent until proven guilty and that the defendant must, in a criminal trial, be proven guilty beyond a reasonable doubt. There's room for discussion about what "reasonable doubt" means exactly, but the implication of this idea is very clear: When the jury is genuinely uncertain about the verdict, they cannot vote "guilty." Nonetheless, juries seem sometimes to misunderstand this point and seem to adopt a rule of "If in doubt, then be careful, and that means don't risk letting the defendant go free—and so, if in doubt, convict."

What can we do about this? Studies of language processing tell us that people understand more when *participating* in a conversation rather than merely *hearing* a conversation. It is troubling, therefore, that jurors are expected to sit passively as the judge recites the instructions; jurors are almost never allowed to ask questions during the instructions about things they do not understand. And if the jurors realize, during their subsequent discussion, that they didn't understand the instructions, there is often little they can do. Requests for clarification often result in the judge's simply repeating the same words that caused the confusion in the first place.

The instructions themselves are also a problem, but psycholinguistic studies provide guides for how the instructions can be simplified. For example, we know that people generally have an easier time understanding active sentences than passive ones, affirmative sentences rather than negative ones. We also know that sentence understanding often depends on certain strategies (e.g., minimal attachment); sentences are easier to understand, therefore, if they have a structure that is compatible with these strategies. Using principles such as these, a number of researchers have developed jury instructions that still reflect the law correctly but are much easier to understand.

We also know that *vocabulary* matters, and language comprehension suffers if the vocabulary is abstract or unfamiliar. It's troubling, therefore, that instructions for juries often contain a lot of legal jargon. Another forward step, then, is simply to seek ways to replace this vocabulary with easier, more concrete, more familiar words!

Where does this leave us? It is of paramount importance that jurors understand the law; otherwise, the jury system cannot function properly. It is therefore worrisome that jury comprehension of their instructions is so limited. But it is encouraging that by using what we know about language processing, we can make easy adjustments to improve the situation markedly.

FOR DISCUSSION

Researchers often want to ask whether juries understand the instructions they have received, but how should this understanding be evaluated? Is there a "correct way" to evaluate understanding? In truth, there are several ways we might try to assess people's understanding of instructions, and we can also assess their understanding either immediately or after some delay.

Imagine that you wanted to carry out a study of jury instructions—perhaps with the goal of comparing two different versions of the instructions, to ask which version led to greater comprehension. First, what would your options be for various ways to measure jurors' understanding of the instructions? Second, what option would you prefer—what do you think is the best way to evaluate someone's understanding?

For more on this topic

Want to see what actual jury instructions look like? The recommended instructions for
criminal cases are available online. You can find many of them, for example, at this
website: http://federalcriminaljuryinstructions.com/ (The "Circuits" mentioned on the
website refer to different regions of the country; my home state of Oregon, for example,

is in the 9th circuit. You might click your way through some of the instructions, though, to decide whether you find them comprehensible or not!)

Lieberman, J., & Sales, B. (1997). What social science teaches us about the jury instruction process. *Psychology, Public Policy, and Law, 3*, 589–644.

Ogloff, J., & Rose, V. (2005). The comprehension of judicial instructions. In N. Brewer & K. Williams (Eds.), *Psychology and law: An empirical perspective* (pp. 407–444). New York, NY: Guilford Press.

Cognitive Psychology and the Law: Remembering Conversation

Many legal cases hinge on a witness reporting the details of how a conversation unfolded. For example, did the shooter say, "It's time to die, fool," just before pulling the trigger? If so, this provides evidence that the shooter had the intention to kill, and hence the murder was (at least briefly) premeditated. Did Fred tell Jim about the new product when they were together at the business meeting? If so, this might indicate that Jim is guilty of insider trading. How exactly did Nikki question her daughter when Nikki was worried about child abuse? Were Nikki's questions suggestive and leading, or were they neutral? The difference here is crucial when we try to interpret her daughter's recollection.

So how accurate is memory for conversation? The answer flows naturally from points we raised in earlier chapters: You remember what you paid attention to; you generally don't remember aspects of your experience that you didn't think much about. (Author Daniel Goleman captures this idea in a wonderfully pithy phrase: *Memory is attention in the past tense.*) We need to ask, therefore, what people pay attention to in ordinary conversation, and the answer is straightforward: They typically pay attention to the meaning, or gist, of what is being expressed, and not to the phrasing. As a result, they typically remember the gist (or, at least, they remember their understanding of the gist) and not the actual words used. (For some of the evidence on this point, look back at Demonstration 7.2.)

In one study, for example, mothers had a conversation with their 4-year-old daughters and then, three days later, were asked to recall exactly how the conversation had unfolded. The mothers' memories for the exact words spoken were quite poor, so they had difficulty recalling (among other points) whether their children's statements were spontaneous or prompted by specific questions; they also had difficulty recalling which utterances were spoken by them and which by the children.

Of course, sometimes in a conversation, the exact phrasing does catch your attention: Sometimes, you hear a phrase that is particularly elegant, or perhaps somewhat rude. In such cases, you do notice the phrasing and so you remember the exact words. However, those occasions are rare, and the fact remains that your memory for conversational details is generally quite poor.

These results are, in a way, unsurprising, and, as we have already noted, simply confirm the broader claim that, overall, memory is selective, and that we tend to remember what we have paid attention to. At the same time, these results are troubling for the legal system, because the simple fact is that we usually cannot rely on someone's recollection of the exact words spoken in a conversation. Also important, though, is the fact that these results provide further evidence for your skill in using language: You easily and quickly derive the meaning from the words you hear, with the consequence that you have no need to ponder the exact words, or the specific phrasing. This is problematic if we focus on what you'll remember later, but it is also a testimonial to how efficient you are in decoding the language that you hear!

FOR DISCUSSION

This essay mentions that you *will* remember conversational details if the exact phrasing, within the conversation, catches your attention. Can you generate a catalogue of the circumstances, or the types of phrasing, that will catch your attention in this way? Can you identify certain speakers (or certain authors) whose phrasing is notable enough so that it consistently catches your attention?

For more on this topic

Bruck, M., Ceci, S., & Francoeur, E. (1999). The accuracy of mothers' memories of conversations with their preschool children. *Journal of Experimental Psychology: Applied, 5,* 89–106.

David, D., & Friedman, R. (2007). Memory for conversation: The orphan child of witness memory researchers. In M. Toglia, J. D. Read, D. Ross, & R. C. L. Lindsay, (Eds.), *The handbook of eyewitness psychology, Volume 1: Memory for events.* Mahwah, NJ: Erlbaum Associates.

Keenan, J. M., MacWhinney, B,. & Mayhew, D. (1977). Pragmatics in memory: A study of natural conversation. *Journal of Verbal Learning and Verbal Behavior, 16,* 549–560.

The Most Commonly Used Words in English

1	the	21	this	41	so	61	person	81	back
2	be	22	but	42	up	62	into	82	after
3	to	23	his	43	out	63	year	83	use
4	of	24	by	44	if	64	your	84	two
5	and	25	from	45	about	65	good	85	how
6	a	26	they	46	who	66	some	86	our
7	in	27	we	47	get	67	could	87	work
8	that	28	say	48	which	68	them	88	first
9	have	29	her	49	go	69	see	89	well
10	I	30	she	50	me	70	other	90	way
11	it	31	or	51	when	71	than	91	even
12	for	32	an	52	make	72	then	92	new
13	not	33	will	53	can	73	now	93	want
14	on	34	my	54	like	74	look	94	because
15	with	35	one	55	time	75	only	95	any
16	he	36	all	56	no	76	come	96	these
17	as	37	would	57	just	77	its	97	give
18	you	38	there	58	him	78	over	98	day
19	do	39	their	59	know	79	think	99	most
20	at	40	what	60	take	80	also	100	us

Source: http://en.wikipedia.org/wiki/Most_common_words_in_English#cite_note-langfacts-0

See Demonstration 9.4.

Visual Knowledge

Demonstrations

10.1 Imaged Synthesis

There is no question that people can "see" things in their mental images that they hadn't anticipated, and, in this way, mental images can plainly be a source of new discoveries. Indeed, the history of science, technology, and the arts is filled with examples of inventions inspired by something the inventor saw in a mental image and only later translated into an external object, formula, or theory.

We can demonstrate a miniature version of this process by relying on a procedure sometimes used in the laboratory to study image-based problem solving. The procedure involves *imaged synthesis*:

- Imagine a capitalized letter D. Lay this image down on its back, so that the vertical side lies flat and the rounded side bulges upward. Underneath it, position a capital letter J, centered underneath the D and just touching the side that is lying flat. What have you produced?

- Imagine the number 7. Make the diagonal line into a vertical. Move the horizontal line down to the middle of the vertical line. Now, rotate the figure 90 degrees to the left. What have you produced?

- Imagine the letter B. Rotate it 90 degrees to the left so that it's lying on its back. Put a triangle directly below it having the same width and pointing down. Remove the horizontal line. What have you produced?

- Imagine the letter Y. Put a small circle at the bottom of it. Add a horizontal line halfway up. Now, turn the figure upside down. What have you produced?

- Imagine the letter K. Place a square next to it on the left side. Put a circle inside of the square. Now, rotate the figure 90 degrees to the left. What have you produced?

■ Imagine the letter *D*. Rotate it 90 degrees to the right so that the bulge of D is at the bottom. Put the number 4 above it. Now, remove the horizontal segment of the 4 that's to the right of the vertical line. What have you produced?

How many of these led you to recognizable forms? Did you find (in this sequence) an umbrella, the letter *T*, a heart, a stick figure of a person, a TV set, and a sailboat?

Most people find these exercises relatively easy, and this provides a compelling demonstration that people really can "inspect" their images to find new forms and can make unanticipated discoveries from their images.

One question still to be asked, however, is whether this sort of "image-based creativity" involves the same processes that great scientists, artists, and inventors use. This is a difficult question, but it is worth noting that laboratory procedures involving imaged synthesis do sometimes produce discoveries that seem quite creative. For example, in one study, participants were told to use these forms in any way they liked to produce something interesting or useful: a capital *P*, the number 8, and a capital *T*. One participant combined these forms (in imagery) to produce this snapshot of a croquet game:

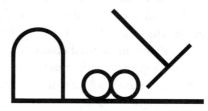

Apparently, then, imaged synthesis in the lab can produce interesting sparks of creativity!

Demonstration adapted from Finke, Ronald A., Pinker, Steven, & Farah, Martha J., "Reinterpreting Visual Patterns in Mental Imagery," *Cognitive Science*, Vol. 13, Issue 1, January–March 1989, pp. 51–78, Table 2, Copyright © 1989 Elsevier Science, Inc., with permission from Elsevier.

10.2   Mnemonic Strategies

Mental imagery plays a central role in many mnemonic strategies, including the peg-word systems we discussed in the textbook's Chapter 5. To use this type of mnemonic, first you memorize the peg words themselves. Then, you "hang" the words you're trying to remember onto these now-memorized "pegs."

Let's make this concrete, via a demonstration. Our first step involves the peg words: Read the following rhyme (which you first met in Chapter 5) out loud twice; that will probably be enough for you to memorize the rhyme.

One is a bun.	Six are sticks.
Two is a shoe.	Seven is heaven.
Three is a tree.	Eight is a gate.
Four is a door.	Nine is a line.
Five is a hive.	Ten is a hen.

Got it? We're now going to use the words in this sequence (bun, shoe, tree, and so on) as "pegs," and we're going to "hang" each of the to-be-remembered items on its own peg.

The first word for you to remember is "ashtray." Take just a moment to form a mental picture that somehow links this word with the first peg word, "bun." It's okay if your mental picture is bizarre or comical; no one will ask you what your picture is!

Now take a moment to form a mental picture somehow linking the second peg word "shoe" with "firewood."

Got it? Now take a moment to form a mental picture somehow linking the third peg word, "tree," with "picture."

Next, take a moment to form a mental picture somehow linking the fourth peg word, "door," with "cigarette."

Now do the same for the remaining pairs:

> Five is a HIVE . . . TABLE
>
> Six are STICKS . . . MATCHBOOK
>
> Seven is HEAVEN . . . GLASS
>
> Eight is a GATE . . . LAMP
>
> Nine is a LINE . . . SHOE
>
> Ten is a HEN . . . PLATE

You probably found this task easy—and, depending on the images you formed, perhaps even fun. But, in addition, you've now memorized the list. Look away from the page and see if you can recall the first four words on the list: What went with bun? shoe? tree? door?

You can also, if you like, try reciting the list backward: What went with hen? Line? Gate?

Odds are good that you've now got this list well under control, and, in fact, you'll probably still remember the list if you test yourself again *tomorrow*. Tomorrow, or even the next day, write down the numbers 1 through 10, and try to remember the ten words you just placed in these mental pictures. If you created adequate mental pictures, you'll probably remember most of them. This provides an excellent argument that imagery can have a powerful effect on memory.

But mnemonics also have a downside. Quickly: What was eighth on the list? Fifth? These questions are probably easy for you. Now: What was the word you memorized that came *after* "picture"? This last question is surprisingly difficult, and you're likely to stammer a bit before spitting out the answer. Why is this? Think about what retrieval paths you *did* establish when you were learning the list, and what paths you *didn't* establish. From that base, you might also think about the *dangers* created if you only establish one or two retrieval paths; what will this imply for the flexibility of your retrieval?

Overall, then, mnemonics are both valuable in classroom learning and potentially harmful. They're valuable if you don't need to think about what the materials mean or imply. (Thinking about the link between "bun" and "ashtray" probably didn't lead you to deep thoughts about either item.) They're also valuable if you're sure, in advance, *how you'll retrieve the information later.* If you know the cue will be "bun," then it's fine if your only access path to "ashtray" is a path that runs from "bun" to "ashtray." But mnemonics can throw you off if, later, you have to be flexible in how you access materials. In that case, having just one retrieval path creates a risk that this won't be the path you'll need!

10.3   Auditory Imagery

This chapter has been about visual imagery, but imagery also exists in other modalities. For example, talented cooks often rely on their imagery to adjust the seasoning in a dish they're preparing: How would these brownies taste, for example, if a little kumquat jelly were mixed into the batter? By imagining the combination, the cook can leap forward to a great variation on a classic dessert. Or, on a more ambitious scale: Ludwig van Beethoven was entirely deaf when he wrote some of his great compositions; apparently, he relied on his auditory imagery to imagine what the music would sound like. And guided by imagery, he produced extraordinary works.

Auditory imagery also gets used for mundane purposes, including any task in which you need to figure out what something would sound like, or need to make some *judgment* about sound. For example, imagine that you saw a car with this license plate:

NE1 4 10 S

You might not get the joke until you read the symbols out loud: "Anyone [NE1] for tennis [10 S]?"

In the same spirit, try to figure out what familiar word or phrase is conveyed by the following sequences. But do this without making a sound. Figure these out, in other words, by *imagining* the sounds.

1. 2 6E 4 U	5. I M D 1 4 U	9. X L R 8
2. U NV ME	6. EZ 4 U 2 C	10. U4EA
3. I M A DV8	7. I M L8	11. AV8R
4. BCNU	8. I M 2 BZ	12. NML

Now, try a simple experiment. Get a friend to try this task, asking your friend to write down his or her interpretations of each of these sequences. How many does your friend get right? Now, get another friend to try the task, but *for the entire time he or she is working on the task*, ask your friend to repeat "Tah-Tah-Tah" quietly out loud. This will tie up your friend's mouth so that he or she will not be able to "mime" the articulation of each stimulus item. How many does this friend get right? His or her performance is likely to be lower than that of your first friend, suggesting that auditory imagery often relies on the support provided by subvocalization: We imagine sounds by (silently) pronouncing them to ourselves and somehow "listening" to what we just "said."

Demonstration adapted from Smith, D., Wilson, M., & Reisberg, D. (1996). The role of subvocalization in auditory imagery. *Neuropsychologia, 33,* 1433–1454.

The answers are at the end of the workbook entry for this chapter (p. 139).

Applying Cognitive Psychology

Research Methods: Expectations, Motivations, and Demand

In most research, we're trying to study how people behave under natural circumstances—how they behave when they're just being themselves. As a result, it is crucial that we take steps to minimize the *demand character* of the study.

As the textbook chapter describes, demand character refers to any cues in a procedure (including an experiment, a survey, or an interview) that might signal to participants how they "ought to" behave. In some cases, these cues can indicate to participants what results the researcher hopes for (i.e., results that would confirm the researcher's hypothesis), and this may encourage participants to make the hoped-for response, even if they're inclined toward some other option. In other cases, a procedure's demand character somehow suggests that certain responses are more desirable than others—so that, for example, participants perceive some responses as indicating greater intelligence or greater sensitivity. It's then plausible that participants will choose these responses to avoid appearing stupid or insensitive.

What can we do to avoid these effects, so that we don't guide participants toward some particular response, and instead observe them as they normally are? Researchers use several strategies. First, we do all we can to make sure that demand character never arises in the first place. Thus, we make sure that the procedure contains no signals about what the hypothesis is. Likewise, we do what we can to phrase our questions and cast the response options so that no response seems preferable to any others.

Second, it's often a good idea to direct participants' attention *away from* the study's main comparisons, or, if the study is an experiment, the procedure's key manipulation. That way, the participants won't spend their efforts thinking about the crucial comparison, and this makes it more likely that they'll respond naturally and spontaneously to the variables we hope to understand. Likewise, by diverting attention away from the manipulation, we make it less likely that participants will try to guard against (or somehow tune) their response to the manipulation.

How do we divert the participants' attention, to achieve these goals? Many procedures contain some sort of "cover story" about what the study is addressing. The cover story is designed, of course, to draw the participants' thinking away from the key aspects of the procedure. But, in addition, a good cover story encourages participants to take the study seriously, and also makes it less likely that they'll spend their minutes, during the study, speculating about the procedure's true purpose.

Third, we do what we can to make sure that all participants in all conditions receive exactly the same treatment. Thus, we encourage all participants in the same way, give them similar instructions, and so on. In some cases, we rely on a *double-blind procedure*, in which neither the participant nor the person administering the procedure knows what the study is about, or whether a particular trial (or a particular test session) is in the experimental condition or the control condition. All of these steps ensure that the administrator won't be more encouraging or more forceful with one group in comparison with the other, or in one condition rather than another. The steps also guarantee that all participants will have the same expectations about the study.

With all these safeguards in place, can we be sure that participants' expectations, goals, and hypotheses play *no role* in shaping our data? Probably not, and this is one more reason why replications (with other participants and other procedures) are so important. Even so, we do what we can to minimize the contribution of these factors, making it far more likely that our results can be understood in the terms we intend.

FOR DISCUSSION

In one of the studies discussed in the textbook chapter, participants were asked yes-or-no questions about a cat: "Does it have a head? Does it have claws? Does it have whiskers?" If participants based their answers on a mental image of a cat, their yes answers were faster for "head" than for "claws" or "whiskers," simply because the head is large and prominent in the mental picture. If, instead, participants based their answers on some other form of mental description (e.g., if they were just thinking in an abstract way about the idea of "a cat"), the pattern reversed—with faster answers for "claws" and "whiskers" than for "head."

Imagine that you wanted to replicate this experiment. You would need two groups of participants: one asked to answer your questions based on a mental picture, and one simply told to "think about cats." What would you tell the two groups, right at the start, about the purpose of the experiment or the nature of their task? Bear in mind that you wouldn't want to tell them your hypothesis; that could, by itself, create a strong demand character. You also probably wouldn't tell them what *question* you're after ("I'm interested in studying how quickly people can draw information from a mental image"), because this might invite participants to generate their own hypotheses, which could somehow distort their performance. But you do need to tell them *something* to make sure they are taking your task seriously. What instructions would you give them?

Cognitive Psychology and Education: Using Imagery

Visual imagery often entertains us—in a wonderful daydream, for example, or in an exciting dream at night. But imagery is also useful in many settings. For example, the textbook chapter discusses the fact that imagery is a powerful aid to memory: We see this in the role of imagery in mnemonic strategies (see Demonstration 10.2), and also in the fact that materials that are easily visualized tend to be easier to remember.

However, we offer one point of caution about image-based strategies for memorizing. As the chapter makes clear, mental imagery does an excellent job of representing what something *looks like*, so imagery mnemonics can help you a lot if you want to remember appearances—how a visualized scene looked, and what it included. These simple points, though, have powerful implications. Let's say that you are using the mnemonic described in Demonstration 10.2, and let's say that you're working on the tenth item on the to-be-remembered list (that was the word "plate") and therefore using the tenth peg word, "hen." To remember this word, you might form a mental picture of a dinner plate underneath a delicious-looking roast chicken, with a helping of mashed potatoes alongside it. Later, when you're trying to recall the list, you'd recite the peg-word rhyme, and so you'd be led to the peg, "Ten is a hen." This might call the mental picture to mind, but now what happens? Thinking about this picture, you might confidently announce, "I remember—the tenth word was 'dish'" or "was 'potatoes.'" Both responses are consistent with the picture—but they don't provide the word you're trying to remember. In this way, the "mental pictures" formed in a mnemonic might not be specific enough to provide the information you need!

Likewise, in forming a mnemonic picture, you're likely to think about what the to-be-remembered items look like, and this may distract you from thinking about what these items *mean*. Imagine, for example, that you want to remember that a hypothesis was offered by the important psychologist Henry Roediger. To remember this name, you might playfully convert it to "rod-digger" and form a mental picture of someone digging into the earth with a fishing rod. This will help you remember the name, but it will encourage no insights into what Roediger's hypothesis was, or how it relates to other aspects of his theorizing, or to other things you know. Images, in other words, are excellent for remembering some things, but often what you need (or want) to remember goes beyond this.

These points are certainly not meant to warn you against using image-based mnemonics. In fact, we've emphasized how *effective* these mnemonics are. However, it's important to understand why these mnemonics work as they do, because with that knowledge you can avoid using the mnemonics in circumstances in which they might actually work against you.

In the same fashion, imagery can be a powerful aid to *problem solving*. Demonstration 10.1 is designed to underline this point, by making it clear how new discoveries can flow from mental pictures. But, again, there are limits on image-based problem solving: Mental images are understood within a certain framework—a framework that indicates the imager's understanding of the image's figure/ground organization, its orientation in space, and so on. This framework helps the imager interpret the depicted form but can also *limit* what the imager will discover from a given mental picture. (This is, for example, why imagers routinely fail to find a "duck" in a "rabbit image" and vice versa, as described in the chapter.)

There is, however, a way to escape these limits. People can often make new discoveries about a form by *drawing a picture*, based on their own mental image. The picture depicts the same form as the mental image; but because the picture is not linked to a particular reference frame, it will often support new discoveries that the original image would not. We can demonstrate this in the laboratory (e.g., in people discovering the duck in their own drawing of the duck/rabbit form, even though they failed to make the discovery from their image). We can also demonstrate this point in real-world settings (e.g., in architects who cannot reconceptualize a building plan by scrutinizing their own mental image of the plan, but who can then make striking new discoveries once they draw out the plan on paper).

The message should be clear for anyone seeking to *use* an image as an aid to problem solving: No matter how clear the image before the mind's eye, it is sometimes useful to pick up a pencil and draw the image out on paper or on a blackboard; this will often facilitate new discoveries.

Again, therefore, we see the benefits of understanding the limits of your own strategies. Once you understand those limits, you can find ways to make full use of these strategies in order to maximize your problem-solving skills, your memory, and your comprehension of new materials—but without falling into traps created by the strategies' limits.

FOR DISCUSSION

The ancient Greeks and Romans put a high value on public speaking, and we still celebrate the skill of great orators like Demosthenes or Cicero. These speakers generally spoke from memory, without notes, and some of the mnemonics still in use were developed in these ancient times to help these orators remember their speeches. One mnemonic involved a familiar place—such as a building the orator knew well, or a path the orator often took. To use the mnemonic, the orator would form some mental picture linking the first topic for a speech with a particular object or location within this familiar place, the second topic with another object or location, and so on. When it was time to deliver the speech, the orator would (mentally) "walk through" the familiar scene.

As he "reached" each landmark, he'd be reminded of the appropriate mental picture and hence the topic, and could deliver that portion of the oration.

This technique works just like the peg word system described in Demonstration 10.2, but it uses the building or path, rather than a silly rhyme, to knit together the to-be-remembered material. And the technique does work: In Greece and Rome, speakers used this strategy to memorize lengthy, complex, many-step speeches. So we can now ask: Is there a way to adapt this ancient mnemonic for modern use? In what educational settings might you use this mnemonic? What sorts of things could you memorize in this way? What might some of the *hazards* be in using this mnemonic?

Cognitive Psychology and the Law: Lineups

There are now almost 300 cases of DNA exoneration in the United States—cases in which DNA evidence, available only after a trial was over, has shown incontrovertibly that the courts had convicted the wrong person. In each case, the actually guilty person walked around free while someone totally innocent spent years in jail. In many cases, the innocent person, now exonerated, had been on death row awaiting execution. If the DNA evidence hadn't been available, the wrong person might have been executed.

In the vast majority of these cases, the mistaken conviction can be traced to bad eyewitness evidence: The juries had (understandably) been persuaded when an eyewitness confidently pointed to the defendant and said, "That's the man who raped me" (or "robbed me" or "shot my friend"). But in case after case, the witnesses were wrong, and the jury's decision was correspondingly mistaken.

These cases are, of course, tragic, with jurors and the courts doing their best—but misled by bad evidence. It's crucial, therefore, to ask what we can do to avoid these incorrect identifications, and we can be guided here by what we know about memory's operation in general and about memory for faces in particular. Specifically, research has identified a number of factors that can undermine the accuracy of an identification, and we can use these factors as a basis for deciding which identifications need to be treated with special caution. As just one illustration, we mentioned in the Cognitive Psychology and the Law essay for Chapter 3 that eyewitness identifications tend to be less accurate when the witness and the perpetrator are of different races. This suggests a need for greater caution when interpreting a cross-race identification, and this point by itself can help the courts make better use of eyewitness evidence.

Other research has asked what steps we can take to diminish the chance of eyewitness error. For example, psychologists have offered advice on how a police lineup should be constructed—that is, what faces should be included in addition to the suspect's—to minimize the chance of error. Evidence makes it clear that a well-chosen lineup can markedly decrease the chance of witness error, and so it is crucial, for example, that the other faces in the lineup be consistent with the witness's initial description of the perpetrator. Otherwise, some lineup members may not be taken seriously as real choices for the witness, and this can guide the witness's attention to the suspect's picture, increasing the risk of a false (incorrect) identification.

We can also change the instructions given to witnesses. It is important, for example, to remind witnesses before viewing a lineup that they are under no obligation to make a choice, and that the perpetrator's face may or may not be among those presented. This instruction seems to have little effect if the perpetrator is actually present in the lineup—in essence, if he's there, you're likely to spot him. But if the perpetrator is *not* present in the lineup (i.e., if clues have led police to the wrong person), then this instruction is remarkably effective in protecting the innocent: Merely telling the witness that "the perpetrator may or may not be shown here" and that "you're under no obligation to choose" seems, in some studies, to cut the risk of a false identification in half.

A different proposal concerns how the faces are shown. In a standard lineup, the witness is shown all six faces at once and must choose from among the group. In a *sequential lineup*, the witness is shown the faces one by one and must make a yes or no judgment about each one before seeing the next. This procedure has been controversial, but even so, it does seem to decrease the number of false identifications, so it may be an improvement on the standard (simultaneous) presentation.

These various points—including the procedural improvements—offer a considerable potential for improving eyewitness accuracy. It is therefore gratifying that law enforcement is taking these steps seriously with a real prospect that we can use what we know about face memory and eyewitness behavior to improve the criminal justice system.

FOR DISCUSSION

On television shows, you often see the eyewitness standing behind a one-way mirror and watching as six people shuffle in and stand against a wall. The detective asks, "Is one of these men the person who robbed you?" However, this sort of *live lineup* is increasingly rare. In the United States, lineups are typically carried out with photographs—with the witness looking at six head-and-shoulder photos and trying to identify the perpetrator from this *photo lineup* (or *photomontage*). In England, lineups increasingly rely on *videos*—with the witness being shown a video of each person first looking straight ahead, then turning to the left, then turning to the right.

Think through the advantages and disadvantages of each of these three systems—live lineups, photomontages, and video lineups. Which system do you think is likely to yield the most accurate identifications? Are there considerations beyond accuracy (efficiency? speed? convenience? safety?) that might favor one of these procedures over the others?

For more on this topic

Innocence Project. (2012). www.innocenceproject.org

Steblay, N. K., Dietrich, H. L., Ryan, S. L., Raczynski, J. L., & James, K. A. (2011). Sequential lineups and eyewitness accuracy, *Law and Human Behavior*, 35, 262–274.

Technical Working Group on Eyewitness Evidence. (1999). *Eyewitness evidence: A guide for law enforcement*. Washington, DC: U.S. Department of Justice, Office of Justice Programs.

Wells, G. L., Malpass, R. S., Lindsay, R. C. L., Fisher, R. P., Turtle, J. W., & Fulero, S. (2000). From the lab to the police station: A successful application of eyewitness research. *American Psychologist, 55,* 581–598.

Wells, G. L., Steblay, N., & Dysart, J. (2011). Seventy-two tests of the sequential lineup superiority effect: A meta-analysis and policy discussion. *Psychology, Public Policy and Law, 17,* 99–139.

Answers to Demonstration 10.3

1. "Too sexy for you"
2. "You envy me"
3. "I am a deviate"
4. "Be seein' you"
5. "I am the [de] one for you"
6. "Easy for you to see"
7. "I am late"
8. "I am too busy"
9. "Accelerate"
10. "Euphoria"
11. "Aviator"
12. "Animal"

Judgment and Reasoning

Demonstrations

11.1   Sample Size

Research on how people make judgments suggests that their performance is at best uneven, with people in many cases drawing conclusions that are not justified by the evidence they've seen. Here, for example is a question drawn from a classic study of judgment:

> In a small town nearby, there are two hospitals. Hospital A has an average of 45 births per day; Hospital B is smaller and has an average of 15 births per day. As we all know, overall the proportion of males born is 50%. Each hospital recorded the number of days in which, on that day, at least 60% of the babies born were male.
>   Which hospital recorded more such days?
>   a. Hospital A
>   b. Hospital B
>   c. both equal

What's your answer to this question? In more formal procedures, the majority of research participants choose response (c), "both equal," but this answer is statistically unwarranted. All of the births in the country add up to a 50-50 split between male and female babies, and, the larger the sample you examine, the more likely you are to approximate this ideal. But, conversely, the smaller the sample you examine, the more likely you are to stray from this ideal. Days with 60% male births, straying from the ideal, are therefore more likely in the smaller hospital, Hospital B.

If you don't see this, consider a more extreme case:

Hospital C has 1,000 births per day; Hospital D has exactly 1 birth per day. Which hospital records more days with at least 90% male births?

This value will be observed in Hospital D rather often, since on many days all the babies born (one out of one) will be male. This value is surely less likely, though, in Hospital C: 900 male births, with just 100 female, would be a remarkable event indeed. In this case, it seems clear that the smaller hospital can more easily stray far from the 50-50 split.

In the hospital problem, participants seem not to take sample size into account. They seem to think a particular pattern is just as likely with a small sample as with a large sample, although this is plainly not true. This belief, however, is just what we would expect if people were relying on the *representativeness heuristic*, making the assumption that each instance of a category—or, in this case, each subset of a larger set—should show the properties associated with the entire set.

Try this demonstration with a couple of your friends. As you'll see, it's easy to find people who choose the incorrect option ("both equal"), underlining just how often people seem to be insensitive to considerations of sample size.

Demonstration adapted from Kahneman, D., & Tversky, A. (1972). Subjective probability: A judgment of representativeness. *Cognitive Psychology*, 3, 430–454.

11.2   Relying on the Representativeness Heuristic

Demonstration 11.1 indicated that people often neglect (or misunderstand the meaning of) *sample size*. In other cases, people rely on heuristics that are not in any way guided by *logic*, so their conclusion ends up being quite illogical. For example, here is another classic problem from research on judgment:

Linda is 31 years old, single, outspoken, and very bright. She majored in philosophy. As a student, she was deeply concerned with issues of discrimination and social justice, and she also participated in anti-nuclear demonstrations.
    Which of the following is more likely to be true?
    a. Linda is a bank teller.
    b. Linda is a bank teller and is active in the feminist movement.

What's your response? In many studies, a clear majority of participants (sometimes as high as 85%) choose option (b). Logically, though, this makes no sense. If Linda is a feminist bank teller, then she is still a bank teller. Therefore, there's no way for option (b) to be true without option (a) also being true. Therefore, option (b) couldn't possibly be more likely than option (a)! Choosing option (b), in other words, is akin to saying that if we randomly choose someone who lives in North America, the chance of that person being from Vermont is greater than the chance of that person being from the United States.

Why, therefore, do so many people choose option (b)? This option makes sense if people are relying on the representativeness heuristic. In that case, they make the category judgment by asking themselves: "How much does Linda resemble my idea of a bank teller? How much does she resemble my idea of a *feminist* bank teller?" On this basis, they could easily be led to option (b), because the description of Linda does, in fact, encourage a particular view of her and her politics.

There is, however, another possibility. With options (a) and (b) sitting side-by-side, someone might say: "Well, if option (b) is talking about a bank teller who *is* a feminist, then option (a) must be talking about a bank teller who is *not* a feminist." On that interpretation, choosing option (b) does seem reasonable. Is this how you interpreted option (a)?

You might spend a moment thinking about how to test this alternative interpretation—the idea that research participants interpret option (a) in this narrowed fashion. One strategy is to present option (a) to some participants and ask them how likely it is, and to present option (b) *to other participants* and ask them how likely it is. In this way, the options are never put side by side, so there's never any implied contrast in the options. In this situation, then, there's no reason at all for participants to interpret option (a) in the narrowed fashion. Even so, in studies using this alternative procedure, the group of participants seeing option (a) still rated it as *less likely* than the other group of participants rated the option they saw. Again, this makes no sense from the standpoint of logic, but it makes perfect sense if participants are using the representativeness heuristic.

Demonstration adapted from Tversky, A., & Kahneman, D. (1983). Extension versus intuitive reasoning: The conjunction fallacy in probability judgment. *Psychological Review, 90,* 293–315.

11.3 Applying Base Rates

Chapter 11 documents many errors in judgment, and it is deeply troubling that these errors can be observed even when knowledgeable experts are making judgments about domains that are enormously consequential. As an illustration, consider the following scenario.

Imagine that someone you care about—let's call her Julia, age 42—is worried that she might have breast cancer. In thinking about Julia's case, we might start by asking: How common is breast cancer for women of Julia's age, with her family history, her dietary pattern, and so on? Let us assume that for this group the statistics show an overall 3% likelihood of developing breast cancer. This should be reassuring to Julia, because there is a 97% chance that she is cancer free.

Of course, a 3% chance is still scary for this disease, so Julia decides to get a mammogram. When her results come back, the report is bad—indicating that she does have breast cancer. Julia quickly does some research to find out how accurate mammograms are, and she learns that the available data are something like this:

	Mammogram indicates	
	Cancer	No cancer
Cancer actually present	85%	15%
Cancer actually absent	10%	90%

In light of all this information, what is your best estimate of the chance that Julia does, in fact, have breast cancer? She comes from a group that only has a 3% risk for cancer, but she's gotten an abnormal mammogram result, and the test seems, according to her research, accurate. What should we conclude? *Think about this for a few moments, and, before reading on, estimate the percentage chance of Julia having breast cancer.*

When medical doctors are asked questions like these, their answers are often wildly inaccurate, because they (like most people) fail to use base-rate information correctly. What was your estimate of the percentage chance of Julia having breast cancer? The correct answer is 20%. This is an awful number, given what's at stake, and Julia would surely want to pursue further tests. But the odds are still heavily in Julia's favor, with a 4-to-1 chance that she is *entirely free of cancer.*

Where does this answer come from? Let's fill in the tables below, but using *actual counts* rather than the *percentages* shown in the previous table. Specifically, let's imagine that we are considering 100,000 women with medical histories similar to Julia's. We have already said that overall there is a 3% chance of breast cancer in this group, and so 3,000 (3% of 100,000) of these women will have breast cancer. Fill that number in as the *top* number in the "Total number" column, and this will leave the rest of the overall group (97,000) as the *bottom* number in this column.

	Mammogram indicates		
	Cancer	No cancer	Total number
Cancer actually present			3,000
Cancer actually absent			97,000

Now, let's fill in the rows. There are 3,000 women counted in the top row, and we've already said that in this group the mammogram will (correctly) indicate that cancer is present in 85% of the cases. So the number for "Mammogram indicates cancer" in the top row will be 85% of the total in this row (3,000), or 2,550. The number of cases for "Mammogram indicates no cancer" in this row will be the remaining 15% of the 3,000, so let's fill in that number—450.

	Mammogram indicates		
	Cancer	No cancer	Total number
Cancer actually present	2,550	450	3,000
Cancer actually absent			97,000

Let's now do the same for the bottom row. We've already said that there are 97,000 women represented in this row; of these, the mammogram will correctly indicate *no* cancer for 90% (87,300) and will falsely indicate cancer for 10% (9,700). Let's now put those numbers in the appropriate positions.

	Mammogram indicates		
	Cancer	No cancer	Total number
Cancer actually present	2,550	450	3,000
Cancer actually absent	9,700	87,300	97,000

Finally, let's put these pieces together. According to our numbers, a total of 12,250 women will receive the horrid information that they have breast cancer. (That's the total of the two numbers, 2,550 + 9,700, in the left column, "Mammogram indicates cancer.") Within this group, this test result will be *correct* for 2,550 women (left column, top row). The result will be *misleading* for the remaining 9,700 (left column, bottom row). Thus, *of the women receiving awful news from their mammogram, 2,550 ÷ 12,250, or 20%, will actually have breast cancer; the remaining 80% will be cancer free.*

Notice, then, that the mammogram is *wrong* far more often than it's right. This is not because the mammogram is an inaccurate test. In fact, the test is rather accurate. However, if the test is used with patient groups for which the base rate is low, then the mammogram might be wrong in only 10% of the cancer-free cases, but this will be 10% of a large number, producing a substantial number of horrifying false alarms.

This is obviously a consequential example, because we are discussing a disease that is lethal in many cases. It is therefore deeply troubling that even in this very important example, people still make errors of judgment. Worse, it's striking that experienced physicians, when asked the same questions, also make errors—they, too, ignore the base rates and therefore give risk estimates that are off by a very wide margin.

At the same time, because this is a consequential example, let's add some caution to these points. First, if a woman has a different background from Julia (our hypothetical patient), her overall risk for breast cancer may be higher than Julia's. In other words, the base rate for her group may be higher or lower (depending on the woman's age, exposure to certain toxins, family history, and other factors), and this will have a huge impact on the calculations we have discussed here. Therefore, we cannot freely generalize from the numbers considered here to other cases; we would need to know the base rate for these other cases.

Second, even if Julia's risk is 20%, this is still a high number, so Julia (or anyone in this situation) might pursue treatment for this life-threatening illness. A 1-in-5 chance of having a deadly disease must be taken seriously! However, this does not change the fact that a 20% risk is very different from the 85% risk that one might fear if one considered only the mammogram results in isolation from the base rates. At 20%, the odds are good that Julia is safe; at 85%, she probably does have this disease. It seems certain that this is a difference that would matter for Julia's subsequent steps, and it reminds us that medical decision making needs to be guided by full information—including, it seems, information about base rates.

Demonstration adapted from Eddy, D. (1982). Probabilistic reasoning in clinical medicine. In D. Kahneman, P. Slovic, & A. Tversky (Eds.), *Judgment under uncertainty: Heuristics and biases* (pp. 249–267). Cambridge, England: Cambridge University Press.

11.4   Frequencies Versus Percentages

This chapter argues that we can *improve* people's judgments by presenting evidence to them in the right way. To see how this plays out, recruit a few friends. Ask some of them Question 1, and some Question 2:

> 1. Mr. Jones is a patient in a psychiatric hospital, and has a history of violence. However, the time has come to consider discharging Mr. Jones from the hospital. He is therefore evaluated by several experts at the hospital, and they conclude: Patients with Mr. Jones' profile are estimated to have a 10% probability of committing an act of violence against others during the first several months after discharge. How comfortable would you be in releasing Mr. Jones?
>
> 1   2   3   4   5   6   7
>
> No way! Keep him in the hospital.   Yes, he is certainly ready for discharge.

2. Mr. Jones is a patient in a psychiatric hospital, and has a history of violence. However, the time has come to consider discharging Mr. Jones from the hospital. He is therefore evaluated by several experts at the hospital, and they conclude: Of every 100 patients similar to Mr. Jones, 10 are estimated to commit an act of violence against others during the first several months after discharge. How comfortable would you be in releasing Mr. Jones?

1	2	3	4	5	6	7

No way! Keep him in the hospital.   Yes, he is certainly ready for discharge.

These two questions provide the same information (10% = 10 out of 100), but do your friends react in the same way? When experienced forensic psychologists were asked these questions, 41% of them *denied* the discharge when they saw the data in frequency format (10 out of 100), and only 21% denied the discharge when they saw the percentage.

Of course, there's room for debate what the "right answer" is in this case. Therefore, we cannot conclude from this example that a frequency format *improves reasoning*. (Other evidence, though, does confirm this important point.) But this example does make clear that a change in format matters—with plainly different outcomes when information is presented as a frequency, rather than a percentage.

For more on this topic

Kahneman, D. (2011). *Thinking, fast and slow*. New York, NY: Farrar, Straus and Giroux.
Slovic, P., Monahan, D., and MacGregor, D. (2000) Violence risk assessment and risk communication. *Law & Human Behavior, 24,* 271–296.

11.5   The Effect of Content on Reasoning

In the textbook chapter, we note that *how* people reason is heavily influenced by the *content* of what they're reasoning about, and this is not what we would expect if people were using the rules of logic. Those rules are guided only by the *form* of the statements being examined, and not by the content. (This is the basis for the term "*form*al logic.") Thus the rules apply in exactly the same way to any of these cases:

"If Sam is happy, I'll shout. Sam is happy. Therefore I'll shout."
"If p is true, then q is true. P is true. Therefore q is true."
"If griss is triffle, then zupie is hockel. Griss is triffle. Therefore zupie is hockel."

All three of these are valid arguments, and there's just one logic rule (called *modus ponens*) that applies to all of them. Obviously, these statements vary in their content, but, again, that's irrelevant for logic. As we said, logic rules only consider the statements' *form*.

The chapter provides several examples, however, indicating that human reasoning *does* depend on a problem's content, and this provides important information about the principles guiding your reasoning. As one more demonstration of this broad point, let's look at a variation on the four-card task discussed in the chapter.

Imagine that you're the *owner* of a large company. You are concerned that your employees have been taking days off even when they're not entitled to do so. The company's rule is:

> If an employee works on the weekend, then that person gets a day off during the week.

Here are employment records for four employees. Each record indicates, on one side, whether the employee has worked on the weekend or not. The record indicates, on the other side, whether that person got a day off or not.

As the owner of this business, which records would you want to inspect to make sure that your rule is being followed? Place an *X* under the cards that you would turn over.

Now, imagine that you are a *worker* in the same large company. You are concerned that your boss is not giving people their days off, even when they have earned the days off. Which records would you want to inspect to make sure that the company's rule is being followed? Place an asterisk under the cards that you would turn over.

Most people give different answers to these two questions. As a *company owner*, they turn over the middle two cards—to make sure that the person who didn't work on a weekend isn't taking an "illegal" day off, and to make sure the person who did take a day off really earned it. As a *worker*, they tend to turn over the first and last cards—to make sure that everyone who earned a day off gets one.

In the textbook chapter, we mention two theories that can be applied to cases like this one. One theory is cast in terms of evolution, with an emphasis on how people reason when they're thinking about "cheaters." A second theory is cast in terms of pragmatic reasoning, on the idea that people have learned, during their lifetime, how to think about situations involving *permission* and situations involving *obligation*. Which of these theories fit with the observation that selections in the four-card problem presented above *change* if your perspective changes (that is changes from the owner's perspective to the worker's perspective)? Can you see how an emphasis on "cheater-detection" might fit with these results, including the flip-flop in responses when your perspective changes? Can you see how an emphasis on permission and obligation also fits with the results?

Demonstration adapted from Gigerenzer, G., & Hug, K. (1992). Domain-specific reasoning: Social contracts, cheating and perspective change. *Cognition, 43,* 127–171.

11.6 Wealth Versus Changes in Wealth

Many economists regard utility theory as a description of how you *should* make choices, and also a description of how you *do* make choices. But psychologists have had an easy time identifying challenges to utility theory. Specifically, ordinary decision makers seem to follow rules rather different from those proposed by this theory.

For example, utility calculations focus on where a decision will leave you—will you choose to end up with Outcome #1, or with Outcome #2? In making choices, however, people don't just look at the outcomes; they also *compare* the outcomes to their current status and are heavily influenced by the *change* that might result from their decision. This is a problem for utility theory, because current status is actually irrelevant to utility calculations.

To make this point concrete, first consider this comparison (from Nobel Prize winner, Daniel Kahneman):

> Today Jack and Jill each have a wealth of 5 million dollars.
> Yesterday, Jack had 1 million and Jill had 9 million.
> Are they equally happy?

For most people, this is an easy question—Jack is likely to be much happier than Jill, because of the *change* he has experienced. How might this influence their decision making? Here's a different comparison, again from Kahneman:

> Anthony's current wealth is 1 million.
> Betty's current wealth is 4 million.
> They are both offered this choice; would they rather have
> 　　A gamble, with equal chances to end up winning 1 million or 4 million
> 　**OR** A sure thing: End up owning 2 million

How will Anthony choose? How will Betty choose? You've probably answered differently for these two people, because you're alert to the *changes* in wealth, and not just the outcome levels.

Or, as one more example (and, again, adapted from Kahneman), imagine two contestants on a TV game show:

> Contestant 1 has just won $1000.
> She now has a choice: Receive another $500 (and so end up with $1500) **OR** toss a coin.
> 　　If the coin comes up "heads," she wins another $1000 (and so has $2000).
> 　　If the coin comes up "tails," nothing happens (and so she stays at $1000).
>
> Contestant 2 has just won $2000.
> She now has a choice: Give up $500 (and so end up with $1500) **OR** toss a coin.
> 　　If the coin comes up "heads," nothing happens (and so she stays at $2000).
> 　　If the coin comes up "tails," she loses $1000 (and so drops to $1000).

What would you do if you were Contestant 1? Contestant 2? Again, you're probably very sensitive to the *changes* in wealth state, and not just the outcomes.

For more on this topic

Kahneman, D. (2011). *Thinking, fast and slow*. New York, NY: Farrar, Straus and Giroux.

11.7　Probabilities Versus Decision Weights

Does utility theory describe how ordinary people make decisions—in the marketplace, or in their lives? According to the theory, people should be influenced by *probabilities*. (The chapter describes the formula for calculating the *expected value* of a decision's outcome, and probabilities are a key part of the formula.)

However, it's easy to show that people don't respect the laws of probability in their decision making. Among other points, people overinterpret the difference between a 0% probability and, say, a 5% probability—because they perceive a huge difference between "can't happen" and "might happen." Kahneman and Tversky refer to this as the "possibility effect." (In other words, people are keenly sensitive to whether something is a possibility or not.) Likewise, people overinterpret the difference between 100% and, say, 95%—because here they perceive a huge difference between "will happen" and "might happen." This is called the "certainty effect."

These effects show up in many settings. People are willing to pay for lottery tickets because they are impressed by the notion that they *might* win (the possibility effect). People will likewise pay a lot to increase their chances of a gain from 99% to 100%—because of the high value they put on certainty.

To see these effects in action, consider the following pair of questions:

- A friend of yours is going in for surgery. You've heard that the surgery has risks attached to it, so you do a bit of research on the Internet and discover that, for people with your friend's profile, the risk is actually 0%. But then you find a more recent bit of news, and you realize that the risk is actually 5%. How much would this increase your level of anxiety?

- A different friend of yours is going in for surgery. You've heard that the surgery has risks attached to it, so you do a bit of research on the Internet and discover that, for people with your friend's profile, the risk is actually 5%. But then you find a more recent bit of news, and you realize that the risk is actually 10%. How much would this increase your level of anxiety?

Alternatively, imagine two scenarios:

- You're the director for a small company, and you've heard an illness is likely to affect the city in which your company is located. You decide to vaccinate all of your employees to protect them against the illness. You do a bit of research and discover that you can buy enough doses of Vaccine A for $30,000. But Vaccine A is only 90% effective; Vaccine B is 93% effective. How much more would you be willing to pay for Vaccine B?

- Again, you're the director for a small company, and (as before) you've heard an illness is likely to affect your city. You decide to vaccinate all of your employees to protect them against the illness. You do a bit of research and discover that you can buy enough doses of Vaccine X for $30,000. But Vaccine X is only 97% effective; Vaccine Y is 100% effective. How much more would you be willing to pay for Vaccine Y?

What are your intuitions about these cases? Is the difference between 0% and 5% risk larger than the difference between 5% and 10%? Is the difference between 90% and 93% smaller than the difference between 97% and 100%?

For more on this topic

Kahneman, D. (2011). *Thinking, fast and slow.* New York, NY: Farrar, Straus and Giroux.

11.8   Framing Questions

What are the factors that influence your decisions? What are the factors that *should* influence your decisions? Evidence suggests that the "frame" of a decision plays an important role; should it?

Recruit four friends for this demonstration. Ask two of them this question:

> Imagine that you are part of a team, working for a medium-sized company, trying to decide how to invest $10 million. You have just learned about a new stock market fund that has, in the last 5 years, outperformed 75% of its competitors.
>   What percentage of the $10 million would you want to invest in this stock market fund?

Ask two other friends this question:

> Imagine that you are part of a team, working for a medium-sized company, trying to decide how to invest $10 million. You have just learned about a new stock market fund that has, in the last 5 years, been outperformed by 25% of its competitors.
>   What percentage of the $10 million would you want to invest in this stock market fund?

According to a straightforward economic analysis, the two versions of this question provide identical information—outperforming 75% of a group is, of course, the same as being outperformed by 25% of the group. According to the points in the textbook chapter, though, this difference in frame may change how people react to the questions. Can you predict which group will be more likely to invest heavily in the fund?

In making your prediction, bear in mind that physicians are more likely to recommend a new medication if they've been told that the treatment has a 50% success rate, rather than being told that it has a 50% failure rate. People are more likely to buy ground meat that is 90% fat-free rather than meat that is 10% fat. It seems likely, therefore, that your friends will invest more heavily in the fund in the first frame described here, rather than the second!

Demonstration adapted from Tversky, A., & Kahneman, D. (1981). The framing of decisions and the psychology of choice. *Science, 211,* 453–458.

11.9   Mental Accounting

In the textbook chapter, we consider evidence that people seek *reasons* when making a decision, and they select an option only when they see a good reason to make that choice. But *how* do people seek reasons, and what reasons do they find persuasive? We can get some insights into this problem by looking at various decisions that people make. For example, imagine that you are at an electronics store and about to purchase a pair of headphones for $180 and a calculator for $20. Your friend mentions, though, that the same calculator is on sale for $10 at a different store 20 minutes away.

Would you make the trip to the other store? Think about it for a moment. Poll a few friends to find out if they decide the same way.

Now, imagine a different scenario. You are at an electronics store and about to purchase a pair of headphones for $20 and a calculator for $180. Your friend mentions that the same calculator is on sale for $170 at a different store 20 minutes away.

In this case, would you make the trip to the other store? Think about it and decide, and again poll a few friends.

Most people *would* go to the other store in the first scenario, but they *would not* go in the second scenario. Of course, in either of these scenarios, your total purchase will be $200 if you buy these two items at the first store, and $190 if you buy both items at the second store. In both cases, therefore, the decision depends on whether you think a savings of $10 is enough to justify a 20-minute trip. Even so, people react to the two problems differently, as if they were dividing their purchases into different "accounts." If the $10 savings comes from the smaller account, then it seems like a great deal (the calculator is 50% cheaper!). If the savings comes from the more expensive account, it seems much less persuasive (merely a 5% savings on that item).

It seems clear, then, that our theories of decision making must include principles of "mental accounting," principles that will describe how you separate your gains and losses, your income and your expenses, into separate "budget categories." These principles are likely to be complex, and, in truth, it's not at all obvious why, in our example, people seem to regard the calculator and the headphone purchases as separate (rather than, say, just thinking about them under the broader label "supplies"). But the fact is that people do think of these purchases as separate, and this influences their decision making. Therefore, complicated or not, principles of mental accounting must become part of our overall theorizing.

Demonstration adapted from Thaler, R. (1999). Mental accounting matters. *Journal of Behavioral Decision Making, 12,* 183–206.

11.10 Seeking Reasons

As you can see, we've offered a long list of demonstrations for this chapter—because the phenomena in play here involve the sort of real-world thinking that we all do all the time. Therefore, it's easy to find demonstrations that link the research in this domain to our everyday experience! Here's one last demonstration. For this one, you'll need to recruit some friends.

Ask your friends to imagine they're shopping for a specialized dictionary, one that covers the technical vocabulary in a field that they're especially interested in. Ask them to imagine that they're in a used-book store, and find . . .

- *For some of your friends:* They find a copy of the highly respected Brown Dictionary. The copy they discover was published in 1993 and has 10,000 entries. Its condition is like new. *How much would they be willing to spend for the dictionary?*

- *For other friends:* They find a copy of the highly respected White Dictionary. The copy they discover was published in 1993 and has 20,000 entries. Its cover is torn, but it is otherwise like new. *How much would they be willing to spend for the dictionary?*

- *For a third group of friends:* They find a store that offers both the highly respected Brown Dictionary, and also the highly respected White Dictionary. The copy of the Brown Dictionary that they find was published in 1993 and has 10,000 entries. Its condition is like new. The copy of the White Dictionary that they find was also published in 1993 but has 20,000 entries. Its cover is torn, but it is otherwise like new. *Which copy seems more attractive, and therefore worth a higher price?*

Odds are good that the first group of friends will offer a higher price than the second group of friends. If each dictionary is evaluated on its own, the Brown Dictionary looks better. But odds are good that people in the third group, evaluating the two dictionaries side by side, will prefer the White Dictionary! Is this the pattern of your data? If so, can you explain this in terms of reason-based choice?

For more on this topic

Hsee, C., & Zhang, J. (2010). General evaluability theory. *Perspective on Psychological Science, 5,* 343–355.

Kahneman, D. (2011). *Thinking, fast and slow.* New York, NY: Farrar, Straus and Giroux.

Applying Cognitive Psychology

Research Methods: Systematic Data Collection

In your daily life, you frequently rely on judgment *heuristics*—shortcuts that usually lead to the correct conclusion but that sometimes produce error. As a direct result, you sometimes draw inappropriate conclusions, but one might argue that the errors are simply the price you pay for the heuristics' efficiency. To avoid the errors, you'd need to use reasoning strategies that would require much more time and effort than the heuristics do.

For scientists, though, efficiency is less of a priority; it's okay if we need months or even years to test a hypothesis. And, of course, accuracy is crucial for scientists: We want to make certain our claims are correct and our conclusions fully warranted. For these reasons, scientists need to step away from the reasoning strategies we all use in our daily lives and to rely instead on more laborious, but more accurate, forms of reasoning.

How exactly does scientific reasoning differ from ordinary day-to-day reasoning? The answer has many parts, but one part is directly relevant to points prominent in

Chapter 11: In ordinary reasoning, people are heavily influenced by whatever data are easily available to them—the observations that they can think of first when they consider an issue, or the experiences that happen to be prominent in their memory when they try to think of cases pertinent to some question. This is any easy way to proceed, but risky, because the evidence that's easily available to someone may not be representative of the broader patterns in the world. Sometimes, evidence is easily available simply because it's easier to remember than other (perhaps more common) observations. Sometimes, evidence is more available because it's been showcased by the media.

Yet another problem is that evidence is sometimes more available to someone because of the pattern known as *confirmation bias*. This term refers to the fact that when people search for evidence they often look only for evidence that might *support* their views; they do little to collect evidence that might challenge those views. This can lead to a lopsided collection of facts—and an inaccurate judgment.

Scientists avoid these problems by insisting on *systematic data collection*: either recording *all* the evidence or at least collecting evidence in a fashion carefully designed to be independent of the hypothesis being considered (and hence neither biased toward the hypothesis nor against it). Systematic data collection surely rules out consideration of *anecdotal evidence*—evidence that has been informally collected and reported—because an anecdote may represent a highly atypical case, or may provide only one person's description of the data, with no way for us to know if the description is accurate or not. Anecdotal evidence is also easily swayed by confirmation bias: The anecdote describes just one observation, raising questions about how this observation was selected. The obvious worry is that the anecdotal case was noticed, remembered, and then reported merely because it fits well with prejudices the reporter had at the outset!

These points seem straightforward, but they have many implications, including implications for how we choose our participants (we can't just gather data from people likely to support our views) and for how we design our procedures. The requirement of systematic data collection also shapes how the data will be recorded. For example, we cannot rely on our memory for the data, because it's possible that we might remember just those cases that fit with our interpretation. Likewise, we cannot treat the facts we like differently from the facts we don't like, so that, perhaps, we're more alert to flaws in the observations that conflict with our hypotheses or less likely to report these observations to others.

Clearly, then, many elements are involved in systematic data collection. But all of these elements are crucial if we are to make certain our hypotheses have been fully and fairly tested. In this regard, scientific conclusions are on a firmer footing than the judgments we offer as part of our daily experience.

FOR DISCUSSION

Imagine that a friend of yours comments: "You know, strange things influence human behavior. For example, in most cities, the crime rate goes up whenever the moon is full. Why do you think that is?" You might, in conversation, try to seek explanations for this curious phenomenon. Before you do, though, you might ask a question of your own: "Are we sure we've got the facts right? Is it really true that crimes are more common at certain phases of the moon?"

If you really wanted to check on this claim—that crime rates are linked to the moon's phase—what sys-tematic data would you need? How would you collect and record the data, making certain to avoid the problems discussed in this essay?

Research Methods: The Community of Scientists

Our Research Methods essays have described many of the steps scientists take to ensure that their data are persuasive and their claims are correct. We need to add to our discussion, though, another important factor that keeps scientific claims on track—namely, the fact that scientists do not work in isolation from each other. To see how this matters, consider the phenomenon of *confirmation bias*. This broad term refers to a number of different effects, all of which have the result of protecting our beliefs from serious challenge. Thus, for example, when we're evaluating beliefs, we tend to seek out information that might confirm the belief rather than information that might undermine it. Likewise, if we encounter information that is at all ambiguous, we are likely to interpret the information in a fashion that brings it into line with our beliefs. And so on.

Individual scientists do what they can to avoid this bias, but even so, scientists are, in the end, vulnerable to the same problems as everyone else, and so it's no surprise that confirmation bias can be detected in scientific reasoning. Thus, when scientists encounter facts that fit with their preferred hypothesis, they tend to accept those facts as they are; when they encounter facts that don't fit, they scrutinize the facts with special care, seeking problems or flaws.

Some scholars, however, have argued that confirmation bias can be a *good thing* for scientists. After all, it takes enormous effort to develop, test, and defend a scientific theory and, eventually, to persuade others to take that theory seriously. All of this effort requires considerable motivation and commitment from the theory's advocates, and confirmation bias may help them to maintain this commitment: Thanks to this bias, the advocates remain certain that they're correct, and this certainty sustains their efforts in developing and promoting the theory! Perhaps it makes sense, therefore, that, according to some studies, the scientists most guilty of confirmation bias are often those who are considered most important and influential by their peers.

These points, however, do not diminish the serious problems that confirmation bias can create. How, therefore, do scientists manage to gain the advantages (in motivation) that confirmation bias creates, without suffering the negative consequences of this bias? The answer lies in the fact that science depends on a *community* of scientists, and, within this community, there is almost always a diversity of views. As a result, the confirmation bias of one researcher can be counteracted by the corresponding bias of other researchers. To put it bluntly, I'll be gentle with the data favoring my view, but harsh in scrutinizing the data favoring your claims. You'll be gentle with your data, but harsh in scrutinizing mine. In the end, therefore, both your data and mine will receive careful examination—and that's precisely what we want.

To promote this scrutiny, scientists rely on a *peer-review process*. Before a new finding is taken seriously, it must be published in a scientific journal. And before any article can be published, it must be evaluated by the journal's editor (usually, a scientist with impressive credentials) and three or four experts in the field. (These are the "peers" who "review" the paper, and hence the term "peer review.") The reviewers are chosen by the editor to represent a variety of perspectives—including, if possible, a perspective likely to be critical of the paper's claims. If these reviewers find problems in the method or the interpretation of the results, the article will not be published by the journal. Thus, any article can appear in print only if it has survived this evaluation—an essential form of quality control.

Then, once the paper is published, the finding is accessible to the broader community and therefore open to scrutiny, criticism, and—if appropriate—attack. In addition, once the details of a study are available in print, other scientists can try to reproduce the experiment to make sure that the result is reliable. These are significant long-term benefits from publication.

In short, we take a hypothesis seriously only after it has received the scrutiny of many scientists—both during the prepublication formal process of peer review, and in the months after the paper is published. These steps ensure that the hypothesis has been examined both by scientists inclined to protect the hypothesis and by others inclined to reject it. In this way, we can be certain that the hypothesis has been fully and persuasively tested, and thus the scientific community can gain from the commitment and motivation that are the good sides of confirmation bias, without suffering the problems associated with this bias.

FOR DISCUSSION

As this essay describes, confirmation bias is not always a bad thing. A strong commitment to your own beliefs, to your own ideas, can provide you with the motivation you need to pursue your beliefs—testing them, refining them, presenting them to others. Without this commitment, you might end up being too tentative and not at all persuasive when you present your beliefs.

It would seem, then, that what we really need is a balance—a commitment to pursuing and developing your beliefs, but also a willingness, in the end, to admit you're wrong if that's what the evidence indicates. But how should we define that balance? The answer depends on several factors. Imagine, as one example, that you're standing in the supermarket and see a tabloid headline: "Herd of Unicorns Located on Tropical Island." Would you abandon your belief that there are no unicorns? Or would you give in to confirmation bias and overrule this evidence? Imagine, likewise, that a high school physics stu-

dent, in a lab exercise, finds evidence contradicting the Newtonian claim that $F = ma$. Would you abandon your belief that Newton was correct? Or would you give in to confirmation bias and overrule this evidence, too?

Based on these examples, can you develop some ideas or principles that might guide us in thinking about when confirmation bias is more acceptable and when it is less so? Why is it that in these examples you probably gave in to confirmation bias and were not inclined to give up your current ideas? (As a hint: Should confirmation bias be stronger when the challenge to your belief comes from a source of uncertain quality? Should confirmation bias be stronger when the belief being tested is already well supported by other evidence? Should confirmation bias be stronger when you're first trying to develop an idea, so that perhaps the idea isn't ready for testing? Thinking through these points will help you figure out when confirmation bias is a real problem and when it's not.)

For more on this topic

Tweney, R., Dyharty, M., & Mynatt, C. (1981). *On scientific thinking*. New York, NY: Columbia University Press.

Cognitive Psychology and Education: Making People Smarter

Chapter 11 documents the many errors people make in judgment, but the chapter also offers encouragement: We can take certain steps that improve people's judgments. Some of those steps involve changes in the environment, so that we can, for example, ensure that the evidence people consider has been converted to *frequencies* (e.g., "4 cases out of 100") rather than percentages ("4%") or proportions (".04"); this simple step, it seems, is enough on its own to make judgments more accurate and to increase the likelihood that people will consider base rates when drawing conclusions.

Other steps, in contrast, involve *education*. As the chapter mentions, training students in *statistics* seems to improve their ability to think about evidence—including evidence that is obviously quantitative (e.g., a baseball player's batting average or someone's exam scores) and also evidence that is not, at first appearance, quantitative (e.g., thinking about how you should interpret a dancer's audition or someone's job interview). The benefits of statistics training are large, with some studies showing error rates in subsequent reasoning essentially cut in half.

The key element in statistical training, however, is probably not in the mathematics per se. It is valuable, for a number of purposes, to know the derivation of statistical equations or to know the procedures for using a statistics software package. For the improvement of everyday judgment, though, the key involves the new *perspective* that a statistics course encourages: This perspective helps you realize that certain observations (e.g., an audition or an interview) can be thought of as a *sample* of evidence, drawn from a larger pool of observations that potentially you could have made. The perspective also alerts you to the fact that a sample may not be representative of a broader population and that larger samples are more likely to be representative. For purposes of the statistics course itself, these are relatively simple points; but being alert to these points can have striking and widespread consequences in your thinking about issues separate from the topics and examples covered in the statistics class.

In fact, once we cast things in this way, it becomes clear that other forms of education can also have the same benefit. Many courses in psychology, for example, include coverage of methodological issues. These courses can also highlight the fact that a single observation is just a sample and that a small sample sometimes cannot be trusted. These courses sometimes cover topics that might reveal (and warn you against) confirmation bias or caution against the dangers of informally collected evidence. On this basis, it seems likely that other courses (and not just statistics classes) can actually improve your everyday thinking—and, in fact, several studies confirm this optimistic conclusion.

Ironically, though, courses in the "hard sciences"—chemistry and physics, for example—may not have these benefits. Obviously, these courses are immensely valuable for their own sake and will provide you with impressive and sophisticated skills. However, these courses may do little to improve your day-to-day reasoning. Why not? These courses plainly do involve a process of testing hypotheses through the collection of evidence, and then the quantitative analysis of the evidence. But, at the same time, let's bear in mind that the data in, say, a chemistry course involve relatively homogeneous sets of observations: After all, the weight of one carbon atom is the same as the weight of other carbon atoms; the temperature at which water boils (at a particular altitude) is the same on Tuesday as it is on Thursday. As a result, issues of *variability* in the data are much less prominent in chemistry than they are, say, in psychology. (Compare how much *people* differ from each other to how much *benzene molecules* differ from each other.) This is, to be sure, a great strength for chemistry; it is one of the (many) reasons why chemistry has become such a sophisticated science. But this point means that chemists have to worry less than psychologists do about the variability within their sample, or, with that, whether their sample is of adequate size to compensate for the variability. One consequence of this is that chemistry courses often provide little practice in thinking about variability or sample size—issues that are, of course, crucial when confronting the (far messier) data provided by day to day life.

In the same way, cause-and-effect sequences are often much more straightforward in the "hard sciences" than they are in daily life: If a rock falls onto a surface, the impact depends simply on the mass of the rock and its velocity at the moment of collision. We don't need to ask what mood the rock was in, whether the surface was expecting the rock, or whether the rock was acting peculiarly on this occasion because it knew we were watching its behavior. But these latter factors are the sort of concerns that do crop up in the "messy" sciences—and, of course, also crop up in daily life. So here, too, the hard sciences gain enormous power from the "clean" nature of their data but, by the same token, don't provide practice in the skills of reasoning about these complications.

Which courses, therefore, should you take? Again, courses in chemistry and physics (and biology and mathematics) are important and teach you sophisticated methods and fascinating content. These courses will provide you with skills that you might not gain in any other setting. But, for purposes of improving your day-to-day reasoning, you probably want to seek out courses that involve a trio of traits: (a) the *testing of hypotheses* through (b) *quantitative evaluation* of (c) *messy data*. These courses will include many of the offerings of your Psychology Department, and probably some of the offerings in sociology, anthropology, political science, and economics. These, it seems, are the courses that may genuinely make you a better, more critical thinker about the conclusions you're likely to weigh in your daily existence.

FOR DISCUSSION

How can we make people smarter? It's a bit embarrassing that the answer, offered by psychologists, seems to be: "People should take psychology courses; that will make them smarter." More bluntly, there is a substantial worry here that our conclusions, and our pragmatic advice, may have been colored by some amount of nar- cissistic self-congratulation, with psychologists shamelessly promoting the value of their own discipline!

Is there a response to this concern? As one approach, what might we look for, in the research done so far, as a way of asking whether the research is somehow biased to favor psychologists? Or, looking forward, what further tests might we do to determine whether psychology courses are, in fact, particularly helpful in improving critical thinking skills? And, finally, will *all* psychology courses have this benefit? Do all psychology courses involve the (allegedly crucial) trio of (a) hypothesis testing with (b) quantitative evaluation of (c) messy data? Could we use differences among the various psychology courses as a way of checking on whether this trio is indeed the key to improving people's judgment?

For more on this topic

Fong, G., & Nisbett, R. (1991). Immediate and delayed transfer of training effects in statistical reasoning. *Journal of Experimental Psychology: General, 120,* 34–45.

Lehman, D. R., Lempert, R. O., & Nisbett, R. E. (1988). The effects of graduate training on reasoning: Formal discipline and thinking about everyday-life events. *American Psychologist, 43*(6), 431–442.

Lehman, D., & Nisbett, R. (1990). A longitudinal study of the effects of undergraduate training on reasoning. *Developmental Psychology, 26,* 952–960.

Cognitive Psychology and Education:
The Doctrine of Formal Disciplines

Most universities have some sort of college-wide graduation requirements. Students are often required to take a certain number of courses in mathematics, or perhaps a foreign language. They are often required to take courses in the humanities or in laboratory science.

How should we think about these requirements? One widely endorsed view is the *doctrine of formal disciplines.* The idea, roughly, is that your reasoning and judgment rely on certain formal rules—akin to the rules of logic or mathematics—so you'll think best (most clearly, more rationally) if you are well practiced in using these rules. Therefore, education should emphasize the academic disciplines that rely on these formal rules: math, logic, and, according to some people, linguistics and the study of languages. (This is presumably because the study of languages sensitizes students to the formal properties of language.)

Chapter 11, however, challenges this doctrine. There are, to be sure, excellent reasons for taking courses in math, logic, and language. But it's a mistake to argue that these disciplines somehow strengthen the mind in a fashion that improves thinking in general. Why is this? First, the chapter makes it clear that reasoning and judgment do not rely on formal rules (i.e., rules, like those of math or logic, that depend only on the *form* of the argument being considered). Instead, reasoning and judgment depend heavily on the *content* that you're thinking about. It's therefore wrong to claim that formal disciplines give you training and exercise in the rules you use all the time; you do not, in fact, use these rules all the time.

Second, a number of studies have asked directly whether training in logic, or training in abstract mathematics, improves reasoning in everyday affairs. It does not. We mentioned in the chapter that training in *statistics* improves judgment, but (as we discussed in the previous essay) the key aspect of this training is likely to be the exercise in "translating" everyday cases into statistical terms, and not knowing the mathematical formulations themselves.

Likewise, some studies do suggest that the study of languages is associated with improved academic performance, but these studies are potentially misleading. For example, it is true that students who take Latin in high school do better on the Scholastic Aptitude Test and often do better in college. But this is probably not because taking Latin helped these students; instead, it is probably because the students who choose to take Latin are likely to be more ambitious, more academically motivated, in the first place.

How, therefore, should we design students' education? What courses should the university recommend, and what courses should you seek out if you want to improve your critical thinking skills? Part of the answer was offered in the previous essay: Your ability to make judgments does seem to be improved by courses that rely on quantitative *but somewhat messy* data—disciplines such as psychology, sociology, courses at the quantitative end of anthropology, and so on. And part of the answer is suggested by another issue that arose in the chapter: We mentioned there that people often seem to rely on pragmatic, goal-oriented rules—rules involving permission or obligation, and also rules tied to the pragmatic ways you try to figure out cause-and-effect relationships ("If this broken switch is causing the problem, my car will work once I replace the switch").

One might think, therefore, that reasoning will be improved by practice in thinking in these pragmatic terms—and evidence suggests that this is right. Short episodes of training, reminding people of the procedures needed for thinking about permission or encouraging people to think through different cause-and-effect relationships, do seem to improve reasoning. Likewise, *professional* training of the right sort also helps. Lawyers, for example, get lots of practice in thinking about *permission* and *obligation*; studies suggest that this training helps lawyers think through a variety of pragmatic, day-to-day problems that have little to do with their legal practice.

Notice, then, that there are two messages here. The broad message is that we can use our studies of how people *do* think to start generating hypotheses about how we can *train* people to think more effectively. The more specific message is that the data allow us to start making some recommendations, as we've illustrated in this essay.

FOR DISCUSSION

One might think that courses in *logic*, offered in some universities by the Math Department and in some by the Philosophy Department, would be a great way to improve someone's critical thinking skills. After all, these courses teach students to make good (valid, compelling) arguments and to avoid making invalid arguments. Evidence suggests, though, that courses in logic do little to improve day-to-day reasoning, and it's interesting to think through why this is.

One problem is that logic courses often contain few "everyday" examples. Instead, these courses rely almost exclusively on abstract symbols—and so students are likely to encounter the proposition "p⊃q" but unlikely to encounter "If I study hard, then I will get a better grade." As a result, these courses are valuable for many purposes but provide students with little practice in "mapping" the rules of logic onto the sorts of arguments they'll encounter outside of the classroom.

In addition, the way logicians use the "if . . . then . . ." sequence is somewhat different from the way this expression is used in ordinary speech. (Logicians are alert to this point, and in more advanced materials they carefully distinguish different types of conditional sentences.) To make this concrete, consider these two sentences:

If Jacob passed his driver's test, then it is legal for him to drive.

If Solomon is eligible for jury duty, then he is over 21.

These two sentences seem to have the same structure, but is the relationship the same, in the two sentences, between the "if" and "then" clauses? To think this through, think about what you'd conclude in each case if the "if" part of the sentence was *false*. Can you think of "if . . . then . . ." sentences that contain relationships that are different from either the "Jacob" or the "Solomon" sentences? (Actually, in ordinary speech there are four different ways we use the "if . . . then . . ." sequence; can you think of them all?)

Cognitive Psychology and the Law:
Juries' Judgment

Part of our focus in Chapter 11 was on how people draw conclusions based on the evidence they encounter, and, of course, this is exactly what a judge or jury needs to do in a trial—reach a conclusion (a verdict) based on the trial evidence. Can we therefore use what we know about judgment in other contexts to illuminate how judges and juries perform their task?

Consider, as one example, the separation between System 1 and System 2 thinking: System 1 thinking, we've argued in the chapter, is fast and automatic, but it can sometimes lead to error. System 2 thinking, in contrast, is slower and more effortful, but it can often catch those errors, leading to better judgment. The problem, though, is that people often rely on System 1 even for deeply consequential judgments. System 2, it seems, enters the scene only if appropriately triggered.

How does this play out in the courts? Consider, as one crucial case, the problem of racial prejudice in the legal system. It turns out that Blacks are more likely to be convicted than Whites, even if we focus our attention on cases in which the crimes themselves are the same in the comparison between the races, and if the evidence and circumstances are quite similar. Then, once convicted, Blacks are also likely to receive more severe punishments than Whites—including the death penalty.

What produces these race differences? One troubling hypothesis is that many people involved in the criminal justice system—including police, judges, and juries—are influenced by an easy and automatic association, provided by System 1 thinking, that links Blacks to thoughts of crime. This association may not reflect a belief, in the person's mind, that Blacks are often guilty of crimes. Instead, the association may indicate only that the ideas of "Blacks" and "crime" are somehow linked in memory (perhaps because of images in the media or some other external influence). As a result of this linkage, activating one of the ideas can trigger the other, and this association may be enough to shape a System 1 judgment. This is because, after all, System 1 typically relies on the ideas that come effortlessly to mind; and so, if the idea of "Blacks" triggers the idea of "crime," this can lead to a biased conclusion.

Can we use System 2 to override this effect? In a number of studies, researchers have simply called participants' attention to the fact that a particular trial defendant is, in fact, a Black and that considerations of race may be pertinent to the case. Surprisingly, this is sometimes enough to put participants on their guard, so that they resist the easy conclusion that might be suggested by memory associations. As a result, merely making race explicit as a trial issue can sometimes diminish juror prejudice.

However, it is absurd to think we could somehow erase all the effects of prejudice merely by calling jurors' attention to the defendant's race. The situation is more complicated than this! In some cases, in fact, alerting jurors to the issue of race may *increase* prejudice rather than diminish it. (This would be true if, for example, the jurors were overtly racist; in that case, highlighting race might encourage the jurors to take their own racism into account in evaluating the case.) In still other cases, the jurors might suspect that the *police* are racist; if so, then highlighting the issue of race might prejudice the jury against law enforcement and so might create a bias *in favor of* the defendant. In light of these (and other) complications, there is surely no simple step that works in a general way to guarantee courtroom procedures that are free of bias.

Even so, the research certainly reminds us that we do need to consider how courtroom judgments can be shaped by System 1 thinking. What steps we can take to deal with this (and how, for example, we can ensure that System 1's prejudices are overruled by the more careful thinking of System 2) is an urgent matter for future research.

FOR DISCUSSION

Some people would argue that the distinction between System 1 and System 2 is *irrelevant* for the legal system. They would suggest that judges and juries know they are making enormously important decisions, and this would, by itself, be enough to motivate judges and juries to use the more careful, more accurate System 2. For judgments as important as a courtroom verdict, it would be irresponsible to rely on System 1's "shortcuts." Likewise, some people would suggest that judges are experienced and skilled in thinking about courtroom issues; this should virtually guarantee that judges would "rise above" the shortcuts inherent in System 1 and rely instead on the more accurate processes of System 2.

Unfortunately, though, the textbook chapter provides indications that these arguments are wrong and that System 1 is likely to play a role in the courts—no matter how consequential the issues or how experienced the judges. What is the evidence, within the chapter, that might be relevant to these crucial points?

For more on this topic

Correll, J., Park, B., Judd, C. M., & Wittenbrink, B. (2002). The police officer's dilemma: Using ethnicity to disambiguate potentially threatening individuals. *Journal of Personality and Social Psychology, 83,* 1314–1329.

Dovidio, J. F., Kawakami, K., & Gaertner, S. L. (2002). Implicit and explicit prejudice and interracial interaction. *Journal of Personality and Social Psychology, 82,* 62–68.

Sommers, S. R., & Ellsworth, P. C. (2001). White juror bias: An investigation of prejudice against black defendants in the American courtroom. *Psychology, Public Policy, and Law, 7,* 201–229.

Cognitive Psychology and the Law: Pretrial Publicity

As Chapter 11 describes, reasoning can be pulled off track by many factors, so that our conclusions are sometimes less logical, less justified, than we would wish. How does this apply to the courts?

In many trials, potential jurors have been exposed to media coverage of the crime prior to the trial's start, and this pretrial publicity can have many effects. One concern is the pattern called *belief bias*. In the lab, this term refers to a tendency to consider an argument "more logical" if it leads to a conclusion that the person believed to begin with. In the courtroom, this could translate into a juror's evaluating the trial arguments not on their own terms, but in terms of whether the arguments led to the conclusion the juror would have endorsed (based on the media coverage) at the trial's start. This influence of information from outside the courthouse is contrary to the rules of a trial, but jurors may be unable to resist this powerful effect.

As a related concern, consider *confirmation bias*. As the chapter discusses, this bias takes many forms, including a tendency to accept evidence favoring your views at face value but to subject evidence challenging your views to special scrutiny, seeking flaws or weaknesses in these unwelcome facts. This tendency can easily be documented in trials. In one study, participants were first exposed to a newspaper article that created a bias about a particular murder trial. These pretend "jurors" were then presented with the trial evidence and had to evaluate how persuasive each bit of evidence was. The results showed a clear effect of the newspaper article: Evidence consistent with the (biased) pretrial publicity was seen as more compelling; evidence inconsistent with the publicity was seen as less compelling. And, of course, this effect fed on itself. Each bit of evidence that the "jurors" heard was filtered through their confirmation bias, so the evidence seemed particularly persuasive if it favored the view the "jurors" held already. This led the "jurors" to be more confident that their view was, in fact, correct. (After all, the evidence—as they interpreted it—did seem to favor that view.) This now-stronger view, in turn, amplified the confirmation bias, which colored how the "jurors" interpreted the next bit of evidence. Thus, around and around we go— with confirmation bias coloring how the evidence is interpreted, which strengthens the "jurors'" belief, which creates more confirmation bias, which colors how later evidence is interpreted, which further strengthens the belief.

In this study, the pretrial publicity had a powerful effect on the "jurors'" verdict, but we need to be clear that the publicity did not influence the verdict directly. Indeed, the odds are good that the "jurors" weren't thinking of the publicity at all when they voted "guilty" or "not guilty." Instead, their verdicts were based (as they should be) on the participants' evaluation of the trial evidence. The problem, though, is that this evaluation was itself powerfully shaped by the pretrial publicity, via the mechanisms we have just described.

In light of these results, we might worry that the courts' protections against juror bias may not be adequate. In some trials, for example, jurors are merely asked: "Can you set aside any personal beliefs or knowledge you have obtained outside the court and decide this case solely on the evidence you hear from the witness stand?" Such questions seem a thin shield against juror prejudice. As one concern, jurors *might not know* whether they'll be able to set aside their prejudices. They might not realize, in other words, that they are vulnerable to belief bias or confirmation bias, and so they might overestimate their ability to overcome these effects. As a related point, jurors might be determined to vote, in the jury room, based only on what they heard during the trial. As we have now seen, though, that's no protection at all: In the study we described, the jurors' ultimate decision *was* based on the evidence, but that doesn't change the fact that the decision was based on the evidence as viewed through the lens provided by pretrial publicity.

Belief bias and confirmation bias are powerful effects that often work in a fashion that is completely unconscious. This strongly suggests that the courts need to seek more potent means of avoiding these influences in order to ensure each defendant a fair and unbiased trial. Possible solutions include stricter screening of jurors, and procedures that would make it easier to change a trial's location. In any case, it seems clear that stronger precautions are needed than those currently in place.

FOR DISCUSSION

Often research data force us to rethink policy issues. For example, democratic governments are usually committed to the principle of freedom of the press, so that newspapers and television are allowed to report on whatever topics they choose. At the same time, though, it appears that some forms of news coverage—namely, pretrial publicity—can be damaging to the judicial process. How should we think about this apparent conflict between the desirability of a free press and the desirability of a fair legal system?

Setting these policy issues to the side, though, the psychological question remains: What might we do to provide remedies for the influence of pretrial publicity? Bear in mind that changing the location of a trial—to some other county or some other state—is often quite expensive, and also requires some time (and so conflicts with a goal of providing speedy trials). Note also that selecting just those jurors who don't follow the news at all might produce a jury that's not representative of the community. In light of these concerns, what should we do about the effects of pretrial publicity?

For more on this topic

Hope, L., Memon, A., & McGeorge, P. (2004). Understanding pretrial publicity: Predecisional distortion of evidence by mock jurors. *Journal of Experimental Psychology: Applied, 10*, 111–119.

Cognitive Psychology and the Law:
Confirmation Bias in Police Investigation

In the criminal justice system, a *confession* from a suspect is powerful evidence, and juries rarely fail to convict someone who has confessed to a crime. It turns out, though, that sometimes people confess to crimes they did not commit, so we need some means of separating genuine confessions from false confessions.

How often do false confessions occur? No one really knows, but one insight comes from the cases (mentioned in Chapter 7) of men who have been convicted in the United States courts but then exonerated, often years later, when DNA evidence finally showed that they were actually not guilty at all. Scrutiny of these cases indicates that roughly 25% of these men had offered confessions—and, since the DNA evidence tells us they were not guilty, we can be sure that these confessions were false.

Police officers understand that not all confessions are true, so the police usually seek further evidence to corroborate (or, in some cases, undermine) a confession. The problem, though, is that this collection of further evidence can be biased by the confession itself. In other words, the confession can lead the police officer to believe the suspect is guilty, and then confirmation bias enters the scene, shaping the subsequent investigation, and perhaps even producing *errors* in the investigation.

One recent study indicates that the concern here must be taken seriously. The researchers examined all of the DNA exoneration cases that included a confession (and, again, the DNA evidence makes it clear that these confessions are *false*) and found that these cases tended to contain other errors as well. Specifically, these confession cases tended also to include invalid or improper forensic evidence, mistaken eyewitness identifications, and false testimony from snitches or informants. Each of these types of errors were more common in the false-confession cases than in cases without confessions. And, troubling, in the cases involving multiple errors, police records indicate that the confessions were obtained early in the case, before the other errors occurred. The suggestion, then, is that the false confessions may have caused (or invited, or encouraged) these other errors.

Other studies indicate a similar pattern. For example, hearing about a confession can influence the judgment of experienced polygraph examiners and also latent-fingerprint experts: These trained investigators, once they have heard about a confession, are more likely to interpret their evidence (the polygraph results or a fingerprint) as indicating guilt, just as we might expect based on confirmation bias.

What should we do with these results? At the least, it seems important to get these findings into the view of the police, in the hope that they can somehow guard against this type of bias. It's also important to get these findings into a jury's view, with the goal of helping the jury interpret confession evidence. More broadly, these results highlight the dangers of false confessions, and urge us toward a closer examination of the procedures through which confession evidence is obtained in the first place. In addition, these findings provide a compelling reminder of how confirmation bias can shift how even a trained professional perceives the world, pays attention to evidence, and evaluates that evidence.

FOR DISCUSSION

Most colleges and universities have some sort of judiciary process that investigates and adjudicates allegations of on-campus offenses—including allegations of academic dishonesty, sexual misconduct, offenses tied to illegal substances, and more. What procedures would you recommend to your institution's judiciary, to protect it against confirmation bias? What protections would you recommend to ensure that an error at one point in an investigation doesn't encourage other errors (that might compound and confirm the first mistake)?

For more on this topic

Kassin, S., Bogart, D., & Kerner, J. (2012). Confessions that corrupt: Evidence from the DNA exoneration case files. *Psychological Science, 23,* 1–5.

Kassin, S., Drizin, S., Grisso, T., Gudjonsson, G., Leo, R., & Redlich, A. (2010). Police-induced confessions: Risk factors and recommendations. *Law and Human Behavior, 34,* 3–38.

CHAPTER 12

Problem Solving and Intelligence

Demonstrations

12.1   Analogies

Analogies are a powerful help in solving problems, but they are also an excellent way to convey new information. Imagine that you're a teacher, trying to explain some points about astronomy. Which of the following explanations do you think would be more effective?

Literal Version

Collapsing stars spin faster and faster as they fold in on themselves and their size decreases. This phenomenon of spinning faster as the star's size shrinks occurs because of a principle called "conservation of angular momentum."

Analogy Version

Collapsing stars spin faster as their size shrinks. Stars are thus like ice skaters, who pirouette faster as they pull in their arms. Both stars and skaters operate by a principle called "conservation of angular momentum."

Which version of the explanation would make it easier for students to answer a question like the following one?

What would happen if a star "expanded" instead of collapsing?

   a. Its rate of rotation would increase.

   b. Its rate of rotation would decrease.

   c. Its orbital speed would increase.

   d. Its orbital speed would decrease.

Does your intuition tell you that the analogy version would be better as a teaching tool? If so, then your intuitions are in line with the data! Participants in one study were presented with materials just like these, in either a literal or an analogy version. Later, they were asked questions about these materials, and those instructed via analogy reliably did better. Do you think your teachers make effective use of analogy? Can you think of ways they can improve their use of analogy?

Demonstration adapted from Donnelly, C., & McDaniel, M. (1993). Use of analogy in learning scientific concepts. *Journal of Experimental Psychology: Learning, Memory and Cognition, 19*(4), 975–987. Copyright © 1993 by the American Psychological Association. Adapted with permission. *Also,* Donnelly, C., & McDaniel, M. (2000). Analogy with knowledgeable learners: When analogy confers benefits and exacts costs. *Psychonomic Bulletin & Review, 7,* 537–543.

12.2   Incubation

Many people believe that an "incubation" period aids problem solving. In other words, spending time *away from the problem* helps you to find the solution, because, during the time away, it's claimed, you are unconsciously continuing to work on the problem.

Is this belief warranted—an accurate reflection of how problem solving truly proceeds? To find out, psychologists study problem solving in the lab, using problems like these.

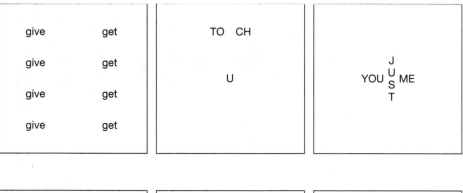

Each of the figures shown here represents a familiar word or phrase. Can you decipher them? (To get you started, the first figure represents the common phrase "forgive and forget." We'll give you the other solutions in a moment.) In one study, participants were more likely to solve these puzzles if they worked on them for a while, then took a break, then returned to the puzzles. This result seems to indicate an "incubation" benefit, but the explanation for the result probably doesn't involve any sort of "unconscious problem solving." Instead, the break helped simply because it allowed the participants to lose track of the bad strategies they'd been trying so far, and this in turn allowed them to get a fresh start on the problem when they returned to it.

Support for this interpretation comes from the fact that, in this study, a helpful clue was provided for some of the figures (thus, the sixth picture shown here might be accompanied by the word "first"). For other figures, the clue was actually misleading (e.g., the first picture here might be accompanied by the clue "opposites"). The participants were helped much more by the break if they'd been misled at the start. This pattern is just what we'd expect if the break allowed the participants to set aside (and maybe even to forget) the misleading clue, so that they were no longer derailed by it. On this basis, the break didn't allow unconscious problem solving; it instead allowed something simpler: a bit of rest, a bit of forgetting, and hence a fresh start.

The remaining solutions, by the way, are "you fell out of touch," "just between you and me," "backwards glance," "three degrees below zero," and "first aid."

Demonstration adapted from Smith, S., & Blankenship, S. (1989). Incubation effects. *Bulletin of the Psychonomic Society, 27*, 311–314. *Also*, Smith, S., & Blankenship, S. (1991). Incubation and the persistence of fixation in problem solving. *American Journal of Psychology, 104*, 61–87. *Also*, Vul, E., & Pashler, H. (2007). Incubation benefits only after people have been misdirected. *Memory and Cognition, 35*, 701–710.

12.3 Verbalization and Problem Solving

Research on problem solving has attempted to determine what factors *help* problem solving (making it faster or more effective) and what factors *hinder* problem solving. Some of these factors are surprising.

You'll need a clock or timer for this one. Read the first problem below, and give yourself 2 minutes to find the solution. If you haven't found the solution in this time, take a break for 90 seconds; during that break, turn away from the problem and try to say out loud, in as much detail as possible, everything you can remember about how you've been trying to solve the problem. Provide information about your approach, your strategies, any solutions you tried, and so on. Then go back and try working on the problem for another 2 minutes.

Problem 1: The drawing below shows ten pennies. Can you make the triangle point downward by moving only three of the pennies?

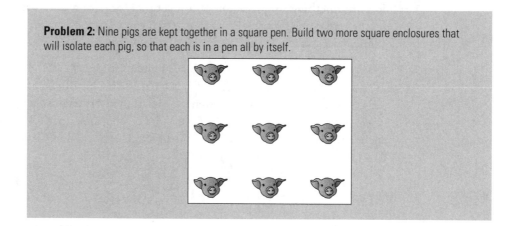

Now do the same for the next problem—2 minutes of trying a solution, 90 seconds of describing out loud everything you've thought of so far in working on the problem, and then another 2 minutes of working on the problem.

Problem 2: Nine pigs are kept together in a square pen. Build two more square enclosures that will isolate each pig, so that each is in a pen all by itself.

Do you think the time spent describing your efforts so far *helped you*, perhaps by allowing you to organize your thinking, or *hurt* you? In fact, in several studies this sort of "time off, to describe your efforts so far" makes it *less likely* that people will solve these problems. In one study, participants solved 36% of the problems if they had verbalized their efforts so far, but 46% of the problems if they didn't go through the verbalization step. Does this fit with your experience?

Why might verbalization interfere with this form of problem solving? One likely explanation is that verbalization focuses your attention on steps you've already tried, and this may make it more difficult to abandon those steps and try new approaches. The verbalization will also focus your attention on the sorts of strategies that are conscious, deliberate, and easily described in words; this focus might interfere with strategies that are unconscious, not deliberate, and not easily articulated. In all cases, though, the pattern makes it clear that sometimes "thinking out loud" and trying to communicate your ideas to others can actually be counterproductive! Exactly why this is, and what this implies about problem solving, is a topic in need of further research.

The solutions appear at the bottom of p. 185.

Demonstration adapted from Schooler, J., Ohlsson, S., & Brooks, K. (1993). Thoughts beyond words: When language overshadows insight. *Journal of Experimental Psychology: General, 122,* 166–183.

12.4 Remote Associates

Can creativity be measured? Some researchers believe that it can and design tests that (they believe) tap into the processes that are essential for creativity. For example, some people believe that creativity depends on the ability to detect unanticipated, perhaps distant relationships among ideas. One test designed to measure this ability is the Remote Associates Test. In this test, you're given three words, and you need to come up with a word that can be combined with each of the three. Thus, you might be given "cottage, swiss, cake," and you need to come up with "cheese" (as in cottage cheese, swiss cheese, and cheesecake).

Below you'll find a number of these test items. If you wish, time yourself, allowing 2 seconds to work on each item; how many can you solve? The answers are on p. 174.

cream / skate / water	cracker / fly / fighter	flower / friend / scout
loser / throat / spot	safety / cushion / point	river / note / account
show / life / row	cane / daddy / plum	print / berry / bird
night / wrist / stop	dream / break / light	pie / luck / belly
duck / fold / dollar	fish / mine / rush	date / alley / fold
rocking / wheel / high	political / surprise / line	opera / hand / dish
dew / comb / bee	measure / worm / video	cadet / capsule / ship
fountain / baking / pop	high / district / house	fur / rack / tail
preserve / ranger / tropical	sense / courtesy / place	stick / maker / point
aid / rubber / wagon	worm / shelf / end	hound / pressure / shot
flake / mobile / cone	piece / mind / dating	

On the following page are the answers, and the number alongside each answer is the percent of research participants who, in one study, were able to solve each problem within two seconds of trying.

ice	34	fire	17	girl	9
sore	22	pin	24	bank	2
boat	31	sugar	19	blue	10
watch	38	day	24	pot	15
bill	31	gold	17	blind	13
chair	37	party	7	soap	16
honey	30	tape	10	space	18
soda	34	school/court	18	coat	2
forest	18	common	8	match	1
band	22	book	17	blood	4
snow	9	game	6		

Demonstration adapted from Bowden, E., & Jung-Beeman, M. (2003). Normative data for 144 compound remote associate problems. *Behavior Research Methods, Instruments & Computers, 35,* 634–639.

12.5   IQ Testing

Many students are curious to know their own IQ scores, but we will not provide a full and formal IQ test in this workbook. There are several reasons, including the fact that IQ tests, to be valid, need to be administered under carefully set up, carefully standardized circumstances. Nonetheless, we can at least point you toward some websites that offer reasonable tests that will provide you with an approximation of your IQ score.

First, though, let's be clear that many of the intelligence tests available on the Internet have no validity: They are not standardized tests; there is no evidence indicating we should take these tests seriously. However, other tests on the Internet do resemble the tests actually used by researchers and educators. For example, the chapter mentions the Raven's Progressive Matrices as a nonverbal intelligence test that (supposedly) has no cultural bias because it involves no prior knowledge, and no language skills. (This claim of "no bias" must be viewed skeptically, though, because the Raven's test certainly requires familiarity with the idea of putting things into a "table," in the appropriate rows and columns, and this idea is by no means universally shared across cultures.) The Raven's test is, in any case, often used and does have some validity.

You can, if you wish, enter these words into an Internet search engine: "Raven's Progressive Matrices Online Test." This step will bring you to several websites offering approximations of the Raven's test, and this will give you one rough estimate (and we emphasize a *rough* estimate) of your IQ score. In interpreting this score, though, you'll want to bear in mind that IQ scores—while generally stable across the lifespan—can change and, in fact, can change by as much as 15 points as the years go by. If your score is high, therefore, don't decide you can relax in your efforts to get a good education; and if your score is low, don't decide that all is lost. (Indeed, the chapter emphasizes at several points why your IQ score does not define your destiny!)

Other intelligence tests take very different forms. For example, the chapter mentions that the standard IQ tests usually involve many subtests and that some of these subtests rely heavily on how much *g* the person has, while other subtests rely less on *g*. Verbal analogies, for example, depend strongly on *g* and also depend on the person's verbal skills. If you're curious to see how well you do with analogies, therefore, you can point your browser at "Miller Analogies practice test." The Miller test is not designed as an intelligence test; it is instead designed as a test of "high-level analytical reasoning" and is used by many graduate schools as part of their admissions screening. Even so, this test will give you a glimpse of what analogy problems look like, and how well you do on them. Once again, though, let's be clear: Your IQ score is an important fact about you, but it does not define your destiny.

Applying Cognitive Psychology

Research Methods: Defining the Dependent Variable

In the Research Methods essay for Chapter 1, we discussed the importance of testable hypotheses—that is, hypotheses that are framed in a way that makes it clear what evidence will confirm them and what evidence will not. Sometimes, though, it's not obvious how to phrase a hypothesis in testable terms. For example, in Chapter 12 we discuss research on creativity, and within this research investigators often present hypotheses about the factors that might foster creativity or might undermine it. Thus, one hypothesis might be: "When working on a problem, an interruption (to allow incubation) promotes creativity." To test this hypothesis, we would have to specify what counts as an interruption (5 minutes of working on something else? an hour?). But then we'd also need some way to measure creativity; otherwise, we couldn't tell if the interruption was beneficial or not.

For this hypothesis, creativity is the *dependent variable*—that is, the measurement that, according to our hypothesis, might "depend on" the thing being manipulated. The presence or absence of an interruption would be the *independent variable*—the factor that, according to our hypothesis, influences the dependent variable.

In many studies, it's easy to assess the dependent variable. For example, consider this hypothesis: "Context reinstatement improves memory accuracy." Here the dependent variable is accuracy, and this is simple to check—for example, by counting up the number of correct answers on a memory test. In this way, we would easily know whether a result confirmed the hypothesis or not. Likewise, consider this hypothesis: "Implicit memories can speed up performance on a lexical decision task."

Here the dependent variable is response time; again, it is simple to measure, allowing a straightforward test of the hypothesis.

The situation is different, though, for our hypothesis about interruptions and creativity. In this case, people might disagree about whether a particular problem solution (or poem, or painting, or argument) is creative. This will make it difficult to test our hypothesis.

Psychologists generally solve this problem by recruiting a panel of judges to assess the dependent variable. In our example, the judges would review each participant's response and evaluate how creative it was, perhaps on a scale from 1 to 5. By using a panel of judges rather than just one, we can check directly on whether different judges have different ideas about what creativity is. More specifically, we can calculate the *inter-rater reliability* among the judges—the degree to which they agree with each other in their assessments. If they disagree with each other, it would appear that the assessment of creativity really is a subjective matter and cannot be a basis for testing hypotheses. In that case, scientific research on this issue may not be possible. But if the judges do agree to a reasonable extent—if the inter-rater reliability is high—then we can be confident that their assessments are neither arbitrary nor idiosyncratic.

Let's be clear, though, that this is a measure of *reliability*—that is, a measure of how consistent our measurements are. As the text describes, reliability is separate from validity (i.e., whether we've succeeded in measuring what we intended to measure). It's possible, for example, that all of our judges are reacting to, say, whether they find the responses humorous or not. If the judges all have similar senses of humor, they might agree with each other in this assessment (and so would have a high level of inter-rater reliability), but, even so, they would be judging humor, not creativity (and so would not offer *valid* assessments). On this basis, measures of inter-rater reliability are an important step toward establishing our measure—but we still need other steps (perhaps what the chapter calls a "predictive validation") before we're done.

Notice, in addition, that this way of proceeding doesn't require us to start out with a precise definition of creativity. Of course, a definition would be very useful because (among other benefits) it would allow us to give the judges on our panel relatively specific instructions. Even without a definition, though, we can just ask the judges to rely on their own sense of what's creative. This isn't ideal; we'd prefer to get beyond this intuitive notion. But having a systematic, nonidiosyncratic consensus measurement at least allows our research to get off the ground.

In the same way, consider this hypothesis: "College education improves the quality of critical thinking." This hypothesis—and many others as well—again involves a complex dependent variable, and might also require a panel of judges to obtain measurements we can take seriously. But by using these panels, we can measure things that seem at the outset to be unmeasurable, and in that way we appreciably broaden the range of hypotheses we can test.

FOR DISCUSSION

A number of television shows have centered on talent competitions: Who is the best singer? The best dancer? The funniest stand-up comedian? Who should be the next American Idol? In some cases, these television shows let the *viewers* decide: People call in and vote for their favorite singer or dancer or comic. For some shows, people can call as many times as they wish and cast as many votes as they want to. For these shows, the phone lines are often jammed when the time comes to vote, so people who are less persistent (less willing to dial and redial and redial) end up not voting; only the persistent viewers vote. Is this a reasonable way to judge talent? Using the points made in this essay (concerned with how researchers assess a dependent variable) and the points made in previous essays (e.g., the Research Methods essay on systematic data collection for Chapter 11), can you evaluate this voting procedure as a means of finding the best singer or the best dancer?

On other TV shows, things run differently: A panel of (supposedly expert) judges does the voting and decides who stays on the show and who goes away. Is this a reasonable way to judge talent?

Finally, on still other shows, there is just *one* judge— one expert chef, for example, who decides which of the contestants is the worst cook that week and so is removed from the show. Is this a reasonable way to judge talent?

Research Methods: Correlations

Often in psychology, data are analyzed in terms of *correlations*, and this is certainly true in the study of intelligence. We say that intelligence tests are reliable, for example, because measures of intelligence taken, say, when people are 6 years old are correlated with measures taken from the same people a dozen years later. Likewise, we say that intelligence tests have some validity because measures of intelligence are correlated with other performance measures (grades in school, or some assessment of performance in the workplace). Or, as one more example, we conclude that g exists because we can observe correlations among the various parts of the IQ test—and so someone's score on a verbal test is correlated with their score on a spatial test.

But what does any of this mean? What is a correlation? The calculation of a correlation begins with a list of *pairs*: someone's IQ score at, say, age 6 and then the same person's score at age 18; the *next person's* scores at age 6 and age 18; the same for the next person and the next after that. A correlation examines these pairs and asks, roughly, how well we can predict the second value within each pair once we know the first value. If we know your IQ score at age 6, how confident can we be in our prediction of your score a dozen years later?

Correlation values—usually abbreviated with the letter r—can fall between +1.0 (a so-called "perfect correlation") and −1.0 (a perfect *inverse* correlation). Thus the strongest possible correlation is *either* +1.0 *or* −1.0. The weakest possible correlation is zero—indicating no relationship. As some concrete examples, the correlation between your height, measured in inches, and your height, measured in centimeters, is +1.0 (because these two measurements are obviously assessing the exact same thing). The correlation between your current distance from the North Pole and your current distance from the South Pole is −1.0 (because each mile you move closer to one pole necessarily takes you one mile away from the other pole). The correlation between your height and your IQ, in contrast, is zero: There's no indication that taller people differ in their intelligence from shorter people.

Most of the r values you'll encounter in psychology, though, are more moderate. For example, the chapter mentions a correlation of roughly $r = +.50$ between someone's IQ and their GPA in college; the correlation between someone's IQ score and the score of their (nontwin) brother or sister is about $r = +.60$. What do these values mean? The full answer is complicated, but here's an approximation.

Researchers routinely report r values, but the really useful statistic is r^2—that is, $r \times r$. Bear in mind here that (as we noted early on) correlations are based on *pairs* of observations, and the r^2 value literally tells you how much of the overall variation in one measure within the pair can be predicted, based on the other measure in the pair. Thus, let's look at the correlation between IQ and school performance (measured in GPA). The correlation is +.50, and so r^2 is +.25. This means that 25% of the variation in GPA is predictable, if you know students' IQ scores. The remaining 75% of the variation, it seems, has to be explained in other terms.

A different way of thinking about these points hinges on the "reduction of uncertainty." To assess this reduction, you might compare how good your prediction of someone's school performance will be if you know the person's IQ, and how good your prediction would be if you didn't know their IQ. Equivalently, you can compare how uncertain you were in your predictions initially, and how much *less* uncertain you would be, once you know the person's IQ score.

But what does "uncertainty" mean in this context? Once again, let's be clear that correlations allow you to make predictions: If you know someone's IQ at age 6, a correlation allows you to predict the person's score at age 18. But predictions, in turn, have two elements: You might predict that the 18-year-old's IQ will be, let's say, 110, but you'll also want to express your degree of uncertainty, so you might say "110 plus-or-minus 8," or "plus-or-minus 5%," or something like that. That "plus-or-minus" clause reflects the unexplained variation, and, as correlations grow stronger, your predictions become more precise, and the plus-or-minus bit gets smaller. (If you have a math background, the notion here is that, with stronger correlations, the individual observations are more tightly clustered around the regression line.) These details aren't crucial, though. What is crucial is the idea that correlations allow predictions, and that stronger correlations allow more precise predictions.

Finally, let's step away from the nature of correlations in general and consider one last point about correlations in psychology: In psychological research, we find only modest correlations. We've said, for example, that the correlation between IQ scores and academic performance is roughly +.50, and, we've now said, this means that 25% of the variation from student to student is predictable based on IQ, and the remaining 75% of the variation needs to be explained in other terms. Thus, IQ is a major contributor to performance, but even so, a very large amount of the observed variation—the differences between an A student and a C student, and so on—is produced by the effect of *other* variables, separate from IQ. Some of these other variables, on their own, matter a lot (including the amount of studying, or choice of strategy in studying). Other variables contribute only a little to the overall pattern, but there are many of these variables, and so, in combination, they too have an impact on the 75% of the variation *not* accounted for by the IQ score. All of this is, again, a way of saying that IQ is a major factor in determining life outcomes, but a long list of other factors also play a role. This is one of the reasons that, as we've repeatedly said, IQ scores do not shape your destiny.

Psychologists are impressed when they find that the relationship between IQ scores and school performance is $r = +.50$. In our field, this is considered a solid finding. A skeptic might respond, however, by saying that this r value means that $r^2 = +.25$, and hence this "solid" finding explains only a tiny slice of the overall data pattern. With this r^2, 75% of the margin for error, 75% of the variation within the data, remains unexplained! Why should researchers chase after this small piece of the puzzle?

Is there a response to this challenge? In truth, there are many ways to think about this issue. As one option, you might explore this line: If your goal is to *improve* students' school performance, you might hope to remove *every obstacle*, and to provide *every possible* source of aid; in that way, you'd optimize students' performance. But, of course, that grand strategy isn't realistic. What would a more realistic strategy look like, and how might that bear on the skeptic's challenge?

Can you come up with other ways to think about the skeptic's challenge?

Cognitive Psychology and Education:
Improving Intellectual Performance

The material in this chapter is rich with practical suggestions about how you can improve your performance in academic settings and in a wide range of other settings as well. For example, we know that people often rely on a hill-climbing strategy and therefore get bogged down when a problem requires them to "move backward" briefly in order to "move forward." Simply knowing this—and, specifically, knowing the limitations of hill climbing—is likely to be useful and might encourage you to continue your efforts even when (unexpectedly) your strategy does seem momentarily to be moving you away from your goal.

Likewise, we know that people underutilize analogies, largely because they tend to focus on the superficial features of the problems they encounter rather than on the problems' underlying dynamic. You can therefore improve your problem solving by doing more to focus on the deeper structure of the problems you meet. Thus, when thinking about already-solved problems, you might ask yourself why exactly the solution gets the job done, and what this solution has in common with other problem solutions. That perspective will better prepare you to use the current problem as a basis for a productive analogy at some later point.

Related, research indicates that analogy use is more likely if you've seen multiple analogues in the past, not just one or two. Presumably, this exposure to multiple examples encourages you to think about what the examples have in common; this in turn will lead you to think about the examples' underlying dynamic—exactly the right path toward promoting analogy use. This is, by the way, why homework exercises are often useful. The exercises sometimes seem redundant, but the redundancy turns out to have a function.

Perhaps more important, though, the chapter makes it clear that intellectual performance is often shaped by factors that don't seem, strictly speaking, to be "intellectual" in nature. Concretely, performance in intellectual pursuits is often undermined by expectations of failure and fears that your poor showing will only confirm people's worst beliefs about you. Guided by these fears, you're likely to become anxious, which by itself can undermine your performance. You're also likely to interpret early frustrations, or slow progress, as "proof" that the problems you're working on are actually beyond your abilities. This interpretation can lead you to abandon your efforts, or perhaps just try less hard, if you encounter these early obstacles.

The factors just described are, of course, what the chapter discusses under the heading of *stereotype threat*. In the chapter, we focused on how these factors influence groups (and so lead African Americans to underperform on intelligence tests and lead women to underperform on math tests). But the same factors, and the same destructive dynamic, apply to individuals—and so many of us, guided by these expectations, do less well on intellectual tasks than we might.

How can we defeat these forces? Research points the way toward several suggestions. In one study, women performed less well on a math test if they came into the test believing that differences between men and women in math abilities are rooted in genetics and therefore unchangeable. Women performed better if they came into the test with *the correct belief* that, in truth, the gender difference is largely rooted in environmental factors and, no matter what the source of the difference, is certainly changeable. In this case, then, knowing the actual facts is helpful!

Another study, discussed in the chapter, asked middle-school students to write a few sentences, at various points during the school year, about things they valued—athletic ability, or being good at art, or creativity, or whatever. This simple exercise was enough to reaffirm for these students values other than academic achievement, and this was apparently enough to provide a sense of perspective that diminished academic anxieties and improved academic performance.

These and other studies suggest that rather modest steps can shift students' attitudes toward achievement and testing and thereby undercut the harmful effects of stereotype threat. There's nothing magic about these steps, and they won't help poor performance that's the result of not getting enough sleep or inadequate training. If someone had poor nutrition and lousy health care as a child, these shifts in attitude cannot erase the earlier harms. Nevertheless, the research is clear that working toward a broader perspective and more positive attitude can have a remarkable impact on how well you do in many cognitive arenas!

FOR DISCUSSION

Discussions of stereotype threat tend to showcase two examples: African Americans taking intelligence tests, and women taking math tests. These examples are deeply important, but researchers have pointed out that stereotype threat is relevant to many other cases as well. This notion is relevant whenever there is a stereotype about a particular group's performance—for example, the stereotype that Asians do well in mathematics, or that the elderly have bad memories. Can you think of other places in which stereotype threat might arise? Bear in mind that you don't need to limit yourself to intellectual performance; the same logic should apply to athletic or artistic performances. For that matter, don't limit yourself to *negative* stereotypes: The case of Asians doing well in mathematics reminds us all that sometimes people have positive stereotypes. How would stereotype threat apply to those cases?

Cognitive Psychology and the Law:
Problem Solving in the Courts

In many trials, judge and jury are trying to make a straightforward decision: The defendant is either innocent or guilty; the lawsuit should be decided for the plaintiff or for the defendant. These decisions can be enormously difficult, but at least the task is clear: Gather and evaluate the evidence; make a choice between two outcomes.

In other cases, though, the court's role is different. The court has a goal and must figure out how to reach the goal. In a divorce case, for example, the goal is to reach a settlement that is fair for both husband and wife; if the couple has dependent children, the goal must also include a living arrangement for the children that will be sensitive to their needs. Likewise, in a bankruptcy case the goal is to arrive at a distribution of resources that is fair for everyone.

These cases suggest that we should sometimes think of the courts as engaged in problem solving, rather than decision making. As the textbook chapter describes, problem solving begins with an initial state (the circumstances you are in right now) and a goal state (the circumstances you hope to reach). The task is to find some path that will lead you from the former to the latter. And, in many court cases, the problem is an *ill-defined* one: We know roughly what the goal state will involve (namely, a solution that is fair for all parties concerned), but the specifics of the goal state are far from clear.

In addition, some people argue that solutions to legal disputes should, as much as possible, promote the health and well-being of all parties involved. This emphasis, sometimes called "therapeutic jurisprudence," adds another goal in our search for a problem solution.

The search for these solutions can be difficult. The judge (or other mediator) needs to be fair and pragmatic but in many cases also needs to be insightful, creative, and perhaps even wise. How can we help people to find these King Solomon–like solutions? Legal scholars, therapists, social workers, and others have all offered their advice, but it also seems plausible that we might gain some insights from the study of problem solving.

As an illustration, many courtroom settlements can be guided by *analogy*. A judge, for example, might find an equitable resolution for a child-custody dispute by drawing an analogy from a previously decided case. Likewise, a mediator might find a fair divorce or bankruptcy settlement by appealing to some suitable analogy. Of course, judges already use analogies; this is built into the idea that legal decisions should be guided by appropriate legal *precedents*. But we know that in general people often fail to find and use appropriate analogies, and also that there are steps we can take to promote analogy use. It seems likely, therefore, that we can use these steps to help legal decision makers become better problem solvers and, in that fashion, provide real benefit for the justice system. However, little research investigates this specific point, and cognitive psychology's potential contribution to this important area is largely underexplored. It is therefore an area that we can recommend to students and to colleagues as being in need of research and further development.

What sorts of training would you propose to teach judges and mediators how to be better problem solvers? What sorts of materials would you expose them to? What perspective or attitude would you encourage them to bring to this training material?

In thinking this through, bear in mind that research provides some guidance on these issues—including the sort of training materials that promote analogy use, as well as the attitudes during training that make subsequent analogy use more likely.

For more on this topic

Winick, B. J. (1998). Sex offender law in the 1990s: A therapeutic jurisprudence analysis. *Psychology, Public Policy, and Law, 4*, 505–570.

Winick, B. J., & Wexler, D. B. (2003). *Judging in a therapeutic key: Therapeutic jurisprudence and the courts.* Durham, NC: Carolina Academic Press.

Cognitive Psychology and the Law:
Intelligence and the Legal System

Whether we measure intelligence with an IQ test or in some other way, there's no question that people vary in their intelligence: Common sense tells us that some people are wonderfully smart, while others are stunningly slow. And the rest of us, of course, are somewhere in between. These differences are real and are important for the legal system for several reasons.

Let's start with the fact that the individuals who are swept up in the legal system— people who are arrested, defendants who are on trial—tend, on average, to be lower in intelligence than citizens not swept up in the system. There are many reasons for this. People who are less smart are more likely to drop out of school, more likely to get low-level jobs (or no jobs at all), and these factors are themselves statistically associated with criminality. (If your best option for employment is some unrewarding, unsatisfying, minimum wage job, then the "income" from crime looks all the more enticing.) In addition, people who are low in impulse control are likely *both* to do poorly on intelligence tests *and* to consider criminal activities. Then, as a further concern, people who are less intelligent are not just likely to commit crimes, they're also more likely to get *caught* by the police, which makes it all the more probable that the people in jail, and the people on trial, will be (again, on average) less intelligent than the typical citizen.

Once someone is arrested, there are other complications attached to lower intelligence. In the United States, the police must remind a suspect of his or her "Miranda Rights"—the right to remain silent, the right to have an attorney present during questioning, and so on. There are several studies, however, making it clear that low-intelligence individuals often misunderstand these rights, and fail to exercise their rights properly. As a result, low-intelligence individuals don't receive some of the essential protections that the government offers to all citizens.

In many investigations, police don't just question a suspect (to learn what happened); they also *interrogate* a suspect, trying to persuade the suspect to confess (or, at least, to make some self-incriminating statement), so that the police will then have firm evidence to provide for the prosecution. Many people—political leaders, attorneys, journalists, researchers—have expressed the concern that sometimes police obtain a *false confession*, so that the suspect admits to some actions that, in truth, he or she didn't do! Evidence suggests that one of the factors making a false confession more likely is low intelligence—perhaps because a less intelligent suspect misunderstands the entire process. Specifically, some suspects "confess" because they are convinced that, once they have given the police "what they want," the police will be satisfied and release them. This is, of course, a serious mistake, and certainly increases the danger of a false confession.

Once on trial, citizens in the United States are guaranteed (by the Sixth Amendment to the U.S. Constitution) the right "to be informed of the nature and cause of the accusation; to be confronted with the witnesses against him." Courts have long held the view that this right is empty if the defendant does not understand this information—i.e., does not understand "the nature and cause of the accusation," and this is one of the reasons that someone cannot be tried if the person lacks "legal competency." Related, the Sixth Amendment guarantees the right "to be confronted with the witnesses against him; to have compulsory process for obtaining witnesses in his favor," and this right, too, is empty if the person cannot understand the legal process, or what the witnesses are saying.

What defines "competency" to stand trial? The U.S. Supreme Court set out its standards in a 1960 ruling in *Dusky v. United States*, and (among other points) insisted that the defendant must have "sufficient present ability to consult with his lawyer with a reasonable degree of rational understanding" and a "rational as well as factual understanding of the proceedings against him." Sometimes someone fails to meet these requirements because of mental illness (the defendant in the *Dusky* case had been diagnosed with schizophrenia), but a defendant can also lack competence to stand trial because of low intelligence.

Questions about "competency" also emerge in other settings. If defendants want to act as their own attorney (that is, to "represent themselves"), they must be competent to do so. And if someone wants to plead guilty, they must be competent to do so. Do these steps require the same sort of functioning as competency to stand trial? In 1993, the U.S. Supreme Court (in *Godinez v. Moran*) said that one standard can be used for all of these decisions, so if someone is competent for one of these issues, that person is competent for all. However, this remains a matter of ongoing debate. A separate question is *competency to be executed*. For jurisdictions still using the death penalty, a defendant can be put to death only if capable of understanding why he is being executed.

Plainly, then, the legal system needs to worry about intelligence levels, and about procedures for evaluating intelligence. There can be no question, therefore that the topics of defining and measuring intelligence are crucial for anyone in the judicial system to understand.

You've probably watched the scene on TV dozens of times: A suspect is arrested, and a police officer reads him his Miranda rights. In most jurisdictions, the rights go like this:

> You have the right to remain silent. Anything you say or do can and will be held against you in a court of law. You have the right to speak to an attorney. If you cannot afford an attorney, one will be appointed for you. Do you understand these rights as they have been read to you?

Does this statement of a person's rights seem clear enough so that we can count on everyone understanding it? If your intelligence level were well below the population average, do you think you would have trouble with these rights? With which bits? What "repairs" might we make to avoid confusion? How could we find out if a particular suspect does or does not understand the rights? Is the final question ("Do you understand these rights . . . ?") a good check?

For more on this topic

Godinez v. Moran, 509, U.S. 389 (1993). Like all of the Court's rulings, this one is available on line.

Greene, E., & Heilbrun, K. (2010). *Wrightsman's Psychology and the Legal System* (7th ed.). Belmont, CA: Wadsworth.

Kassin, S., Drizin, S., Grisso, T., Gudjonsson, G., Leo, R., & Redlich, A. (2010). Police-induced confessions: Risk factors and recommendations. *Law & Human Behavior, 34,* 3–38.

Here are the solutions to Demonstration 12.3:

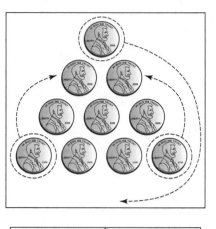

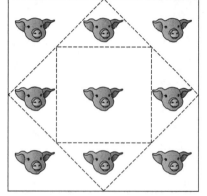

CHAPTER 13

Conscious Thought, Unconscious Thought

Demonstrations

13.1 Practice and the Cognitive Unconscious

People can perform remarkably complex, sophisticated actions on "autopilot"—that is, without any conscious monitoring of these actions. There are several ways an action can reach this status—that is, can get to the point where autopilot is possible—but one common path simply involves lots and lots of practice.

No matter how an action becomes automatic, however, both a gain and a loss are produced by this "automaticity." On the positive side, you can perform automatic actions easily, swiftly, and without any thought. On the negative side, though, you have difficulty focusing on, or adjusting, these automatic actions even if you want to. As an illustration, take a piece of paper and write down step-by-step instructions for *how to tie your shoes*. Assume that the person you're writing for has the basic vocabulary (and so knows what a "lace" is, what "left" and "right" mean, what a "loop" or a "cross" is, and so on). But assume this person has never tied shoes before and will need complete, detailed instructions.

Once you have done this, recruit a friend. Give him or her an untied shoe to work with, and then read your instructions out loud, one sentence at a time. Ask your friend to follow your instructions exactly. Make sure that your friend doesn't just rely on his or her own knowledge; instead, your friend must do exactly what you say in your instructions—no more and no less!

Will the shoe end up tied? Odds are good that it will not, and you're likely to end up with your friend's arms tied in knots, and not the laces.

Of course, you know perfectly well how to tie your shoes; you do it every day. But the sequence of steps is so well practiced that it's now something you barely think about. Indeed, this demonstration suggests that even when you *want* to think about this everyday activity, you can't—the steps are so automatic that they've become largely inaccessible to your conscious thinking.

13.2 The Quality of Consciousness

One of the remarkable things about consciousness is that people seem to differ from each other in the very nature of their inner experience. Of course, people think different things and have different ideas. What's amazing, though, is that people also differ in the fundamental texture of their mental lives—so that some people routinely have experiences that are utterly foreign to other individuals. To make this concrete, ask the following questions of several friends. (You'll want to pause, of course, after each question, to give your friends time to answer.)

Imagine a girl carrying an umbrella. Can you see her in your mind's eye? Now, is the umbrella open or closed? Is it on her shoulder or held in front of her? Is she facing you or standing in profile? What is she wearing? What color is her jacket, or is she not wearing a jacket? What color are her boots? What's in the background behind the girl?

What sorts of responses do you get from your friends? It's inevitable that the answers will differ in the details. (Some people might imagine a blue jacket; others might imagine yellow; and so on.) But what's striking is that your friends' answers will probably indicate that they are having different *types* of experiences. At one extreme, some of your friends are likely to have an immensely detailed visual picture and will give you fast and complete answers to every question. In describing their image, they'll sound as if they are effortlessly reading off information from an *actual* picture, not a mental picture.

At the other extreme, though, some of your friends may describe a very different experience. When you ask them about the umbrella, they'll say something like: "I wasn't thinking about the umbrella's position until you mentioned it." When you ask them about colors, they may say: "What I'm thinking isn't in color *or* in black and white; it's just a thought, and I don't have a sense of it being in any way colored or not colored." In short, they may describe an experience that's not in any fashion picture-like. Remarkably, they may insist that they *never* have picture-like inner experiences and never feel as though they can see a "mental picture" with their "mind's eye." Surely, they will have heard these (often-used) phrases, but they will think of them as loose metaphors and will insist that "mental seeing" doesn't feel in any fashion like "actual seeing." (You may need to question several friends until you find someone at this extreme.)

What should we make of these variations? Is it possible that some people routinely have conscious experiences ("mental pictures") that are totally different from the types of conscious experiences that other people have? Do these differences from one person to the next *matter*—for what they can do or what they can do easily? If so, this becomes a powerful argument that the experience of being conscious really does matter—does change how we act, what we say, and how we think or feel.

Applying Cognitive Psychology

Research Methods: Introspection

In Chapter 1, we discussed some of the limits on introspection as a research tool, and, in fact, our discussion throughout the textbook has rarely relied on introspective evidence. This is because, as one concern, introspection relies on what people *remember* about their own mental processes, and we cannot count on these memories being reliable. In addition, introspections are usually reported verbally: The person uses words to describe what happened in his or her own mind. But as we discussed in Chapter 10, some thoughts are nonverbal in content and may not be captured adequately by a verbal description.

As a further problem, your introspections, by definition, involve an "inspection" of your mental life, and so this method necessarily rests on the assumption that your mental state is "visible" to you. (You can't inspect something that's invisible!) As Chapter 13 describes, however, a great deal of mental activity goes on outside of awareness, and so it is, in fact, "invisible" to introspection. This provides yet another limit on introspection as a source of scientific evidence—because introspective data will necessarily be incomplete in what they tell us about mental processes.

Let's be careful, though, not to overstate these claims, because unmistakably, introspective reports sometimes do have value. For example, in the study of problem solving, researchers sometimes ask people simply to "think out loud" as a means of discovering what strategies the people are using as they work on the problem. Likewise, in Chapter 10 we acknowledged the complexities attached to someone's introspective reports about the vividness of his or her own mental images, but we also argued that these vividness reports can be an important source of data about images. (Also see Demonstration 13.2.) And in Chapter 6, we explored the nature of implicit memories; an important source of data there was people's introspective reports about whether a stimulus "felt familiar" or not.

How can we reconcile these uses of introspective data with the concerns we've raised about introspection? How can we argue that introspective data are of questionable value but then turn around and use introspective data? The answer lies in the simple fact that *some* thoughts *are* conscious, memorable, and easily verbalized; for thoughts like these, introspection can provide valuable data. The obvious challenge, therefore, lies in determining which thoughts are in this category—and so available for introspectively based self-report—and which thoughts are not.

How does this determination proceed? Let's say that "think out loud" data indicate that participants are relying on a certain strategy in solving problems. We then need to find *other* evidence that might confirm (or disconfirm) this introspection. We can ask, for example, whether people make the sorts of errors that we'd expect if they are, in fact, using the strategy suggested by the self-report. We can also ask whether people have trouble with problems that can't easily be solved via the strategy suggested by the self-report. In these ways, we can *check on* the introspections and thus find out if the self-reports provide useful evidence.

Likewise, in Chapter 10 we discussed some of the evidence indicating that self-reports of image vividness do have value. Specifically, we described evidence that reveals a relationship between these reports, on the one hand, and how well people do in certain imagery tasks, on the other hand. Other evidence indicates a link between these imagery self-reports and activation levels in the visual cortex. So here, too, we can document the value of the introspective evidence by checking the introspections against other types of data, including behavioral data and data from neuroscience.

The point, then, is that introspection is neither wholly worthless nor wonderfully reliable. Instead, introspection can provide fabulous clues about what's going on in someone's mind—but we then need to find other means of checking on those clues to determine whether they are misleading. But let's also note that introspection is not unique in this regard. Any research tool must prove its worth—by means of data that in one fashion or another validate the results obtained with that tool. (Consider, for example, our discussion in Chapter 12 of the steps needed to assess the validity of intelligence tests.) In this way, we use our research methods to build our science, but we also use our science to check on and, where possible, refine our research methods.

FOR DISCUSSION

In many settings outside the lab, you are asked to introspect: A close friend asks you, "Do you love me?" A teacher asks, "Why did you choose that answer?" A marketing survey asks, "Why did you decide to buy a Japanese car rather than one from Europe or the United States?" A therapist asks, "Why do you think your room-mate annoys you so much?" Or you ask yourself, "Why can't I keep my attention focused on my studies?" or "What do I really want to major in?"

In light of the points raised in this essay about introspection, and in light of the points raised in the textbook, how much confidence should we have in your ability to answer these questions accurately and completely? And if your answers might be inaccurate or incomplete, does that mean we should stop asking these questions? In thinking about these points, be alert to the fact that your response may depend on exactly what you're being asked to introspect about and who is doing the asking. You might also want to consider the possibility that introspections—even if incomplete or inaccurate—might nonetheless be useful for many purposes.

For more on this topic

Stone, A., Turkkan, J., Bachrach, C., Jobe, J., Kurtzman, H., & Cain, V. (Eds.) (2000). *The science of self-report: Implications for research and practice.* Mahwah, NJ: Erlbaum.

Cognitive Psychology and Education: Mindfulness

As the chapter discusses, you're able to accomplish a great deal through unconscious processing, and in many ways *this is a good thing.* With no attention paid to the low-level details of a task, and with no thought given to the exact processes needed for the task, you're able to focus attention instead on other priorities—on your broader goals, or on the products (the ideas, memories, and beliefs) resulting from these unconscious, unnoticed processes.

The chapter also makes it clear, though, that there's a cost associated with these benefits, because this state of affairs leaves you less able to *control* some of your own mental processes. The role of unconscious processes also guarantees that you end up *less well-informed*, and less insightful, about why you believe what you believe, perceive what you perceive, feel what you feel. As a result, with less control and less information about your own mental life, you end up more likely to rely on habit or routine, and more vulnerable to the pressures or cues built into the situations you encounter. You're also more likely to be influenced by chance associations and by the relatively primitive thought processes that, in Chapter 11, we referred to as System 1 thinking.

It's not surprising, therefore, that some people urge us all to be more *mindful* of our actions and, in general, to seek a state of *mindfulness*. Sports coaches, piano teachers, writing instructors, and many others urge us to "pay attention" to what we're doing—on the sports field, at the piano, at the word processor—with the clear notion that by paying attention we'll be able to rise above old habits and adjust (and improve) our performance. In the same spirit, instructors sometimes complain about their students performing a task in a "mechanical" fashion or "on autopilot," with the broad suggestion that a thoughtful, more mindful performance would be better—more alert to the circumstances, better tuned to the situation. Likewise, commonsense wisdom urges us to "Look before you leap" or sometimes just to "Think!"—apparently based on the idea that some forethought, or some thought during an action, might help us to be more aware of, and therefore wiser about, what we are doing.

These various suggestions—all celebrating the advantages of mindfulness—fit well with the argument that unconscious processes tend to be inflexible and too rigidly controlled by situational cues or prior patterns. But how should you use this information? How should you try to be more mindful? You might start by asking yourself: "What is my usual practice in taking notes in class? What is my usual strategy when the time comes to prepare for an exam? What does the rhythm of my typical day look like?" In each case, you might pause to ask whether these practices and strategies developed for good reasons or simply out of habit. In each case, you might ask yourself whether, on reflection, you might want to modify your practices to take advantage of suggestions you've read about in these essays or found in other sources. In these ways, some thoughtful, mindful, and *conscious* reflection on your thoughts and behaviors may lead you to some improvements in how you think, what you think, and how you act.

FOR DISCUSSION

This essay describes ways in which you might "fight against" your habits and ways in which you might try to be more mindful about your own behaviors. Ironically, though, it's sometimes possible to go in the other direction—and to *use* automaticity as a means for changing your life.

Specifically, there are settings in which you can take steps to establish new habits, ones that are better in tune with your goals. To do this, some authors recommend creating rigidly defined rituals and then giving yourself no option about following these rituals. In this way, you're sacrificing some moment-to-moment control of your own life, but you're also relying on these rituals to create new habits that will serve you well.

Imagine, for example, that you're concerned about spending too many minutes on computer games and not enough time studying. In this case, you might decide: You'll devote a specific, clearly defined interval each day to computer games, and you'll design explicit rules for how you'll end this interval and step away from the games. Do not allow yourself compromise or flexibility. Instead, count this as a firm obligation, and stick to it. It may also help to announce this obligation to friends,

and encourage them to scold you if you violate your own rule.

Will this work for you? Many people are convinced that it will. You're relying on a mix of habit, social pressure, and (sometimes) explicit incentives to change your life. Above all, though, you're relying on the fact that your behavior is often controlled by habits and circumstances, and you're using that fact to make your life better!

Can you design a specific example, or a specific circumstance in which you might create one of these "life-improving" rituals? What steps might you take, at least initially, to enforce the ritual? How might you find out, after a while, if the ritual truly has created a new and largely automatic behavior?

For more on this topic

Brown, K., Ryan, M., & Creswell, J. (2007). Mindfulness: Theoretical foundations and evidence for its salutary effects. *Psychological Inquiry, 18,* 211–237.

Cognitive Psychology and the Law: Unconscious Thinking

Chapter 13 argues that much of your thinking goes on unconsciously, and, like many of the observations we've encountered throughout the text, this fact has important implications for the legal system. In many trials, for example, the judge knows that jurors have been exposed to prejudicial pretrial publicity. The judge may ask the jurors, therefore, whether they'll be able to set aside what they've heard prior to the trial and decide a verdict based only on the trial evidence. But how accurately can the jurors answer this question? Can the jurors forecast what they'll be influenced by? Then, at the time of the verdict, will the jurors know whether they were influenced by the pretrial publicity? Research on the cognitive unconscious suggests pessimistic answers to these questions—because the relevant influences are likely to be unconscious, and so not something the jurors could ever assess. On this basis, the judge's initial question to the jury ("Will you be influenced by . . .") and the judge's subsequent instruction ("Make sure that you only consider . . .") provide little protection against the effects of pretrial publicity.

Similar concerns apply to the trial's witnesses. Imagine, for example, that the police show you six photographs and ask you to pick out the man who robbed you. After you make your choice, the police officer smiles and says, "Yes, that's who we suspected. By the way, how certain are you in your selection?" Then the officer asks some additional questions: "How good a view did you get of the perpetrator? How far away was the perpetrator? For how many seconds was the perpetrator in view?"

In this situation, notice that you received a bit of confirming feedback right after the identification ("Yes, that's who we suspected"), and research tells us that this feedback has a powerful influence. As we mentioned in Chapter 7, study participants given this sort of feedback report that they are more confident in their choice, compared with participants not given feedback. (And similar effects have been observed with actual witnesses to actual crimes!) Participants given this feedback also end up remembering that they paid closer attention, had a better view, and were able to see more of the perpetrator's face, in comparison to people not given this feedback. Of course, these recollections are mistaken—because, in the experiments, the feedback and no-feedback groups got exactly the same view and could see exactly the same details.

Why does feedback have these effects? It is as if research participants were saying to themselves, "I guess I can set my doubts to the side, because the officer told me that I did get it right. With my doubts now suspended, I suppose I can say that I'm certain. And since I apparently chose the right guy, I guess I must have gotten a good view, been standing close enough, and so on. Otherwise, I'd have no explanation for why I made the right choice and am so confident in my choice."

This certainly sounds as if participants are drawing inferences from the feedback and reaching conclusions about what they did or didn't see. But such reasoning happens unconsciously. Participants are aware only of the *product* that results from these steps: a specific level of confidence in their identification, and a set of recollections about the event. They are entirely unaware of the *process* that led to these products. And as Chapter 13 describes, there is nothing unusual or exotic about this example. Instead, this is the way cognition works in general—with most of your thought process hidden from view. As a result, witnesses will be the unwitting victims of their own unconscious inference and may give misleading evidence because of this inference. And, because the relevant processes are unconscious, witnesses may well *deny* making these inferences, if asked directly, and so make their testimony seem more compelling than it really should be.

Do these steps really happen? I testified in one trial in which a store's security video made it clear that a key witness was looking *away* from the robber for most of the duration of the robbery. This witness did, however, identify the defendant from a police lineup, and the police assured him that he'd selected the "right guy." He then testified in court, telling the jury how clear a view he'd gotten, and how he'd spent most of the robbery staring at the robber's face. In other words, his testimony was completely inconsistent with the security video, and, in my testimony, I suggested that we should put more faith in the video than in the witness's recall. In explanation, I described to the court the effects of feedback, and how feedback can lead to a distorted memory. What happened next? The prosecution re-called this witness to the stand and asked him directly: "Were you influenced in any way by the feedback you received?" The witness confidently said no, and this denial was apparently persuasive to the jury. However, the jury probably got this wrong, because the witness's denial was, in truth, of little value. The denial simply tells us that the witness wasn't *consciously* influenced by the feedback, but that doesn't mean that the witness was immune to the feedback.

These are all troubling points and suggest that we might need to rethink some of our judicial procedures—whether we're talking about procedures for protecting a trial from the influence of earlier publicity, or procedures for deciding how much weight to give to an eyewitness's account. More broadly, we might need to find ways to educate jurors so that they'll be more sophisticated in their thinking about what's conscious and what's not. These steps would, we can hope, help everyone in the justice system to think more accurately about psychological processes, and, with that, to render better, more accurate, more *just* decisions.

FOR DISCUSSION

Judges will not allow experts to testify in a trial if their testimony would only rehash points that the jury already understands. On this point, expert testimony about *memory* is often forbidden, with the judge arguing something like this: "We all have memories. We all use our memories all the time. We all therefore have a wonderful opportunity, across our lives, to learn how memories work. Therefore, we don't need an expert to testify on these points; instead, anything the expert might offer is likely to be just a matter of common sense—and thus already known to the jury."

Is this skepticism about memory research justified? Does our research merely echo common sense?

You might think about this point with a focus on the postidentification feedback effect: The witness is convinced that his or her memories of the past come from one source, but research indicates that these "memories" aren't memories at all; they are instead after-the-fact inferences based on the feedback the witness has received. Are there other examples of unconscious processes influencing memory that also undermine jurors' (commonsense) beliefs about how memory functions and how much faith they can put in witnesses' memories?

For more on this topic

Bradfield, A., et al. (2002). The damaging effect of confirming feedback on the relation between eyewitness certainty and identification accuracy. *Journal of Applied Psychology, 87,* 112–120.

Wells, G. L., Olson, E. A., & Charman, S. (2002). The confidence of eyewitnesses in their identifications from lineups. *Current Directions in Psychological Science, 11,* 151–154.